Theatre Notebook: 1947–1967

JAN KOTT

Theatre Notebook

1947–1967

Translated from the Polish
by Boleslaw Taborski

DOUBLEDAY & COMPANY, INC.
GARDEN CITY, NEW YORK
1968

Library of Congress Catalogue Card Number 68–22632
Translation Copyright © 1966, 1967, 1968 by Boleslaw Taborski
"A Little Treatise on Erotics" Copyright © 1966 by Evergreen Review, Inc.
All Rights Reserved
Printed in the United States of America
First Edition

PREFACE

I was still a schoolboy when I found myself backstage for the first time. The year was 1932. I was enraptured by the Polish actress Lena Zelichowska, so I bought some flowers and went to her dressing room after a performance. I knocked at the door. She said, "Come in, boy," and went on changing. I threw the flowers down and made my escape. Three years later I published my first theatre reviews in a student magazine. After the war I occasionally wrote reviews of plays performed in Łódź theatres. In the last ten years or so, writing theatre reviews has become almost my main occupation.

Theatre has always seemed to me more real than books or film. One goes to the cinema either alone or with someone, and a film is shown. It was made two years ago, a year ago, or a month ago; it does not matter. It is there, once and for all. It has another substance, another reality than that of the audience watching it. It is brought in a tin, and it can be seen in an empty room. But an empty house in a theatre is embarrassing. The audience in a theatre is different from one in a cinema. Theatre is very much like a café. Spectators play a part as well as the actors. And it is a somewhat different performance every time it is given.

Even the best directors cannot be certain of anything until after the first night. At rehearsals, things are different. A performance proves itself only when an audience is present.

Frequently it comes to mean something other than what was intended. The spectators are aware of not only the actors on the stage, but one another. If the performance bores them, they sink into themselves and become isolated, as in a cinema. But if the performance touches them, the spectators become an audience; they begin to play their part, to laugh, clap their hands, engage actively in what goes on. The performance is then a common experience. For this reason the custom of cutting the intermissions short, or having just one intermission, which is prevalent nowadays, is lethal for the theatre. Theatre is a social pleasure. The spectators want to be in their own company for a bit, want to look at one another. Conversation about the play and the acting, everything that is the café part of the theatre, is also part of theatrical enjoyment. Theatre is never a solitary pleasure.

Perhaps that is why I like writing about the theatre. I thrust myself into something that really happened; into something that goes on between the director, the actors, and the audience. When I write about a book, or a film, I feel as if I were writing about something dead. The public does not change anything in a film. In the theatre one watches men who are alive and with whom one can go to supper after the show.

A book is written by a solitary man, then a few hundred or a few thousand people read it in solitude—today, in a month, or in a year's time. A play is attended by five hundred or a thousand people at one time, and they will keep coming for as long as the play runs. When I write about the play, I meddle with their judgment, with something that has really happened in time and place. Every production has its contemporary validity; it may be a short one, but it is definite nonetheless. It began two or three months ago. It was from the outset a collective effort by people whom I know or do not know, whom I like or do not like, but who read the same newspapers as I do. We are in the same boat.

Theatre, particularly in Poland, particularly since the war, has been something of a litmus paper. It has reflected politics,

fashion, snobbery, literary discussion, desire for change. Theatre, especially in Poland, and especially in our time, is
acutely sensitive to all that goes on. It is state-supported
financially, but at the same time it is a nest of vipers,
sometimes very talented vipers. Polish theatre today may be
entertaining, didactic, ideological—sometimes even artistic.
Many persons and institutions meddle with it, assist it, and
hamper it. But it also has to have an audience, who pay
back some of the funds advanced by the state, but who
could equally well go to a cinema, or stay at home and watch
television. All these factors contribute to the pressure under
which the theatre exists; something is continually happening
to it or with it. Thanks to these factors, too, a theatrical
performance in Poland, far more often than in the East or
in the West, can be an event: political, artistic, or social.
Something has happened and has to be noted down, de-
ciphered, pointed at. That is one of the reasons why I prefer
to write about theatre. I take part in the great game, or at
least I think I do.

Theatre people say that a reviewer should know the theatre
from the inside: should come to rehearsals, or at least see
a performance several times. I prefer going backstage to attending rehearsals. Still more I like going to a performance
in the company of an intelligent director or a sensitive actress,
just as I like going to exhibitions of paintings with painters.
They tell me things I did not notice or even suspect before.
But very few of those observations are useful to me when
I get down to writing. On several occasions in my life I
have participated in the production of a play from the first
rehearsal to the first night. I could not write a word about
any of those productions. I knew too much. I knew the
effects that had been intended and did not come off; what
the director, the stage designer, the actors wanted; what
nobody wanted and what still happened. Who cares how
many sheets of paper I have torn up and thrown in the
wastepaper basket while I was writing these words? Only
graduate students writing their theses worry about things

like that. And historians of literature when they write about the great masters. If they deal with lesser writers, the game is boring, and nobody gives a hoot.

Probably the reviewer should know something about theatre, but it is not very clear what. What happens not in but around the theatre is, for the most part, more interesting. A critic should first of all know, and sense, the points at which political and social events, tradition, history, and the present intersect with art. A critic's seat is actually located not in the third, or fifth, row of the orchestra, but in a public square.

I am, of course, mainly interested in dramatic literature. But I hardly ever read a play before seeing it performed, and not very often after that either. I am interested in what of the text has come alive, and how it sounds confronted with the present; in what a play means when the words "first performed on such and such a day" are written on the billboard. I had this kind of experience with Mayakowsky's two well-known plays *Bathhouse* and *The Bedbug*, when they were performed by Polish and Russian theatres before and after the death of Stalin. Sometimes I manage to define the reading the director or the audience has given a play, which is a small but heartening satisfaction for a reviewer.

The great Polish critic Boy-żeleński was most interested in what the theatre showed about "life" and changes in manners and customs. I, too, am mainly interested in "life," but the word means something quite different to me from what it did to Boy in the 1920s. In his day, the basic Polish repertoire consisted of farces and comedies of manners. These plays came from countries where the democratic process was far more advanced than in Poland; they reflected the moral crisis following World War I. Boy was a genius when it came to summarizing those second- and third-rate plays. His summaries were descriptions of new moral situations and new manners. One cannot, however, summarize a play by Dürrenmatt, Ionesco, or Różewicz; just as one cannot summarize or narrate the plot of a circus number with trained seals or a trapeze act. One can, with some difficulty, summarize Hegel, Taine, even Kant, but it is almost impossible to summarize Husserl, Heidegger, or Carnap. One can describe what there is to be seen in Manet's "Luncheon on the grass," but one cannot do so with a painting by Klee. One cannot summarize a handbook of logistics. Sartre is probably the last dramatist of our time whose plays can be summarized fairly satisfactorily. New playwriting is more and more like the training of tigers, and like the handbook of metalanguage or metaphilosophy.

It is, of course, committed, perhaps even more committed than pièces à thèse or bedroom farces were. But the *informel* in painting is also committed, to the conflict about which way to see the world and, more than that, about its concreteness. Informel often reminds me of photographs of the movement of electrons or other particles in physics handbooks. Pictures taken through an electronic microscope do not cease to be realistic, but the word "realistic" comes to mean something different. A microcosm is not "realistic."

To my mind, with Dürrenmatt, Ionesco, Beckett, and Genet, drama crossed the point of no return as far as theatre conceived of as the mirror of manners goes. The new theatre is committed to other matters, and—as in the new novel, poetry, or painting—it often takes the mirror itself as its theme: the mirror's existence, function, chemical composition. Thus the mirror sees itself.

Theatre is politics, didactics, café conversation. If it were not all these things, it would be rather boring. But sometimes, theatre becomes theatre, philosophy, style, or at least the search for theatre, philosophy, style. Then it takes us by surprise. There, as usual, is the stage, the auditorium, people we know sitting here and acting there. And suddenly we are smitten. A new sphere of sensitivity is touched. To write about the theatre means to invoke, or to search for, that sphere. After all, one of our dreams is that at ten P.M. we might leave the theatre different people than we were when entering it at seven. But this does not happen often.

CONTENTS

II: JOURNAL OF A TRAVELING SPECTATOR

I: On the Polish Theatre

A GENEALOGY OF
CONTEMPORARY POLISH DRAMA*

The scene is laid in Poland or nowhere. The scene is laid
in Poland or everywhere. The first of these statements concluded Alfred Jarry's introduction of his play *Ubu Roi* to the
opening night audience in 1896. The second might have been
said by Mrożek of all his plays, and it would also apply to the
play of Gombrowicz, Różewicz, and, particularly, those of
Witkiewicz. The shambles of history in *Ubu Roi* are in
Poland, which is nowhere. Almost fifty years later Jarry's
"nowhere" turned into "everywhere."

 Ubu Roi is undoubtedly one of the three or four plays
that originated the modern theatres of the absurd and of
cruelty. Ubu was at first a stuffed puppet that symbolized
a detestable physics teacher. Then he became respectively a
vindictive father, a cowardly bourgeois, and a cruel monarch.
Jarry discovered that his use of the puppet made it possible
to present within one play a shocking epitome of Shakespearean tragedies. It is not unlikely that his discovery had
a much greater importance. *Ubu Roi* became not only the
epitome of Shakespeare's histories but also the first grotesque
essay on the presentation of the mechanism of history, the
essay condensed into a dramatized two-hour "comic strip."
Ubu the King murders people and collects revenues; his every
other word is merde; he is cruel, greedy, and stupid. The

* This essay was originally prepared as a lecture presented at the
Center for Slavic and Eastern Studies of the University of California
at Berkeley on April 3, 1967.

simplest definition of the contemporary theatre of the absurd is a single sentence: Tragedy turns into horrifying mockery. When the real events of history go beyond the limits of the absurd and horror, then Richard III becomes Ubu the King.

In 1966 a Belgian journalist visited Poland. He left under the spell that my country casts on so many foreign visitors. His impressions of his trip were reprinted by the Polish press: "A visitor to Poland is daily confronted with a unique combination of Kafka, Ubu, and Shakespeare." In Jarry's play the names of two authentic kings of Poland appear. The first is Jan Sobieski, the victor of the battle at the Vienna walls where the Turkish army was defeated; the second is Stanislas Leszczyński, son-in-law to Louis XV of France. Leszczyński, after being banished from Poland, turned up in Lorraine where he ruled and acquired the nickname of "the Philosopher King." These kings lived in the seventeenth and eighteenth centuries, respectively. Ubu also becomes a Polish monarch, who flees across the Baltic to Sweden aboard a ship; he flees before the oncoming troops of the czar.

To the Poles, a fragment of their country's history presented as a comic strip is at once more preposterous and more conceivable than it may be to others. The city of Warsaw spreads over the left and right banks of the Vistula River. The section on the right bank is called Praga. My very first memory—I was not more than three or four years old at the time—is of the blast of an explosion that blew up a bridge over the Vistula. German troops were approaching Warsaw, and the Russians were leaving in a great hurry. Later I witnessed the blowing up of the same bridge on two other occasions: in 1939, when the Germans were entering the outskirts of the city, and in 1945, when the Germans were leaving Warsaw and the Russians were coming in.

Ubu Roi was produced in Poland in 1956, the year of the glorious Polish October and the Hungarian Revolution. It opened in a small theatre run by students of the Warsaw Polytechnic Institute. The theatre is a part of a student club known as The Barn. Several months before the opening night of *Ubu Roi*, the first striptease show in Poland took place there. It was a one-girl show. She was a student at the Polytechnic Institute, and she simply undressed completely. She did it in the most natural way with no tricks and no gimmicks. She was accompanied by music, but not the ordinary strumming that goes with acts of this kind. Originally they had thought of playing the Polish anthem during the show. The censors intervened. So the girl stripped to the music of Beethoven's *Eroica*. I believe that this performance belongs with what is known as the Happening and should be mentioned in the future as such. It was a challenge to the old order, a protest and a provocation. A political provocation, as a matter of fact, rather than social. In Poland even a striptease act may have ideological overtones.

Ubu Roi as presented in The Barn became an important, if not the most important, theatrical event of the time in Warsaw. Naturally, it was a political event as well. It was *Ubu Roi* transformed into a cruel mockery of events that had really happened; events that had their beginnings in 1939. The mockery did not spare anything or anyone. It ridiculed both the stupidity of the usurpers of power and the heroism of their victims. The time of jeers and gibes had come after all the years of heroism and fear. On stage Ubu was running around beating his fat belly and shouting "Merde." He collected revenues and signed death warrants, or he signed deaths warrants and collected revenues. Two Polish poets, Mickiewicz and Słowacki, often referred to by their countrymen as the prophets, in their dramas assigned Poland very specific parts to play among the nations of the world. Mickiewicz saw Poland as the Jesus Christ of the nations; Słowacki, as the first soldier of the great revolution that was to sweep the world and bring freedom to its peoples. *Ubu Roi*, in the Warsaw production, had a comment to make on these particular missions of Poland: Merde. If it is impossible to alter the course of history or to move to another geographical latitude, then all one can do is to laugh at history. At times this laughter is very bitter. The young men who adapted *Ubu Roi* and played in it thought they were extremely anti-romantic. Apparently they did not realize that for the last one hundred and fifty years each generation of the Poles has been learning a lesson of madness and a lesson of common sense, alternately. Both lessons have always proved deceptive. Neither madness nor common sense could have changed the fate of Poland.

The Warsaw production of *Ubu Roi* owed almost equal amounts to Jarry and to Shakespeare. Yet it is the history of the last two decades in Poland that has been so very Shakespearean—in the sense, of course, not of *A Midsummer Night's Dream* but of *Richard III*.

In the well-known Andersen fable the naked Emperor walks on the streets. Nobody dares to speak until one day a child cries out: "The Emperor is naked." In this period in my country and in several other countries, a person would have to be as naïve as a child or as bold as a clown to shout: "The Emperor is naked." The clown plays not only a great theatrical role but a social one as well. The clown who knows that he is a clown is not really a clown. He only pretends to be one. The real clowns are those who are not aware of their identity. The clown makes clowns of others. If wisdom becomes foolery, foolery becomes wisdom. If the world turned upside down, one might rush headlong to the right place. The function of the clown is to discover that the Emperor is naked. The clown tells the truth, but his language is clownish. That is the role played by Shakespearean clowns. Within the period of socialist realism in Poland, the anonymous political anecdote performed this function of a Shakespearean clown.

Several days after Khrushchev's unannounced visit to Warsaw during the stormy days of the October Revolution, the following kind of anecdote circulated widely. Aboard a plane in flight are Khrushchev, Bulganin, Zhukov, Malenkov, and twenty Russian generals. Suddenly the plane bursts into flames. Question: Who was saved? Answer: Poland.

A few years before the new type of Polish drama emerged

or, in other words, before Mrożek, Różewicz, and Herbert made their debuts as playwrights, the student theatres were the cradles of this type of political anecdote, specializing in the blackout, and venomous grotesque—all the elements that differentiate the Polish school of the absurd from the absurd in the West. In fact, the very name, "theatre of the absurd," when applied to contemporary Polish drama, is often misleading. Inmates of a madhouse do not tell jokes about madness. An absurd anecdote rationalizes the absurd; it is the intellectual's attempt to overpower the absurd. "There's a method in this madness." It is the struggle of logic against madness. One of the great masters of aphorism in modern literature is Stanisław Jerzy Lec. Some of his thoughts are condensed, one-line scripts for the modern theatre:

Illiterates must dictate.

Don't shout for help at night. You may wake your neighbors.

It is easy to hang puppets. The strings are already there.

The aphorisms of Lec carry us into the world of Kafka, but it is that world seen from within, through real experience. The first realization resulting from this experience is that the world is closed:

Open Sesame—I want to get out.
I prefer the sign No ENTRY to the one that says No EXIT.

Kafka continues to be read in the West as a writer of the metaphysical horror of human existence. But there are various levels of reading literature. For the reader in Eastern Europe, Kafka provides a different, much more real kind of horror. The term "alienation" has two fundamental meanings: the existentialist and the social. Kafka in his nightmares exposed to us the stuff of the contemporary horror. Erotic dreams have very probably been the same throughout the epochs, but every epoch dreams its own nightmare. "We are such stuff as dreams are made on." I wouldn't be so sure. "Dreams are such stuff as we are made on." But prophetic dreams occur.

Kafka began his *Trial* and *The Castle* before World War I. There was still some time before the era of concentration camps and gas chambers. He was, however, the first of the great writers to show very explicitly the meaning of turning a man into a number, not a number within humankind but a number written on one's back; to be a number among fellow numbers in a camp; to be one's own number.

It seems to me that Lec's aphorisms picture the real nightmare of Kafka's world:

Don't tell your dreams. What if the Freudians come to power?

Only the dead can be resurrected. It is more difficult with the living.

When confronted with his murderer the corpse did not identify him.

In the epilogue of *The Trial* Joseph K. comes to believe in his guilt. He believes in his own trial. Everybody is guilty, according to one interpretation of Kafka, because everybody is human. The very fact of being born makes one guilty. I do not agree with this interpretation. To the reader in Central and Eastern Europe the word "trial" has certain specific associations, or, to use a scholarly term, has a different semantic field from the one accepted in the West. It is more connected with political execution than the Last Judgment. Personally I have always sided with those who never admitted their guilt, who never believed in their "trial." Let me quote two more aphorisms by Lec:

He who has a good memory can forget more, more easily.

How should we train memory to learn to forget?

Modern literary criticism often points out that the difference between satire and the absurd is revealed in their different goals. Satire is didactic in nature; it is meant to improve men or society, and, in fact, it is optimistic since it assumes the world is basically sane and orderly. Grotesque, or the theatre of the absurd, is regarded either as the play of the sophisticated mind or as the philosophical confession that all human existence is senseless and grotesque. Again, I do not agree with these statements. Alfred de Musset wrote "Comedy is the logic of the absurd." Absurdity can be defeated only on its own grounds. Logic has provided an excellent weapon for that purpose: reduction to absurdity. Calling the absurd by its own name, reductio ad absurdum to its pure state—to me, these are the means or tools for an intellectual liberation from the absurd. The captive mind —to use Czesław Miłosz's title—believes in the absurd or at least in its necessity. The liberated mind casts away this necessity. It was not a coincidence that the Polish school of the theatre of the absurd emerged after the Polish October and the Hungarian uprising. Compared to the theatre of Ionesco, Beckett, and Pinter, the Polish theatre of the absurd has been much more realistic or, better put, much more political. The label "political grotesque" seems to apply best to that theatre.

Mrożek's* first play was *Police*. In an unnamed country, opposition to the government in power has ceased to exist. All political prisoners have been released after signing the oath of loyalty. Prisons all over the country are empty. There is, however, one man who is still a prisoner. Years ago he threw a grenade to the chief of the police. It did not explode. Now the man is questioned every day by the chief. It has been going on for years. Each time the chief attempts unsuccessfully to persuade the prisoner to sign the confession. Suddenly the prisoner changes his mind. He wants to sign the oath. The chief is frightened. He will lose his only pris-

---

* Sławomir Mrozek (b. 1930). Polish satirist and playwright. *The Elephant*, New York: Grove Press, 1963, London: Macdonald, 1962; *Six Plays: Police, The Martyrdom of Peter Ohey, Out at Sea, Charlie, The Party, Enchanted Night*, New York: Grove Press, 1967, London: Jonathan Cape, 1967; *Tango*, New York: Grove Press, 1968, London: Jonathan Cape, 1968.

oner; the police will have to be dissolved. The man is insistent, and finally, after signing the oath, he is released. In Act II the chief finds a solution. His old sergeant used to make extra money in his free time by putting on plain clothes and working as an agent provocateur, inciting people to shout anti-regime slogans. This never produced a single scapegoat. But a new prisoner is urgently needed. The chief explains to his sergeant that for the sake of their organization the sergeant must appear in the window and shout, "The president is a pig." Then he will be arrested. The chief assures him of an important change in his career: he will be assigned to the top secret division of the police force. The plan is carried out.

In Act III the routine questioning of the new prisoner is on. But the evidence against the ex-sergeant is too weak. The government wants proof of conspiracy, and a general is sent to take charge of the investigation. The general's aide is the former stubborn prisoner. He has come to like the government so much that he has been made an expert on conspiracies. The expert has an ingenious idea: let the ex-sergeant throw a grenade at the general, the same grenade that is still in the files as evidence. Since it did not explode then, it will not explode now.

The chief approves of the plan. The new prisoner tosses the grenade. It explodes. Now the chief puts the expert under arrest for causing the death of the general. The expert puts the chief under arrest for approving his plan. Then the general, an experienced soldier, who, when the grenade went off, hid in the toilet, enters and arrests both the chief and the expert. They, in turn, arrest the general for being reckless in the face of danger. The whole police staff is arrested by one another, several times in a row. Mrożek has a complete reductio ad absurdum.

An even more Kafkaesque atmosphere and equally sinister metaphors appear in one of Mrożek's next works, the one-act play *Striptease*. The setting is a room with nothing in it but two chairs. Two men enter. They carry briefcases and look like high-ranking officials. The door to the room is open, but neither leaves—one because he thinks he was ordered to come here, the other because he wants to preserve his inner freedom. As long as he is in, he is free to choose. The moment he leaves this freedom will be gone:

> "What is freedom? It's the possibility of choosing. As long as I am sitting here and know I can leave via that door, I am free. On the other hand the moment I get up and go out, I have made a choice, in other words, I have limited my field of action, I've forfeited my freedom. I become a slave of my going out."

An enormous hand appears in the room. The hand is polite, it merely points with the little finger to their brief-cases and then to their clothes. The gesture is gentle but determined. Both men frown at these strange orders, but quietly do what they are told. One believes that the hand must be acting according to some superior plan. Perhaps the hand represents the authorities. One should not irritate the authorities. The other man is equally obedient in his actions, but he keeps repeating very loudly that the absurd and degrading demands of the hand concern only his body. Clarifying their points of view, both men submissively take off their trousers.

MAN B. A fine sight you are now with your inner freedom. Your trousers are falling down.

MAN A. You're no picture yourself. They don't keep any better without a belt.

MAN B. What do you make of all this?

MAN A. I can repeat what I said before: that hand has deprived me, first, of the ability to move around and, secondly, of the ability to wear my trousers. That's true, I grant you. But what of it? All this is on the outside. Inwardly I'm still free. I've not committed myself to any gesture, to any line of action. I didn't so much as lift a finger. Sitting here, I'm at liberty to do any of those things which still

remain within my sphere of possibilities. But not you.
You did something, you made a choice and made a fool of
yourself. Slave!

Both Man A, the follower of inner freedom and, most
likely, a student from the Ketman school described by
Miłosz* in *The Captive Mind*, and Man B, who simply
respects the authorities, are standing now with only their
shorts on. The hand, at first good-natured, begins to grow
angry with the men. The gentlemen in briefs make excuses
to the silent hand. They want to give it flowers, but there
are no flowers in the room. Another hand, dressed in a red
glove, appears. The first hand throws dunce's caps over the
men's heads and leaves the room. The men follow.

The Belgian journalist visiting Poland was struck and enchanted by this combination of Kafka, Alfred Jarry, and
Shakespeare. It is perhaps more admirable for foreign visitors
than for Poles. Professor Daniel C. Gerould of San Francisco
State College who returned from Poland delighted by the
intellectual atmosphere of Warsaw had similar comments
to make. His article "The Non-Euclidean Drama: Modern
Theatre in Poland" begins: "In Poland two and two make
five." True. It seems worth mentioning, however, that in the
same country where two and two make five an extremely
fine group of mathematicians created one of the most famous
schools of thought known as "The Polish School of Mathematics." The Polish school of logic, to which Professor Alfred
Tarski, presently in America, belongs, is one of the best in
the world. A country where two and two make five and where
at the same time great mathematicians and logicians abound
—this is truly a Kafkaesque situation.

* Czesław Miłosz (b. 1911). Polish poet, essayist, novelist and
translator, professor at University of California, Berkeley. *The Captive
Mind*, New York: Knopf, 1953, London: Secker & Warburg, 1953;
Seizure of Power, New York: Criterion, 1955; *The Usurpers*, London:
Faber, 1955; *Postwar Polish Poetry*, New York: Doubleday, 1965;
Native Realm: A Search for Self-Definition, New York: Doubleday,
1968.

State-run religious bookstores [continues Professor Gerould], bouquets of flowers in a shop window displaying ball bearings, kissing the hand of a woman truck driver—surprises and contradictions abound. In a country with such an odd mixture of old and new traditions and with such a confused and fantastic history, the implausible becomes probable. In a modern play about power, politics, and revolutions, Fortinbras suddenly appears in a faded Elizabethan costume; now senile, he falls asleep in his chair listening to radio reports about how the strongman Fortinbras is coming to restore order throughout the world.

The name of the play mentioned by Professor Gerould is *The King the Fourth* by Stanisław Grochowiak, a member of the youngest generation of Polish poets and playwrights. Mrożek belongs to the generation of Osborne and Pinter. Grochowiak is ten years younger.

The King the Fourth is a contemporary version of Shakespeare. Shakespeare in Poland or, rather, Shakespeare and Poland is a subject for one of the most interesting books that has yet to be written. It would be largely a book about not only the translations of Shakespeare into Polish or the history of productions of his plays in Poland, but also the many plays and poems that adapted subjects and plots from Shakespeare to specific Polish conditions. Such a book might be called: "If Shakespeare had been a Pole . . ."

Poland was, quite likely, the second or third country in Europe where Shakespeare was played outside of England. It is possible that he was played in Warsaw during his lifetime, around 1611. The cities on the Baltic, members of the Hanseatic League, were frequently visited by groups of merchants from England. To many of these men these cities were their homes. Ambulatory casts or traveling theatres from England came there with repertoires including Shakespeare, Marlowe, and perhaps Thomas Kyd. One of these casts reached Königsberg in Prussia at the time when the elector of Prussia was ready to leave for Warsaw to pay tribute to the Polish king whose vassal he was. As a gift he brought with him the English cast. Probably the actors played, in English of course, *The Comedy of Errors* and *The Merchant of Venice*. What the Polish audience made of the performance is an entirely different matter.

Hamlet was staged in Polish for the first time in Lwów in 1797, two years after Poland's loss of independence. It was, as far as one can tell today, a very special Hamlet. The actor who had the title role and directed the play, Wojciech Bogusławski (later called the father of the Polish theatre) had been one of the prominent participants in the Kościuszko Insurrection three years earlier. The failure of the insurrection brought about the fall of Poland. In this performance at the end of the eighteenth century, Denmark suddenly became Poland, and Claudius, the usurper of the Crown, stood for Catherine the Great, Frederic, and Maria-Theresa, the three authors of the partition of Poland.

In 1956, over a hundred and fifty years later, I saw the opening of *Hamlet* in Kraków. This date has its particular significance. It was three years after the death of Stalin; the time of the Twentieth Congress in Moscow; the stormy October in Poland; the time of "the thaw." In my country thaw breaks the ice. The première of *Hamlet* was in September, the same September that was followed by the Polish October.

The lines that everyone knew by heart, that were until now only literature, suddenly sounded frightening, almost shocking. "Something is rotten in the state of Denmark" was the first chord of the new meaning in *Hamlet*, and then the dead sound of the words "Denmark's a prison" thrice repeated. *Hamlet* became, from the first scene to the last, a political drama. Of all Shakespearean words the most audible was "watch." At Elsinore Castle someone is hidden behind every curtain. Guildenstern and Rosencrantz, friends of Hamlet, behave like agents of the secret police. I think that is how Shakespeare saw them. He certainly knew well who murdered Marlowe and why. Politics lies heavy over every sentiment and there is no escape from it. Hamlet's "To be

or not to be" may signify "To act or not to act." The
Polish Hamlet of 1956 was both an angry young man and a
rebellious Communist.

If Hamlet had been a Pole . . . The first Polish Hamlet
appeared in *Horsztyński*, a historical drama by Słowacki written in the 1830s. This Polish Hamlet, Szczęsny-Kossakowski
by name, is the central figure of the play. He has a fine
aristocratic lineage; his father commanded the Polish army
and his uncle was a bishop. Both the father and the uncle
are authentic historical figures. Both were hanged during
the Kościuszko Insurrection for treason and servitude to
Catherine of Russia. The time of the play is the eve of the
insurrection. Szczęsny hates his father, the traitor to Poland,
but his Hamlet-like "To be or not to be," "To act or not to
act" is, at the same time, the choice between keeping the tradition of the nobility of old Poland and joining the mob of
cobblers and tailors who, in their admiration for the French
Revolution, are only too eager to hang the aristocrats. The
first Hamlet in Polish drama is unable to make the choice.

In 1967 I saw a performance of *MacBird* in New York. I
was moved by the play since it seemed to me not only truly
Elizabethan in its courage in dramatizing violent contemporary history, but also very Polish in its free, unfettered attitude
toward Shakespeare, in its method of adapting contemporary
politics to plots and images from Shakespeare. The witches
in *MacBird* transformed into the down-with-war and anti-
discrimination pickets prophesy the future of Kennedy and
Johnson. In Słowacki's *Kordian*, a drama written in the early
1830s and one of the outstanding works of Polish romanticism, the witches and the devil pick out of a caldron full of
bubbling sulphur marionettes of the leaders of the current
uprising. In the same play Słowacki sends his hero to the
cliff of Dover, so well remembered from the scene with
Gloucester and Edgar in *King Lear:*

> Oh, Shakespeare! Spirit! You have built a mountain
> Higher than that created by God.
> For you have talked of an abyss to a man blind . . .

These lines ring with equal vividness for us and for Słowacki, whom one may call the greatest forerunner of the
theatre of symbolism and expressionism and perhaps one of
the two greatest playwrights of European romanticism; the
other was Kleist. Słowacki came to realize that the mountain
existed only in the imagination of a blind man and that
words were the stuff of which it is made; that the mountain
exists in poetry but not in the stage set.

From Mickiewicz to Gombrowicz, Shakespeare is ever-
present in Polish drama. His presence there, however, is
different from the perception of him in French and German
literature. The Shakespeare who came to be a Pole is pri-
marily mocking and jeering, always found in what the most
courageous and violent Polish theatre produced, always present in what is best in our drama. Mickiewicz gave his *Dziady*
this motto from *Hamlet:*

> There are more things in heaven and earth, Horatio,
> Than are dreamt of in your philosophy.

Słowacki combined within the elements of *Macbeth* and
A Midsummer Night's Dream, a seemingly impossible
achievement, he wrote an astonishing tragicomedy that is both
a fairy tale about the beginnings of Poland and a stinging
contemporary satire.

In two plays by Gombrowicz,* *Ivonia, the Princess of
Burgundy* (1938) and *The Marriage* (1939), we find brilliant parodies of *Hamlet* and *Macbeth.* These two plays
were written at least a decade before the theatres of existentialism and of the absurd were born in the West. With
his novel *Ferdydurke* they belong to the most important
works of the avant-garde in Polish literature. To Gombrowicz the attitudes of Hamlet or Lady Macbeth are
merely stereotypes, masks forced on them by the situation.

* Witold Gombrowicz (b. 1905). Polish novelist, playwright, and
diarist, awarded the Formentor Prize in 1967. *Ferdydurke*, New York:
Harcourt, 1961, 2nd ed., Grove Press, 1967, London: MacGibbon,
1961, Calder, 1966; *Pornografia*, New York: Grove Press, 1967, London: Calder, 1967.

They are, as Gombrowicz puts it, the form. The heroes feel caught in the trap of these ready-made forms, as if someone had glued masks onto their faces, had in fact made the masks their faces. They revolt against these faces, looking for "the inadequacy of form," for what is not ready-made but instead authentic and spontaneous. "Form," says Gombrowicz, "for its part does not agree with the essence of life."

To Gombrowicz, the matter of *Hamlet* is involved with the problem of the face and the mask. To other Polish playwrights, particularly those who live in Poland, *Hamlet* is basically political in its nature. "The rest is silence." False. The rest, or at least the very end, is the coming of Fortinbras. Zbigniew Herbert, of the same generation as Mrożek, and one of our leading poets, wrote in his *Elegy for Fortinbras*:

> . . . Adieu, Prince. I have tasks, a sewer project
> and a decree on prostitutes and beggars
> I must also elaborate a better system of prisons
> since as you justly said Denmark is a prison.

The situation involving Hamlet and Fortinbras is also introduced very clearly in Mrożek's *Tango*. This play is the first contemporary Polish drama that has entered the repertoires of theatre companies of all kinds: student theatres, experimental theatres and professional theatres, both in England and on the Continent.

Tango is set in the present. A young student, Arthur, is Hamlet. Eddie, a butler and the lover of Arthur's mother, is Fortinbras. It is a family play like Pinter's *The Homecoming*. Arthur's grandmother is a former bluestocking; his great-uncle once owned large estates and excellent stables, of which nothing is left except a stuffed horse and a worn-out saddle. His father is an artist, the rebellious and independent member of the family. His mother has been working all her life to keep abreast of the avant-garde. Both parents represent the generation that rejected bourgeois hypocrisy and prejudice, religion, morality, and the establishment. Social references in Mrożek are impeccable in their exactitude.

Arthur's mother says to her husband with pride: "You possessed me in front of Mummy and Daddy on the first night of *Tannhäuser*, in the first row of the stalls, as a sign of protest. What a scandal that was. Ah, the times when it still made an impression!"

In Arthur's house, where there has been no real housecleaning for years, the principle of total freedom and tolerance rules. Let everybody do what he pleases. The contemporary Hamlet returns home to introduce order and cleanliness, morality, principles, even the bourgeois double standard. He dreams of discipline, of respect for the forms. He wants to marry with full trimmings, with the blessings of his parents and a long train for his bride's dress. He rebels against his parents, against the adults, yet he finds it very difficult to rebel since he is free to do anything.

Arthur puts a top hat on his father's head, a girdle on his great-uncle, a white ball dress about fifty years old on his grandmother. The groom and the bride kneel; an old-fashioned phonograph plays Mendelssohn. Grandmother, radiating utter disgust, gives her blessings to the couple. The taking of a wedding picture ends the ceremony. But there will be no picture. The outdated box camera does not work. Moths fly around and the place reeks of mothballs. The return to the old form turned out to be impossible.

"When tragedy is impossible," says Mrożek, "and mockery bores, the last resort is experiment." But the period of experiment is over, too. The final word in *Tango* belongs to Eddie. His is the future. The true strong man brings in his new order based on sheer terror. With a direct punch he downs Arthur and over his corpse makes a brief speech, very much like Fortinbras' last lines: "You have seen what a blow I can strike. But do not be afraid. So long as you sit quietly, don't move about and pay attention to what I say, you will be all right with me, you'll see. I am a simple man. I like to crack a joke occasionally, I like fun. But I must be obeyed."

Tango ends with a tango. Over the body of Arthur, Eddie

invites the frightened great-uncle to dance. This representative of the class that is gone makes no effort to save the remnants of his own dignity. He dances in Eddie's arms. It is a long, ceremonial, majestic dance. This grotesque, ominous tango takes the place of the trumpets and taps with which Fortinbras bade farewell to Hamlet. During the Warsaw production the music kept pouring out of the loudspeakers long after the curtain was down, growing in force until the last spectator had left the audience.

Contemporary Polish theatre with all its originality seems to foreign visitors to be the Polish equivalent of the theatre of the absurd in the West. Actually, the works of Mrożek, Różewicz and Herbert, even granting their freshness, form a body of drama that has close ties with the traditional Polish romantic and neoromantic theatres. The most original Polish play, perhaps the single greatest Polish drama, *The Wedding* written by Wyspiański in 1900, ends with a similar bloodcurdling and ominous dance. In this play the real persons meet and talk to their symbolic doubles. To music played by one of the symbolic characters called Chochoł (the hogle), all the real persons join hands and begin dancing on stage, as if in a dream or a slow-motion film. Chochoł, a rosebush wrapped in straw for winter, symbolizes the dangerous impact of poetry or, more precisely, the lulling spell of Polish romantic poetry. It is dangerous and lulling because it puts illusions in place of reality.

Grotesqueness or a combination of the tragic and the grotesque is regarded by many critics as the main quality of modern art. This is even more conspicuous in modern drama. Born into the theatre of tragicomedy we are apt to understand better and evaluate more deeply of the mixture of tragedy and the grotesque in the past. After three centuries of disregard, *Troilus and Cressida* has only now been included among the greatest works of Shakespeare. Today the German playwright Kleist seems to live with us. And of all Euripides' plays *Orestes* and *The Bacchae* are nowadays believed to be the richest and the most impressive. One can go further

and describe the grotesque as the ever-present power conquering not only literature but also shaping our outlook on
the world around us, on history, on our own lives, on the
human condition. More and more this outlook resembles
the grotesque.

In 1901, the year after Wyspiański's *Wesele* (*The Wedding*), Chekhov wrote *The Three Sisters*. One of the most
original contemporary critics in Poland, Konstanty Puzyna,
has tried to show the resemblances between *The Wedding,
The Three Sisters,* and Beckett's *Waiting for Godot*. In all
these plays the heroes are waiting, waiting for something that
will not come. They are waiting for something or someone
to change their absurd and hopeless lives. During this waiting
they are constantly thrown back and forth between despair
and hope. In fact, they are waiting for a miracle. Two tramps
are waiting for Godot; isn't it true that he came once? The
sisters are waiting for their trip to Moscow. The people in
The Wedding are waiting for the moment that is bound to
come, the morning of a new Polish uprising. They will fight
and win.

The scene is the night of a wedding in rural Poland. To
the house come people from the village and the town,
bourgeois and peasants. There are also several people from
that curious stratum of society called the intelligentsia.
During the long night they drink and dance and torture
one another with recollections of the past. *The Wedding* is
a drama of waiting, disillusionment, immaturity, and total
inability to do anything. These terms, "immaturity" and
"inability" come back many times in plays by Mrożek and
Gombrowicz.

During the night the wedding guests talk to their doubles
and ghosts. Dreams are interwoven with reality, raw colloquialisms with poetry. As time goes by, the play becomes
a cruel, mocking political pamphlet. For a long time *The
Wedding* seemed to be a drama understandable only to Poles.
But if one reads it as a grotesque play, one finds it rings with

contemporary tones, right from the very beginning. Act one, scene one, line one, a rich peasant talking to a journalist:

CHEPIEZ. Well, sir, what's the latest political news? The Chinese are putting up a good fight, they say.

EDITOR. My dear fellow, I am sick to death of the Chinese.

CHEPIEZ. But you're a politician, aren't you?

Mrożek's drama is continuing the work of Wyspiański. But it is a specific kind of continuation. The repetitive use of Wyspiański's motifs alternates with mockery of the same motifs. In the same way, Wyspiański continued the great Polish romantic drama of Mickiewicz and Słowacki, by both repeating and laughing at them. The hero of *Dziady* (*Forefathers' Eve*) by Mickiewicz returns to the stage, both metaphorically and in person, in Wyspiański's drama *Wyzwolenie* (*The Liberation*), first performed in 1904 . . . In that amazing play, the scene of the action is the actual empty stage of the theatre in which its first production took place. It was the stage of the Julius Słowacki Theatre in Kraków. It was one of Wyspiański's boldest theatrical discoveries, forecasting the theatre of Pirandello. Upon that stage, in front of the hero of *Dziady*, the director puts on a new national tragedy, which is a grotesque picture of contemporary society. Mickiewicz himself has a part in it. He plays the Genius who is forced offstage and into a trap door by the leading character.

Mrożek struggles with Wyspiański. Wyspiański wrestles with Mickiewicz. In fact, all three struggle and wrestle with Polish history. They try to explain it, do something with it. Mickiewicz and Słowacki made efforts to bring God, or at least the angels and Satan, into Polish history. Mrożek sees that history as tragicomedy. I am convinced that it makes little difference whether one calls Polish history "tragic" or "absurd." The fact is one can hardly explain this history in terms of nineteenth-century rationalism or, what is even more difficult, accept it by using the West's deceptive yardstick of progress.

It is very characteristic of Polish drama that any realistic pattern it adopted was always blown to pieces by the struggle with history and the fate of the country.

The periods of realism in Polish literature and drama have always been short and have hardly ever produced important works. The essential and great tradition of Polish drama is its specific combination of poetry, history, and politics. Here the term poetry indicates more than the fact that the majority of Polish romantic and neo-romantic plays were written in verse. Poetic drama is understood here in a very contemporary manner; its poetry is based first of all on parable and metaphor, a mixture of visions and reality. *Dziady* is the best example of this. Its hero writes on the walls of his prison cell with charcoal GUSTAVUS OBIIT CALENDIS NOVEMBRIS HIC NATUS EST CONRADUS ("Gustav is dead; here Conrad is born"). Gustav, the romantic lover, appeared first as a ghost, then as a hermit. The romantic lover now becomes Conrad, the revolutionary hero.

A future historian will certainly find that the majority of the conceits and images of modern Polish drama have their sources in our early nineteenth-century romantic drama. But then Poland was nowhere, so these plays had little chance of entering the world repertoires. This chance has come only now when the globe is so small that it has only one great common history—the history that takes its shape in every place on the globe and can just as easily blow that globe into pieces from here as from there.

Mickiewicz in an historical drama on the Kościuszko Insurrection written in Paris, makes one of the characters, Hetman, an aristocrat who is afraid of revolution, say:

O Lord! O Lord! Poland, Oh you poor country! Prince Ignacy Potocki, His Honor the Deputy of Inflant Niemcewicz —and a shoemaker, a shoemaker, Oh Lord!

To a foreign reader none of these names means anything except the word "shoemaker." The shoemakers took part in the first Polish uprising and quite eagerly hanged the aristocrats. But they entered Polish literature and drama almost one hundred and fifty years later.

The Shoemakers (1934) is Witkiewicz's last play. In it there is a character, Superworker, who speaks to the shoemakers after listening to their complaints that things still look bad for them in spite of the Communist revolution:

> "You picked the wrong ticket. Let it be known once and for all that there is no justice and cannot be—it is good enough that there are statistics—and we all should be happy with that."

Immediately after his words he shoots the leader of the shoemakers.

This quotation and the scene are obvious to all of us. They need no comments since they belong to the great history shared by our globe.

S. I. Witkiewicz, or, to use his pen name, Witkacy, was the most original man of letters in Poland between the wars. He was, I believe, one of the great forerunners of European contemporary literature and drama, who is only now being discovered. His plays are being produced in France, Germany, and Scandinavia, and are being translated into English.

Witkiewicz was a great individual. It is not an exaggeration to call him a Renaissance man, both as a human being and as an artist. He was a philosopher, painter, novelist, and playwright. He created his own theory of aesthetics. Among his friends were Leon Chwistek, an initiator of Polish formism in art who, together with Alfred Whitehead and Bertrand Russell, created modern mathematical logic. The second friend of his youth was the anthropologist Bronislav Malinowski, author of *The Sexual Life of Savages*. Witkacy went with Malinowski on an anthropological expedition to Australia. When the news of the war reached him, he returned to Petersburg to join the army and became an officer in the regiment of the czar's guard, a detachment in which the cream of Russian aristocratic families traditionally served.

He lived through the revolution as a White officer, possibly the only White chosen by the rank and file of his regiment to the post of political commissar, although Witkacy had never had any sentiment for communism. Participating in the revolution as a White officer and a Red commissar gave him an experience that very few European writers shared. We might say that in his youth the finger of history touched him. Compared to him not only the Polish but also the Western writers of the time seem provincial.

Witkacy was a catastrophist. Since Spengler there have been many catastrophists in European literature. But Witkacy was much more violent and far-reaching in his conclusions than the others. The first catastrophy he predicted was the annihilation of personality by the growth of bureaucracy and the mechanization of life. Transformation of society into an ant hill, or, in existentialism terms, the reduction of existence to the essence—this was the castastrophy. As a great forerunner of existentialism he called this catastrophy the loss of conscience and metaphysical experience.

He was convinced that contemporary world religion had long ago lost the power to evoke metaphysical horror, or, using his own words, the mystery of being. The feeling of deep existence can be experienced now only through eroticism and drugs. Witkacy used mescaline and peyote for a time and wrote a treatise on drugs. He might be considered, to some extent, a grandfather of the LSD users.

For him, the experience with drugs and the dive into erotics were not simply a way of escape and an enrichment of the imagination but, first of all, total immersion in the mystery of being. The first duty of art and theatre was to discover the same mystery and fear of being. Art to him was not a mirror reflecting reality, and its goal was not to produce pleasure. Art should be violent and cruel like the plague. Antoni Artaud used to speak of his theatre in a similar way. Witkacy and Artaud did not know each other, but in the late twenties they were probably the two greatest visionaries of the theatre of the future. Witkacy could have been the author of this quotation from Artaud's *Theatre and Its Double:*

> And the question we must ask is whether, in this slippery world, which is committing suicide without noticing it, there can be found a nucleus of men capable of imposing this superior notion of the theatre, men who will restore to all of us the natural and magic equivalent of the dogmas in which we no longer believe.

The combination of cold blood and lunacy had much greater density in Witkacy than in Artaud. To Witkacy, the transformation of people into worms is more than the defeat of metaphysics. His catastrophism predicted the new revolution of levelers which would begin in China and spread all over Europe. Such a vision comes at the end of his greatest novel, *Nienasycenie (Insatiety)*, and in some of his plays. Witkacy shot himself to death with a pistol on September 18, 1939, the day after the Red Army entered Poland's eastern territories. Most probably he concluded that the world he had been a part of was gone forever.

In Witkacy's theatre, corpses get up and continue conversations and suicides jumping out of windows come back through the front door. The real topic of his cruel and absurd grotesque is the agony and decay of the first quarter of the twentieth century. The aristocratic princesses from Poland and Russia in search of perverse pleasure take either artists or plain workers as their lovers. The artists and the politicians want to be the *Übermensch*. Yet even these supermen with fascist tendencies are nothing but a regrettable caricature of the Renaissance usurpers of power. All bourgeois standards go down the drain, from erotic prudery to respect for self-interest and money saving. All ideologies seem either ridiculous or monstrous, from liberalism to the socialist visions of happy humankind. Witkacy's plays stand out among all other dramatic descriptions of the Poles striving desperately with their history as perhaps the most venomous and merciless, yet the most universal in their appeal.

In 1934 Witkacy arranged an evening of playreading in his Warsaw apartment. It was his last play, *The Shoemakers*, and Witkacy himself read it to the invited guests. These consisted of two professors of philosophy from the University of Warsaw, two poets, four shoemakers who had their workshops nearby, the superintendent of his house, the maid, and two students. I was one of the students.

In Act III the scene is Poland after the revolution. But to the revolutionary shoemakers released from prison it is only an illusion that they will share in decision-making from now on. There is somebody else who really governs here. In the last scene two comrades dressed in English suits and accompanied by Superworker come on stage. They are the high officials of the revolution, almost of the Orwellian type, seen by Witkacy in a prophetic vision. They belong with "the new class." One of the gentlemen says:

> Listen, Comrade Abramowski, I'm abandoning the idea of nationalizing agriculture for the time being—not because I'm selling out . . .

The other gentleman replies:

> Of course not! It's too bad that we cannot be automatons ourselves.

Two years ago, in Wrocław, I saw *The Shoemakers*. It was being staged for the first time. In a student theatre. By sheer coincidence in the seats just behind me were two Chinese, probably diplomats newly arrived in Poland. I cannot tell you what they understood of the play and what their impressions were, but it was then that I realized for the first time and with full certainty that this Poland that to Alfred Jarry meant "nowhere" is now everywhere, indeed.

(1967)

PRIMITIVE AND MODERN

Little boys are climbing steep ladders to get on the roof of a shed brought here from a mountain village. They are dressed in gray habits, like monks. The oldest is about twelve, the youngest cannot be more than seven. They have climbed on top and are standing in a row between the beautifully carved pointed wooden towers. It could be the roof of a village church. The leader of the choir, or cantor, arrives, with glowing eyes. He spreads out his long fingers, raises his arms high, starts to conduct his choir in an exaggerated manner. The singing begins.

The boys' choir is the most enchanting, theatrically the best part of the show. The boys do not act. They enjoy being in the big theatre. They stretch their thin necks, look around amusedly. The actor playing Christ, who until now has been sitting with his head resting on his hands, looking like all those sorrowing Christs carved by generations of self-taught sculptors in the villages of Podhale, gets up and climbs down the ladder to the abyss of hell, where devils are holding Adam and Eve, prophets and patriarchs. He bangs the wooden door—so like the door of a Polish barn—hard with his fists, but the devil's generals, Cerberus and Lucifer himself, do not want to admit him. The Lord Jesus gets angry and waving a little red banner—used to this day to decorate icing sugar lambs at Easter—flies into a rage. In his fervor he lands his fist on the back of Archangel

Michael. The youngest boy in the choir, his mouth wide open, cannot contain himself any longer and bursts out laughing so loud that an older choir boy has to bring him to order with a cuff.

The boys enjoy themselves and sing, the actors act. But whom do they act? The actors in this show do not cease to be themselves, that is, modern actors. At the same time, they play at presenting a sixteenth-century mystery play and its cast. Not for a moment do they forget that this is an amusement for the modern audience, and that this amusement is true modern theatre. There is almost no stylization, no painstaking reconstruction. The performance is authentic, just as authentic as the choir boys' laughter when Christ fights with Lucifer. There is sheer joy in this show.

Nearly nine years ago the Piccolo Teatro of Milan toured Europe with their unforgettable *Harlequin, or The Servant of Two Masters*. I still remember the strong, almost physical joy I experienced watching that performance. It was a rare revelation of pure theatre, one that inspired the imagination. The Warsaw National Theatre has performed in a like manner the Polish folk mystery play, *The History of the Glorious Resurrection of Our Lord*, written—or rather written down and arranged from earlier texts—by a monk in Częstochowa toward the end of the sixteenth century.

The Piccolo Teatro's *The Servant of Two Masters* was produced in three different versions. The first subordinated all the action to aesthetic stylization; the second was a painstaking and historically accurate reconstruction of the old dell'arte. The third—the one we admired in Paris and in Warsaw—was a modern interpretation of Goldoni's text and of Italian eighteenth-century comedians. A modern director and modern actors transmitted to a modern audience simultaneously the old dramatic text and the modern attitude to that text—a combination of knowledge, affection, and admiration.

In the same way Kazimierz Dejmek, the director, and Andrzej Stopka, the designer, presented to us and made topical the naïve Easter play by Nikolaj of Wilkowiecko, and the interludes taken from the seventeenth-century Polish plebeian theatre. They did not wink at the audience, nor pretend to be simple and naïve. They frankly enjoyed the naïveté, the anachronisms, the epic character of the text, and the new, topical associations of old words, like "partisans of Christ," and the "red banner sealed with the cross." They also obviously enjoyed the lovely, medieval rhythms—repeating the vowels of the last syllables—and the unexpected poetry, rough and yet tender.

> The trees with their little buds,
> Little leaves and flowers, too,
> Which they of themselves send out
> Each year at this season.

They enjoyed mixing tradition and topicality, worldliness and religious rapture, coarse prose and tender lyricism, the brutal realism of country scenes and the great poetry of Resurrection. The director's finest and most original invention was to let the actors speak the stage directions too. For those naïve remarks about actors' gestures and singing, those simple descriptions of characters contain both the knowledge of the old theatre and its stunning poetry.

The director consciously—I would even say, perversely—used anachronism as the element of artistic experience. The fact that the stage directions were spoken aloud by the actors changed the mystery play into epic theatre; it revealed the ambiguity of a performance in which the primitive is presented together with our modern joy at the discovery of the primitive. After all, anachronisms are continually present in the text itself. In the most precious jewel of Polish medieval art, Wit Stosz's polyptych at St. Mary's Church in Kraków, we find in the splendidly gilded figures of saints and apostles the features, gestures, and dress of Kraków burghers, royal courtiers, and students of the Jagiellonian Alma Mater, which recently celebrated its sexcentenary. Similarly, in the soldiers guarding Christ's tomb we suddenly discover sixteenth-century soldiers, calling to one another on the watch in corrupt German, saluting and treating one another with snuff and alcohol. The three Marys haggle with the chemist about myrrh, perfumes, and sweet smelling ointments just as the townswomen of Kraków must have done. Annas and Caiaphas are presented as Jewish priests and appear dressed in bishops' robes. Lucifer is not unlike Pan Twardowski, the Polish nobleman of the sixteenth century who had made a pact with the devil and eventually found himself on the moon.

It was an excellent idea of Andrzej Stopka's to set the mystery play in a Polish mountain village and to change the late medieval two-level stage with its mansions into a wooden peasant cottage with a view of the mountains through its middle gate. Cerberus was turned into Turoń, a figure of Polish folklore, whom boys in mountain villages still carry about, together with a large star, in their improvised shows. The angel, looking as if he were made of tissue paper, with fiery red hair, could have come out of a Christmas card. He lowered some food from the Easter table—eggs, cheese, and sausage—on a string to the contrite devils. The author, a Pauline monk in the Częstochowa monastery, had a kind heart. He wanted even the defeated devils to enjoy the Lord's Resurrection.

For many years Leon Schiller prepared the Polish theatre for monumental representations of romantic drama. He regarded a conscious return to the primitive, to the forgotten tradition of nativity and mystery plays, to the plebeian theatre and the theatre of the strolling players, as the best way to purify the stage of falsehood and cliché. Dejmek is one of Schiller's last and youngest pupils. He has the same gift for reviving and carefully polishing ancient texts. In this he is unique among the present generation of directors.

There are performances destined for spectators who go to the theatre once, or at most twice, a year. There are performances for spectators who go to the theatre three times a month. There are performances for those who spend three nights a week in the theatre. There are performances for children and for grownups; for those who know the language and for those who do not. *The History of the Glorious Resurrection of Our Lord* was one of those rare shows that are for everybody. It was true theatre. And that is why the seven-year-old boy from the choir craned his long, thin neck to see Adam and Eve shaking their fists at Lucifer.

(1963)

A ROMANTIC PROLOGUE

Having recently seen performances of new Polish plays, one can only give a deep sigh and declare that Słowacki's debut in 1830 was better, even though he was younger than any of the new dramatists when his first play was produced. He wrote *Mary Stuart* at the age of twenty in a month during the autumn of 1830, just a few weeks before the uprising in Warsaw. These biographical data are relevant here. At the age of twenty, one usually writes not so much from experience as from one's reading. Słowacki's *Mary Stuart* is mainly a result of his reading. But one cannot help admiring the artistic maturity of the youthful poet and his qualities as a precursor. Słowacki adopted the right model, the key model, as far as romantic theatre was concerned: the Shakespearean model. It was Shakespeare imitated in a somewhat naïve manner, youthful and Byronic, but Shakespeare nonetheless.

Słowacki's qualities as a precursor are all the more impressive because he had Schiller's *Mary Stuart* to cope with. It was not a model easily dismissed. A noble soul who falls victim to tyranny; liberty personified which falls prey to despotism and court intrigue; the cruelty of force and reasons of state, in the face of which love and beauty are helpless. Schiller's *Mary Stuart* was enthusiastically accepted by young people and conspirators; it was interpreted as a topical play, a contemporary drama. To Słowacki it must have seemed artistically dated. His young boy's tastes were far more refined and sophisticated than those of the majority of his contemporaries. He took in avidly all that was happening in France and England, which was rather remote from what was happening in Wilno or Warsaw. Soaked in preromantic atmosphere, sensitive to Byron and Ossian, but a little deaf to the Decembrist and freedom motives in romanticism, he was the least mature ideologically among the romantic youth, though perhaps the most mature in his tastes. He was a stranger and felt a stranger. In those pre-uprising months, for that matter, neither tastes nor ideological attitudes had as yet been crystallized.

Słowacki had enough artistic courage to oppose Schiller by following the Shakespearean path. He understood, or felt, that Shakespeare meant a theatre of great passions, and foresaw the end of the theatre of noble rhetorical tirades. His Mary Stuart is not only a victim of passions but a criminal. Love is a blind and destructive force, and there is no force that can resist it. There is also another passion, just as dangerous and terrible: the passion for power, which must lead to crime. The mechanism of the world that breaks and destroys the weak is cruel.

So much had Słowacki read in Shakespeare. But his Mary Stuart would remain only an interesting document of literary influences, if Słowacki had written merely an imitative and youthfully cruel Shakespearean drama. In fact, however, he wrote into that royal tragedy of love, intrigue, and crime an altogether different play. Probably he was not even aware of the fact. He wrote a contemporary play about romantic boys in love with a girl a few years older than themselves. He made his youthful love, Ludka Sniadecka, into Mary Stuart and transferred his confession as the child of the age to the court of the Queen of Scots.

It is to this unexpected tangle of reading and personal experience that his youthful Mary Stuart owes its charm, freshness, and even its modern quality that still disturbs us.

On the one hand we have the grim Bothwell, draped in the cloak of the Byronic hero, imperious and demonic with his vial of poison; the conventional astrologer, the vindictive and cowardly chancellor, and another cruel feudal lord who has to avenge the slight to his honor; on the other hand we have four young poetic boys, sad, lyrical, declaiming about death, love, and friendship, infected with the romantic mal du siècle. They have been asked to play the parts of the royal husband, the Italian harpist, the court page, and the clown. Among them all, Ludka Sniadecka sits on her throne.

How old is Mary Stuart? Is she a mature woman, bored by the youth given her as husband? She amuses herself by exciting the youths surrounding her, but she well knows that her partner in love can be only a real man, older than herself, one whom she could obey. Or is she a young girl, who has not yet tasted love, for whom marriage and the worship accorded her by those of her own age have only been a lyrical prelude? She is almost innocent still, but she has read a great deal of Byron and Ossian; love means to her a leap into the abyss and is connected with crime.

The historic Mary Stuart was twenty-four years old at the time of Darnley's death. Słowacki's Mary Stuart is ageless: she is both mature and girlish, innocent and initiated. She is a woman with whom a twenty-year-old youth is in love. She may be his senior by just one year, but she is older by a hundred years. She is his contemporary, his playmate, but she is already a woman. She allows him to adore her, perhaps will even let him kiss her, but she does not treat him seriously. Let us now imagine all this in the scenery of romantic exaltation. Indeed, Słowacki must not have found it very difficult to turn Ludka into a tragic criminal on the throne. That was how the romantics settled their lyrical accounts.

Słowacki wrote to his mother from Paris: "O Mama! I was hurt by Ludka's letter you had sent me, for she used to write to me in quite a different manner. Foolish she is, she would be a poetic being, but is ridiculous—sadness will surely not kill her. I think she is offended a little that in my poems I have not written about myself, that is to say—about her. She did recognize me occasionally, however—she said so herself in the letter—it seems to me she must have recognized herself in the scenes between Rizzio and Mary Stuart—especially in the last scene of the second act."

In his account of the first postwar production of *Mary Stuart*, Tadeusz Breza was struck by how human, common, ordinary this tragic royal story was. Amazing how many "scruples, hesitations, heartbreaks, and pangs of conscience" they all have in that play, he wrote; and how right he was! For, in fact, it was a contemporary drama of romantic youth, set in Shakespearean costume. In this lies the charm and surprising novelty of *Mary Stuart*. In the theatre, costume imposes certain obligations, it becomes a reality. Słowacki endowed his youthful personal drama (which he described more directly in his poem "The Hour of Thought") with a bloody Shakespearean plot. He made three emotional youths and one emotional girl perform a kind of *Macbeth*. And they do perform that *Macbeth* on the stage because they have to. In spite of all its naïveté, the literary drama of youthful friendships and loves is thereby raised in stature, given new perspectives. If one reads it, the Shakespearean perspective is less noticeable and seems artificial. This may be the reason why *Mary Stuart*, ignored by literary scholars, was really discovered by the theatre and has been performed constantly for almost a hundred years. For it is, indeed, good theatre.

The romantics were faced with a great choice: Racine or Shakespeare. Racine meant a set of dead rules and cold aristocratic taste. Shakespeare meant a revelation of the fullness of life and artistic freedom. I do not know—perhaps I am influenced by the most recent Polish production of *Phèdre*—but Racine seems to me like Shakespeare in that he slowly burns his heroes in the fire of their passions, while

Shakespeare seems today like Racine in his moral concern, his terror of life, his incessant tragic tension. However romantic drama seems today to be much closer to both Shakespeare and Racine than to all the bourgeois realism that came later. One should perform it today with this in mind.

(1958)

MASQUERADE AND REALITY

After *Mary Stuart* written by the twenty-year-old Słowacki, the Teatr Polski in Warsaw has given us *Masquerade* written by the twenty-year-old Lermontov. This invites comparisons. But what should we compare? The authors' experience or their reading? The two poets' reading was very similar. If their plays are different, it must mean that their experiences were different.

Their reading was almost the same. Shakespeare struck them both with his vastness and made them dream about the cruel stage of history which liberates and magnifies passions. Schiller, whom they had gone through like measles, seemed too childish, flat and pathetic. Byron's heroes appealed to them more. Lonely, grim rebels, they were psychologically closest to the romantic generation. But when they tried to imitate Byron, all that was left was the costume. One had to find a man of flesh and blood and put that costume on him. Where to find him, where to look for the "hero of our time"? The stage was ready: it was the Shakespearean stage. The costume was ready: the Byronic costume. Twenty-year-old authors were looking for their hero.

Their reading had been the same, their experience different. That applied not only to Słowacki and Lermontov, but to the entire Polish and Russian romantic generation. Their experiences had been different, particularly at the very outset, when they had just turned twenty. How miserably

provincial those youths from Krzemieniec and Wilno, or even
Warsaw, seemed compared with young Griboyedov, Pushkin,
Lermontov. Brought up at some small country manor, or in
a small town, they snatched kisses "under the stairs" from
a cousin and wrote poems to her. There were youthful friendships and picnics, at which they drank milk or a bottle of
wine, bought collectively. They formulated the statutes of
student organizations, or declaimed to lower-grade officials
in clubs and cafés.

What about the others? Petersburg was Palmyra and By-
zantium, a Paris of the North. From their childhood they
had known parades, balls, masquerades. They were guests in
the most brilliant salons. They had seen the splendor and
the terror of the court. They had seen how a man could be
ruined with one joke and killed with one deletion. They had
seen suicides after losses at cards, and murders in provoked
duels. They had been initiated into life by the great ladies
of the court, not by chubby country girls, or by emotional
Ludkas and Marylas. Of course, in the intervals one talked
about literature. But no Baroness Schtral would advise her
Prince Zvezditch to write a new *Werther* with a happy end, as
the good Maryla advised Mickiewicz to do.

Polish provincial youths were moreover very poor. How
often in the letters written by Mickiewicz's young college
friends one finds, directly after a passage in praise of Schiller,
a sentence about some old shoes or a student uniform for
which the author's younger brother is waiting so that he
can go to university. Mickiewicz wrote when he was already a
teacher in Kovno: ". . . finances sad: ten rubles I had to pay
for a month's board, six I have paid for my journey . . .
and I have to send Aleksander urgently three, so I am left
without a sou."

As a teacher, Mickiewicz was paid twenty-five silver rubles
a month. At the same time the tutor who taught Lermontov
English at his grandmother's estate used to get three thousand rubles a year. No wonder that in *Masquerade* more than
a hundred thousand rubles were lost in a single throw.

But were the experiences so very different? The most honored guest at a Russian court ball was Benkendorf, the chief of police; in Warsaw, balls were given by Senator Novosiltsov, the man in charge of secret police investigations. The czar was present everywhere: in Moscow and in Petersburg, in Wilno, Warsaw, and Krzemieniec. That was the common experience of the youth in both countries. It was because of that that Mickiewicz made friends so easily when he reached the Neva in Petersburg.

The young romantics were searching for a modern hero, on whom they could force the Byronic mantle. They were looking for a historical scene that could become a theatre of Shakespearean passions. When they grew up they realized that they were themselves modern heroes performing on a stage no less cruel than Shakespeare's. Then they did not need a masquerade or historical setting any more. But they had to grow up first.

The twenty-year-old Słowacki placed himself and the companions of his youthful disillusionment at the court of the Queen of Scots. He wrote his *Macbeth* and gave it the title *Mary Stuart*. The twenty-year-old Lermontov transferred *Othello* to Petersburg salons; he dressed his Othello in a frock coat gave him three thousand serfs, and had him poison Desdemona with a helping of ice cream during a splendid reception. Słowacki was as yet too young and too inexperienced to write a contemporary comedy about a pair of romantic lovers, as Musset did; he had to dress them in historic costume. Lermontov did the opposite: he took the bloody plot of a Shakespearean tragedy and placed it in a contemporary drawing room.

Lermontov was far more mature than Słowacki. That brilliant officer of hussars of the czar's guard had tasted the fruits of life early. He could have written a psychological and social drama of the Petersburg upper class. Why did he need Shakespeare for that?

Without Shakespeare there would be no *Masquerade*. For there are two themes in Lermontov's play. The first theme is expounded in a social comedy—bitter, sarcastic, venomous, brilliantly punctuating the dialogue, drawing a character in a couple of sentences, mature in solving scenic situations. The second theme is developed in the lyrical and pathetic dialogue between Nina and Arbenin—irritating at times, at other times full of poetic beauty, in fact a great poetic fugue. There is in it a fierce hatred for the world and a painful appeal that there should be room for noble feelings and beauty; there is a violent accusation directed at the misery of human fate and at human baseness; a chasm is shown between ideals and the human condition, between dream and reality. There is in this fugue a personal obstinate note of inner struggle and pain.

In the vibrating dialogue between Nina and Arbenin one can sense long passages that have been subdued. The characters talk about betrayal, love and fidelity, but the violence of the accusations outgrows, it seems, the matter of slighted feelings. Or rather, it concerns another kind of feelings. This dialogue is not really Shakespearean, it is as if the *Othello* theme has been merely a pretext for it. The dialogue is romantic, but in the sense the Poles and the Russians understood the word. There is in it a call for freedom and a great knell for the poetry of the Decembrist uprising. It is impossible not to hear the Decembrist tone in *Masquerade*, in spite of all suppressions, in spite of the conflict having been masqueraded. Count Benkendorf had a good ear, and he knew why he refused permission to perform *Masquerade*.

The internal duality of *Masquerade*, ideological and artistic, is one of the most characteristic qualities of Lermontov's youthful drama. This duality must have its purely theatrical cause too. Lermontov had read Shakespeare in the original, but I cannot help feeling that he visualized his *Othello* indirectly, through contemporary Shakespearean adaptations. Just imagine the scene of the masked ball in opera. Protagonists of the drama emerge for a while from among the dancing couples, before they are enveloped again by the great ballet. They stop at the proscenium to speak their lines. No, they sing their arias.

Lermontov visualized his *Othello* through opera. Nearly all the romantics were tempted by the artistic form of the opera. Mickiewicz discussed the essence of opera in his circle of young friends from the University of Wilno. Opera was anti-classical, spectacular, dramatic; it opened up new possibilities for the theatre. Shakespeare was entering the European theatre in operatic adaptations. Among them was Rossini's *Otello*. I do not know whether Lermontov had seen it, but the very idea of Othello in frock coat, of a masquerade, of poison in ice cream, is operatic in its origins. One other detail. Lermontov substituted for Desdemona's handkerchief a lost golden bracelet. But between Shakespeare's handkerchief and Lermontov's bracelet there was a diamond necklace lost by Desdemona in the adaptation by Ducis. Rossini, when composing his *Otello*, knew Shakespeare from Ducis' adaptation. The wheel turned full circle.

Not that the "proof by bracelet" is necessary. Shakespeare's great tragedies usually end with a cruel and violent slaughter, in which all the protagonists die. But Shakespeare lets them die quickly. The smothering of Desdemona is followed by Othello's death in a matter of minutes. Shakespeare knew that in these scenes every minute weighs heavy and every superfluous word is unbearable. But operatic heroes have to sing their final arias before they die. There are such arias in *Masquerade*, and this is the reason why the last two scenes of Lermontov's drama are so hard for a modern audience to endure.

The greatest surprise in the 1958 Warsaw production of *Masquerade* was Jasiukiewicz, who played what appears to be the least gratifying, most melodramatic part of the Stranger. But how he did it! Who is this Stranger, who watches Arbenin and Nina from afar, appears for a moment during the masquerade and then reappears like the sentence of Fate? Undoubtedly it is another grim Byronic hero. He reeks of literature. But the Stranger has his realistic biography, too.

At one time, when he was a youth, Arbenin asked him in to play cards and robbed him clean of all his money, then laughed at him and turned him out. The Stranger lost the game of life at the threshold of manhood and swore vengeance. But what became of this Byronic avenger, who did he become? I admire the young Lermontov. This is how his hero casts off his costume and shows a familiar face from behind his mask:

> I saw that money was this world's Czar,
> So I worshiped money. Years passed and I chased
> Like a ghost: health, riches, and beauty.
> The door to happiness was slammed in my face forever,
> I made then the final contract with fate
> And became what I am . . .

Who did the Stranger become—he, who is everywhere, who follows Arbenin and Nina's every step, who watches and observes? The Byronic avenger became an agent of Count Benkendorf's and his Secret Police. This is how Jasiukiewicz performed the Stranger, and for this reason his Stranger lived and stole the show. It was one of those sudden and unexpected revelations that happen in the theatre.

(1958)

"AH, THOSE ARE THE ROBBER BOOKS"

I have often tried to visualize the scene. After all, a new era began with it. If I were to write a play about the college years of Mickiewicz and his closest friends—Zan, Czeczot, Malewski nicknamed Jarosz, and a few others—the first Polish romantic generation, who acquired their academic knowledge at the University of Wilno and rebellion from Schiller, I would start with that scene. It was on December 20, 1819, at Wielka Street in Wilno. Czeczot came across Zan, who was hurrying to the university.

"How are you, Tomasz?"

"Oh, Janko, Janko. Go and see Jarosz. He's had a letter from Adam Mickiewicz. Quite a funny letter. He's sent a poem, too, but I could not make anything of it."

"Too high-flown?"

"I don't know. You'll see for yourself."

"And where are you going?"

But Zan was already on his way. Perhaps he was in a hurry to hear a lecture by Lelewel. Czeczot did not go to his law seminars that day. He rushed to see Jarosz (who was at the time Mickiewicz's closest friend in Wilno). It was he who had received the new packet from Kovno. Inside was the *Ode to Youth*. Zan could not understand it. In Malewski's lodgings Czeczot got hold of the sheet.

"I read; the writing is not too legible and this does not make it any easier. I read silently and this, too, is an impedimentum. I read, prejudiced. I think; why does Adam lay it on so, why does he strive to express these high thoughts and phrases? I finished. Jarosz is laughing. I don't understand."

All of a sudden, Malewski, usually so calm, began to shout at his friend:

"None of you understand. Such poems do not grow on trees. No, they don't. He hits the spirit of Schiller exactly, he does. What expressions, what fancy!"

It was the greatest name one could invoke in those days. To those twenty-year-old poets Schiller was a revelation. I have often wondered what a "book of the moment" is—a book that is read with flushed cheeks and a lump in the throat; a book that topples the world and lets it be built anew. In the years 1819–20 such a book for the youth of Wilno and Warsaw was a volume of Schiller's dramas, containing *Maria Stuart, Kabale und Liebe,* and above all, *Die Raüber (The Robbers).*

Some six months before the *Ode to Youth* Mickiewicz wrote from Kovno to his friend Jeżowski: "This morning, while lying in bed, I translated a little poem by Schiller, which you will find enclosed. Schiller has been for a long time my only and favorite reading. About the *Räuber* tragedy I know not how to write. No tragedy has made such an impression on me, or ever will. One must be in heaven or hell all the time when reading it; there is no middle place."

A few days later Malewski wrote back: "I am glad to hear that Schiller has been so much to your liking in your present sadness; in his great thoughts you will find, it seems to me, a true consolation. Schiller's youth was like yours. That thought has firmly struck me; perhaps Kovno will be for you what oppression and misery in the military school were for Schiller . . ."

Toward the end of September of the same year, 1820, Mickiewicz wrote to Jeżowski again: "I have read the last volume of dearest Schiller. How wonderful *Maria Stuart* is.

But they are all amazing. Take pity and send me something
German, for I have nothing to read in my better moments."

In the autumn of 1820 every month was meaningful.
Every month meant a great stride forward. While a literary
revolution is on, a week may mean an era in the development
of awareness. On November 25, Malewski wrote to Mickiewicz: ". . . would you read the translation of Schiller's
Jungfrau? It may prompt you to translate *Carlos* or another of
his tragedies. I have now read his terrifying tragedy, *Braut
von Messina*. I cannot describe to you the impression it
made on me. I am convinced that he who does not know
Schiller's dramatic works, only half knows him. But I agree
that he is dangerous for the young ones . . ."

Indeed Schiller was not safe for the young ones. Mickiewicz
certainly had him in mind when he wrote in *Forefathers'
Eve:*

> Ah, those are the robber books,
> The heaven and the torture of my youth.
> They twisted the roots of my wings
> And forced them upwards,
> So I could never now turn downwards in my flight.

The robber books! It was not a matter of literature alone.
On the title page of the second edition of *The Robbers*,
published in 1782, a young lion is climbing a rock and
tautening for a leap. The inscription underneath says: *In
tirannos*—against tyrants. The youth of Warsaw and Wilno
in the early 1820s were reading Schiller like a political manifesto—almost as, some decades later, *The Communist Manifesto* was read. They were certainly deeply touched by the
tragic fate of Amalia and the unhappy love of Charles Moor,
but above all else they read in *The Robbers* the sentence:
"What drugs will not cure, iron will; what iron will not cure,
fire will."

In vain did the radical Wilno group of intellectuals, talented posthumous children of the Enlightenment, jeer at
the stupid gentry, ridicule obscurantism, drunkenness, pom-

posity. The young generation knew that it was not just a matter of combatting stupidity and coarseness. Sentimental criticism of abuses or persuasion in the manner of the Enlightenment was not enough for them. They were sick of rationalist optimism. Schiller's dramas taught them how to hate oppression and scorn bourgeois philistinism. In them they found not only the impetuosity of their own feelings but the conviction that one cannot go on living in the existing world; that slavery kills dignity and thought; that class prejudice destroys love and happiness. Those noble revolutionaries of the future were immature, just as the twenty-year-old Schiller had been. So what? Reading *The Robbers* was dynamite.

The robber books! They were not just literature. When the police were searching a house, to find Schiller's books among the papers was tantamount to proof that the pernicious ideas of freedom were present there. It was the same with *The Communist Manifesto* a hundred years later. "In June 1819," wrote Askenazy, "it was revealed in Zamość that Second Lieutenant Ignacy Pogonowski, held in arrest there, was planning to capture the fortress, get the garrison on his side, and invade Galicia. That mad idea was soon betrayed . . ." Among Pogonowski's papers *The Robbers* was found. Niemcewicz wrote of him: "That rash youth, whose head was full of the writings of Schiller and other German hotheads and eccentrics, came upon the idea of killing the commander of the fortress, getting mastery of same, then invading Galicia and destroying it."

The robber books! It was not the making of literature. Eighteen-year-old Schiller was being choked by the iron discipline of the military medical academy maintained by the vicious and wild Karl Eugen, prince of Württemberg, one of the three hundred little tyrants oppressing Germany. Warsaw under the rule of Grand Duke Constantine and Senator Novosiltsov must have been like the German dukedoms. Let us read Engels:

"The entire country was a vegetating mass of rottenness

and abhorrent degradation. No one was well off. The local trade, commerce, industry and agriculture dwindled to the utmost limits; peasants, craftsmen, and owners of industrial enterprises felt a double oppression: that of a bloodthirsty government, and that of mismanagement. . . . There was neither education, nor any centres acting on the minds of the masses, nor any free press, civic spirit, or wider commerce with other countries; nothing, except villainy and selfishness. The entire nation was impregnated with the common, crawling, villainous spirit of huckstery. . . ." And on tyranny: "The princes were living only for their pleasures and debauched excesses, and permitted their ministers to do every despotic violence. . . ."

Let us now listen to Niemcewicz. It was not by chance that *The Robbers* was read in Warsaw and in Wilno as a great political pamphlet, as a contemporary book, as a topical drama. In 1821 Niemcewicz noted in his *Journals:*

"Why is it that we can only put down sad and violent adventures? Two journalists, Wyżewski and Dmuszewski, the actor, have been put in prison; the first because he printed a translation from the German papers that there was a suspicion that the Queen of England had been poisoned; the other because he printed an advertisement of a button maker saying he makes civilian and military buttons. 'What insolence!' Duke Constantine exclaimed, 'to put civilian buttons next to the military.'"

I suppose that many an officer of the 4th Regiment, many a cadet and future revolutionary, when back in his quarters from the parade in Saski Square, must have read *The Robbers* as a book about himself.

Novosiltsov's, Kuruta's, and Birnbaum's secret police were right. Schiller served as an identification mark for the revolutionaries. To quote just one other document, a literary one, *Tsarevitch Constantine and Joanna Grudzinska, or The Polish Jacobins* was a fascinating book and an excellent political pamphlet published in the first years after the 1830 Revolution. In it Czyński paints the portrait of a conspirator:

"You shunned amusements that others indulged in. When

your comrades spent long hours at balls and dances, you derived your pleasure from getting to know the Polish people: I saw you often talking to peasants, workers, even Jews. When others avidly read romances and learned alexandrines by heart, you amused yourself with Schiller, memorized passages of the *Jungfrau von Orleans*, and walking in long strides, repeated the words: 'One day truth will shine.' "

The robber books are never just literature. Often there is less literature in them than anything else. Or rather, what is literature happens to be their weakest part. At the recent performance of *The Robbers* I continually thought about the amazing fate of that great play. I tried to kindle in myself the enthusiasm of the romantics; to look at the drama with the eyes of the youth of 1820. I have to admit I could not. There are books so fruitful that every succeeding generation feeds itself on them anew. And there are books so vehement that they burn themselves out, as it were, within half a century. Still, they put the world on fire. Among such books are *La Nouvelle Héloïse* by Jean-Jacques Rousseau and Schiller's *The Robbers*. The influence of no other books written in the eighteenth century can be compared with theirs.

And yet, has the fire of *The Robbers* been extinguished as far as we are concerned? I am not quite sure. In the winter of 1918, when Tsaritsyn was rescued for the second time and the army of the White general Mamontov had been defeated, an amateur troupe of soldiers began reading *The Robbers* in a shed where the wind was blowing snow in through holes in the door. Let me quote Alexey Tolstoy:

"When the candle end had burned itself out and Kuzma Kuzmitch had gloomily spoken the last words of Charles who had recalled a poor workman while going to his terrible execution, Anisya and Agrypina began to wipe their eyes with the sleeves of their army coats. 'Some play,' said Latougin. And all agreed that Charles should not have killed his beloved Amalia in his anger, but should have taken her to his band and changed her. One has to correct this detail in

Schiller, or else the play—because of such a trifle—may not please the Red Army soldiers and bad effects may follow. It was decided not to kill Amalia, that Charles should tell her: 'Go home, you wretch.' And she will go, shedding bitter tears."

I believe what Alexey Tolstoy wrote in his *Way through Hell*. I am even convinced by the corrections introduced by the Red Army soldiers. That would, indeed, be a better ending. It is possible that even in this day and age an amateur group, directed by an inspired producer, might infect us with the vehement pathos of *The Robbers*. It is a play in which genius mixes with melodrama, in which the clarity and pungency of thought borders on naïveté, on every page. There is in it a hell of degraded feelings, but one must believe in that hell. The actors must believe in it. *The Robbers* will either excite and move us deeply, or be a dead play.

(1955)

"WHY DON'T YOU WANT TO WRITE ABOUT IT, GENTLEMEN?"

The production of Mickiewicz's *Forefathers' Eve* in Warsaw in 1955 was the most important event in the Polish theatre for ten years. We all felt this on the first night in the tightly packed auditorium of the Teatr Polski. The greatness of poetry and the presence of poetry are not one and the same thing. Mickiewicz's greatness has been written about by Poles and by foreigners. It is indisputable and has its rightful place in history and in the history of literature. But there is also such a thing as a live presence; a dialogue, going on for a century, with someone who is physically present, like all of us, only greater than any of us.

Every Pole struggles with Mickiewicz as best he can. But every one of us needs Mickiewicz. Mickiewicz is read as no other poet is read. Without Mickiewicz one cannot imagine Polish literature. Without him, we could not imagine ourselves. And in this lies his real presence.

Mickiewicz's presence means the *Sonnets*, the *Lausanne Lyrics*, *Pan Tadeusz* and *Forefathers' Eve*. There are moments when one needs artistic perfection above all else, if only to match oneself with the highest model. The verse of the *Sonnets* is definitive. One can experience the *Sonnets* emotionally, or they may leave one cold, but it is impossible not to experience their perfection. Nothing better has been written in Polish. They are definitive in the artistic order, just as the *Lausanne Lyrics* are definitive in the moral order.

Only the *Sonnets* remain in moments of defeat and utter despair, when all other poetry is dead. Without the *Lausanne Lyrics* things would be harder still. This is the most difficult personal meeting with Mickiewicz; so personal that it is hard to share the experience; happy are those who have not had that meeting.

Pan Tadeusz is different. One reaches for that book after a few months out of Poland. One simply has to read it and send it to every Pole who has gone abroad. It is the only book that can be a substitute for Poland. Maybe that is why it is best to read *Pan Tadeusz* outside Poland. At any rate, one reads it somehow differently. It is a book about a Poland that does not exist and, perhaps, never did exist. And that is why it is a book about a Poland that has always existed, but only in dreams and in longing. *Forefathers' Eve*, on the other hand, is about a Poland that really exists; about Poland in all its greatness and all its tragedy.

At the first night of *Forefathers' Eve* people cried—in the orchestra as well as in the balcony. Government ministers were crying, the hands of the technical crew were shaking, the cloakroom attendants were wiping their eyes. *Forefathers' Eve* moved and shocked and became the subject of discussions going on long into the night. I know of no other drama in the whole of world literature that could move an audience after a hundred and twenty-five years as *Forefathers' Eve* did. *Forefathers' Eve* struck home with greater force than any play written since the war, in its historical aspect as well as in its contemporary relevance.

Forefathers' Eve is the most modern Polish literary work of the first half of the nineteenth century. There, for the first time, the hero of a new era appeared on the stage, without the trappings of historical costume. He had shed his Byronic mantle and spoke his own truth, shouted it rather, and so loudly that the shout is echoing still. Time did not consume the play's modern spirit, and it still haunts us today. There is dynamite in *Forefathers' Eve*, and it exploded on the first night.

The main plot of the play is a dramatic biography of a young revolutionary noble, jotted down by Mickiewicz when the events were still fresh, in large chunks, each of which meant a revolution in poetry and an era in the growing-up of a generation. In France the story of the same generation, people born around 1800, was described by Balzac, Stendhal, and Musset in such detail that we know the cut of the heroes' jabots, the color of their waistcoats, the amount of their laundresses' bills, and the price of conscience. Mickiewicz wrote only the essential things about his generation, but they were enough. *Forefathers' Eve* is a fragmented work, like a rock blown to pieces by an explosion; a work that seems to be the opposite of composition and order, that grew spontaneously, its main parts divided by a decade. And yet, it falls into chapters, each of which contains a complete version of the most important experiences and conflicts of that generation.

Forefathers' Eve meant the experience of folklore, at a time when villages where cottages had no chimneys were being discovered as well as folk songs; peasant grievances as well as old legends; a living source of new poetic truth, a morality more human than the humanism of the libertines and more earthly than the stoicism of the belated successors to the Enlightenment. The social biography of the generation and the romantic's own life story begin with the encounter with the people.

One had to go through love in order to grow up to face one's time. The romantics did not invent unhappy love, they merely experienced it as a struggle with the real world. To them it was the most personal experience of social injustice. In the fire of that love, or rather in its hell, sentimentality melted and turned into vehemence and the true feelings of a free man. A man was free when he had rejected the catechism and learned to despise feudal prejudice. Because of that, Gustaw in *Forefathers' Eve* talks a different language from all the previous lovers in our poetry. He is the first portrait of modern man in our literature. In his great lyric fugue Mickiewicz shows his entire generation's intellectual and emotional coming-of-age, from its first enthusiasm for the "robber books" to its rebellion against the mighty.

The third great chapter in the generation's history was the conspiracy. Only a few of the best took part in it. A historian today can describe all the various stages in the development of youth's political and social awareness before 1830—their illusions and dreams, the immaturity of their revolutionary thought, the naïve republicanism and the loneliness of the conspirators. But the great metaphor of the history of the generation will still remain the inscription chalked on the wall in the prison of the ex-Basilian convent: GUSTAVUS OBIIT—HIC NATUS EST CONRADUS.

Mickiewicz's artistic audacity is amazing. He made his personal experiences into a great chapter of the experience of a generation and then showed in a breath-taking condensation the historical path that led to the conspiracy and to the outbreak of the rising on a November night in 1830. Into his poem he put his friends, without changing their names; he did not shrink from the most brutal facts, but took in huge chunks of real life and spat them out like a volcano. In world literature there is no other drama that has made such a tremendous impression by quoting authentic events. Mickiewicz was grasping history in the raw, as it were, and grappled with its drama without resorting to fiction. And so it was: the heroes he had chosen were making history.

Wilno was too small a stage for Mickiewicz's drama. From there he moved his scene to a Warsaw drawing room and to a country house near Lwów. All Poland was the scene of his drama; his actors—the young, the cadets and writers, the patriots and the traitors, Novosiltsov with his henchmen and spies, and Bestuzhev with an outstretched hand. Carts were taking those condemned by the czar to the north, but north meant also the light from the December night's uprising in Senate Square.

The fourth chapter in the history of his generation consisted of the noble revolutionaries' "road to Calvary" and their attack on Heaven. Here Mickiewicz reached the utmost limits of poetry, enclosing the tragedy and greatness not just of the first generation of revolutionaries but of all generations up to the present. At this point the dynamite of Part III of *Forefathers' Eve* explodes, and we experience the immediacy of the poem. This must be said clearly: we are still attacking the Heaven and in this great attack Mickiewicz is on our side. *Forefathers' Eve* is for revolution and for the vehement champions of justice. In this too lies the greatness of Mickiewicz's "arch-poem."

The most living element of *Forefathers' Eve* in its recent production turned out to be the political drama. It revealed all its force, in spite of a traditional interpretation. For Mickiewicz's contemporaries, *Forefathers' Eve* was a work about themselves. Its hero was a living man who loved, rebelled, struggled, and despaired; who experienced romanticism, friendship and democracy, conspiracy, uprising and defeat just as the best of his generation experienced them at the time.

In *Forefathers' Eve* spirits talk about earthly matters, and people attack Heaven. Mickiewicz is as necessary for our theatres as air; not only as theatre, but also as moral.

"LET THE POLES PRAY, RESPECT THE CZAR, AND BELIEVE IN GOD . . ."

Słowacki wrote *Kordian* in 1833 as his personal reaction to both the Polish Uprising of 1830 and Mickiewicz's *Fore-fathers' Eve*. The play is all literature, splendid literature but only literature, whereas *Forefathers' Eve* is truth itself. To compare the two works does not necessarily mean to put one against the other. Słowacki himself provoked comparisons; he wrote *Kordian* as a challenge to Mickiewicz, as his reply to *Forefathers' Eve*, Part III. Indeed, one cannot help but compare. Looking at *Kordian*, one experiences once again the greatness of *Forefathers' Eve* in all its aspects: erotic, patriotic, revolutionary. The spectre, ghost of Gustaw, "dead for this world," is a hundred times more real, modern and convincing than Kordian, for all his subtle psychological motivation and dramatized personal biography.

How much more compact, full of detail—historical, moral, political—seems the dramatic substance of *Kordian*. And yet it is not so. Mickiewicz is content with the ceremony of village exorcism; a wild, mad soliloquy on the bitter taste of love; the great metaphor of Gustaw's transformation into Konrad (which is only a metaphor, for where is the transformation in the drama itself?); an argument with God, which is like a knife fight; a crude scene in the Wilno prison; two visions; a Warsaw drawing-room scene of a few hundred lines; the mystic raving of Father Piotr; three torture scenes;

the thunder of divine justice, and the image of prison carts going north. From this disordered chaos of fragments arises the complete drama of the first generation of revolutionaries: their love and struggle for freedom, their attack on Heaven, and their road to Calvary. In fact, the drama repeats over and over again the last hundred and twenty years of Polish history. Compared with it, *Kordian* is only literature.

Kordian is an overpoeticized confession of a child of the age, a biography of a Byronic rebel made somewhat concrete, and a fairly realistic history of the youth of a Polish aristocrat. On another level, it is a kind of polemic against Mickiewicz's Messianism and poetic divination, a polemic conducted with big words and gestures, somewhat childish, rather rhetorical, but not without common sense. On yet another level, *Kordian* is a verdict on the leaders of the uprising and those responsible for its defeat, as well as a verdict on the uprising itself and its political immaturity. With amazing insight, Słowacki shows—not directly but through metaphor and sheer dramatic power—the loneliness of the conspirator. On its third level, *Kordian* in its direct dramatic substance is a picture of the so-called Coronation Plot against the czar, a great historical scene and a great lampoon, which spares no one: neither the czar, nor Grand Duke Constantine, nor Niemcewicz, nor the conspirators; not even Kordian, or the people. But the people in *Kordian* are a separate and most difficult problem.

There is also a fourth level in *Kordian*. It is another lampoon, aimed at the Poles:

> I will not be with them!—Let the word Fatherland
> Diminish in its sound to these four letters: Czar;
> Let love, faith and the language of the people
> Be lost in this word, in these letters!
> I will not be with them!—

For there have always been two Polands. *Kordian* is a lampoon on the pro-Czar and the pro-Vatican Poland, the opportunist and servile, praying, believing, and slogan-shout-

ing Poland; it is a lampoon on the Poland of little am-
bitions and big fears; the Poland of patriotic gestures and
acceptance of slavery; the Poland of empty words, easy tears,
and fear of revolution.

A producer must choose his *Kordian*. In 1956, Erwin Axer
chose the lampoon, the non-conformist Słowacki. To my
mind, he chose right. He chose the most modern, topical,
incisive Słowacki. At the same time, Axer's *Kordian* is the
least romantic of all possible *Kordians*, at least in the vulgar
sense of the word "romantic." It is an intellectual, skeptical
and ironic *Kordian*, a literary and very cold *Kordian*. I am not
using the word cold in any derogatory sense. It is merely
deceptive. Can an intellectual lampoon be hot? I do not
know.

(1956)

FREDRO, OR THE NATIONAL COMEDY

In 1809 the Napoleonic eagles entered Galicia with the army of the Duchy of Warsaw commanded by Prince Joseph Poniatowski. The campaign was almost bloodless and soon turned into a march of triumph. Galicia, annexed by the Habsburgs and incorporated into Austria in the first partition of Poland, saw Polish troops with their national emblems for the first time in forty years. Sons of the gentry crowded under the national flag. Young Aleksander Fredro joined the army with his brothers. He came of an old family which, thanks to advantageous leaseholds and purchases of land, was approaching the ranks of the aristocracy. Young Fredro received a commission and became second lieutenant immediately on joining.

He was then sixteen years old. Nothing, however, seems to show that he dreamed of a marshal's baton. In gay and dancing Lwów, where the principal regiments of the army were stationed, he gained quite a different kind of fame for himself. He wrote licentious and bawdy poems, which could have made even old Piron and Crébillon blush. The young second lieutenant must have been very frightened when he was ordered to appear before his major. His poems were, of course, the reason for the major's displeasure. He was not concerned with their subject, however, but reproached their author for a frequent lack of a caesura. "And so," confesses

Fredro in his autobiography, "I learned there and then of the existence of the caesura."

The major was a neo-classicist. That was the first literary education received by Poland's most brilliant comic playwright. His ordinary education had been given him at his far-off country mansion by a succession of tutors and teachers. But the boy had preferred fencing, riding, and hunting to books. It was historical events and his army service that became the school of life for young Fredro.

Fredro went on the 1812 campaign with Napoleon's army and reached Moscow. Then came the shameful retreat, starvation and frost, the hard crossing of the Beresina, typhoid in Wilno, and captivity. Fredro escaped and rejoined the army staff in Saxony. He became an ordnance officer, took part in the battles of Dresden and Leipzig, and with the remnants of the Polish troops accompanied Napoleon until his abdication. In 1814 he returned to Poland, rid of all illusions. From then on he devoted his summers to farming on his estate and his winters to gay carnival amusements in Lwów. Gradually he directed his attention to writing and reading.

By then he had graduated from the great school of life from which a number of excellent writers of the period came. I like to imagine Fredro warming himself by the same fire at a bivouac near Smolensk or by the Beresina as Stendhal, only ten years his senior. After all, they were both ordnance officers.

Those years gave Fredro his sharp and acute vision, his dislike of cant, affectation, and pomposity; imbued him with knowledge of life, bitter and tinged with sarcasm; gave him his unmatched familiarity with all human absurdities. For Fredro, as for Stendhal, n'être pas dupe must have become the most important motto to be obeyed. For a writer of comedies it was not bad training.

What he lacked was literary experience. But even in this respect, the war years had not been quite wasted. What had the young Fredro seen in the Paris theatres? Let him tell us himself:

"The French tragedy, although it boasted the then king of tragedians Talma, left me indifferent. Exaggerated speech, conventional movements, the monotony of alexandrines cooling all warmth could not please one who did not know anything about the three unities. On the other hand, vaudeville and comedy entranced me greatly.

"Some years later a happy chance brought to my house a Jewish antiquary who among his books had the works of Molière. I gave him a ducat for these masterpieces, which until that time had been almost unknown to me as I had had the opportunity to see only one of the master's comedies on the Parisian stage. Having taken such an immortal model for my guide, I began to see more clearly the dramatic author's calling and embarked on serious study."

The model of Molière accompanied the beginnings of Fredro's career as a writer of comedy, as it had accompanied the origins of Polish comedy in the Age of Enlightenment. Contemporary life, its heroes and conflicts had no place in classical comedy. It was Molière who taught the Poles how to depict modern man on the stage, how to mock ignorance, superstitions, and follies, how to educate society through laughter. Molière was the great teacher of the Polish comic playwrights of the Age of Reason. The best of them—Bolomolec, Zabłocki, Bogusławski—were brought up on Molière's realism. They did not, however, translate Molière literally. Often they treated his comedies just as Molière had treated Plautus, the traditional motifs of old French farce, or contemporary Spanish and Italian plays. They adapted him.

They set the action of their plays in Poland and endowed their characters with the realistically observed characteristics of their contemporaries. Tartuffe became a Polish hypocrite and was put in prison, not by Louis XIV but by Stanislas Augustus; Arnolphe from *L'École des femmes*, a petty nobleman who kept his Agnès in a Warsaw suburb; Monsieur

Jourdain, a Warsaw merchant mocked and ridiculed at the famous trade fairs in Dubno, in the Ukraine, where the Turkish envoy stopped on his way from Constantinople to the court of King Stanislas.

The comedies of Aleksander Fredro grew out of the great tradition of the Polish Enlightenment and were a continuation of the rationalist and realist literature of the second half of the eighteenth century, the literature that attacked feudal superstition and strove for social reform. But everything that represented progressive and radical thought before 1789 gradually became an anachronism after 1818, when Fredro's early comedies first appeared on the stage in Warsaw and Lwów.

Conflict between Fredro and the new literary generation was inevitable, for artistic as well as political reasons. Young poets discovered in folk ballads and legends not only new sources of artistic inspiration but also a moral pattern that condemned the feudal lord who lived from the slave labor of the serfs.

Fredro remained a total stranger to romanticism. By his station in life and his political sympathies, he was bound to the Galician aristocracy, which was loyal to the Habsburg monarchy, averse to all reforms, jealous of its privileges, fearful of the danger of revolution everywhere. The old Napoleonic soldier sincerely hated political conspirators and did not believe that any self-constituted rebellion could be successful.

The romantics attacked him in his most sensitive spot: as a writer of comedies. At a time when the national character of literature was regarded as its highest quality, he was accused of writing comedies that imitated foreign writing, and of praising tradition and the feudal past uncritically.

Yet Fredro introduced an immense variety of characters to the Polish theatre, among them, apart from old eccentric noblemen, small usurers and newly appointed counts, home-bred politicians and bourgeois upstarts, old Napoleonic soldiers and bankrupt aristocrats, provincial seducers and foppish scatterbrains—in fact the entire little human comedy of his time drawn with an incomparable irony and humor. No one could depict as well as Fredro gestures and customs, neighbors' conflicts and matrimonial strife, the style of courtship, all the fascinating everyday realities the great romantic drama left out.

Mochnacki, Goszczyński, and others of the generation of romantic revolutionaries were certainly wrong in their estimate of Fredro. But how could they not be? Let us imagine ourselves in their place. I asked myself that question while watching Fredro's *Man and Wife* recently. After all, if we had lived in that period, we would have found a common language far more easily with Mochnacki and Goszczyński than with the embittered count, who was so wise but so reactionary.

For people who devoted whole nights to talking about the spirit of history and peasant rents, about despotism and the republic, about the need to organize conspiracies and the stupidity of the gentry, about those who betrayed the uprising and the revolution in France—Fredro's comedies must have seemed unbearably boring and shocking in their political blindness.

Once more let us imagine ourselves in their place. They asked for great political drama. And, after all, they were right. They wanted a play dealing with the fate of the country. Again they were right. They wanted a tragedy in which the Hegelian triad of history would reveal itself with all its dialectical contradictions, and the spirit of history would appear as eternally revolutionary. In this, too, they were largely right, although their arguments were expressed in very involved language.

They were thrilled by Krasiński's *Undivine Comedy*. And now they were asked to watch two silly country girls who had read some nonsense about the magnetism of the heart and vowed not to get married, or an old feudal swashbuckler wrangling with a paltry provincial lawyer about a fence knocked down in some courtyard, or a count seducing another count's wife and maid. After all, they met those Wacławs and Alfreds, those old noblemen and notaries, Claras and Angelas every day, in every drawing room and in every little village, but they did not see anything interesting in them. Why should such dull figures be shown on the stage?

They wanted to see themselves on the stage, just as we want to see ourselves in the theatre today. They wanted to see on the stage the hero of their own time. They rightly saw such a hero in a noble revolutionary who breaks his ties with his own class. They wanted to share his feelings and passions, his anger, hate, and hopes. But Fredro showed them Mr. Jovial and the feudal museum that had been ridiculed almost a century ago in the comedies of the Age of Enlightenment.

How could they help being bored and shocked? They were blind to Fredro, but so were they to Balzac. Countess Rzewuska in her feudal Wierzchownia could read and admire Balzac, but Mochnacki or Dembowski could not. Balzac meant for them drawing-room romances suitable for the amusement of bored aristocratic women, who were not very moral either.

It is easy to point out what was absent in Fredro's writings. It is easy to show subjective blindness to social questions in that Galician count whom the very word "democrat" moved to anger. It is easy to show Fredro's class limitation and the fact that he did not, and did not want to, see much outside the feudal manor and the people from his "sphere." In Fredro there is not a trace of the romantic mythology that attempted to find an angelic soul under the Polish nobleman's coarse exterior. Fredro did not idealize his heroes, did not take patriots and conspirators out of them. And that was what both the naïve democrats and the defenders of feudalism could not forgive him: that Angela and Clara embroidered on their tambours instead of preparing bandages for the insurgents; that Gustav stole off for debauchery in the Golden Parrot, and did not say one word about the poor captive country.

In spite of the academic boredom of many productions, in

spite of the formalist tendencies Fredro had to suffer from between the two World Wars, the theatre remained far more loyal to the true Fredro than did the literary scholars.

The Warsaw production of *Man and Wife* by Bohdan Korzeniewski in 1954 presented Fredro as an acute observer of his time and his contemporaries, as an inimitable chronicler of the moral standards then prevalent, as a writer who had no illusions about the little world he described. Our theatre comes nearer and nearer now to the new Fredro: to the realistic observer of people and morals.

In all the performances I have seen of *Maidens' Vows*, there was always a sad, gloomy and tearful Albin walking about the stage, a *serious* Albin who, instead of amusing the audience, seemed irritating and annoying. In those performances Albin was brooding out of time, out of history and any authentic style of behavior. And yet the action was taking place in a small country manor near Lublin, three or four years before the 1830 uprising. Why is Albin sad? Why is he a walking fountain of tears? After all, he owns a sizable village and is an eligible bachelor; he has her father's agreement to marry Clara whose odd behavior is not to be taken very seriously. Well, Albin is sad and tearful because he must have read Mickiewicz's *Forefathers' Eve*, Part IV, and presumably also *La Nouvelle Héloïse* and *Werther*. Albin is for Fredro a sentimental and romantic lover who is courting his lady according to the precepts of a new poetic fashion, which Fredro heartily hated and mocked. Albin is the mockery of romantic love as Fredro saw it.

To my mind Fredro chose the name of Gustav with good reason. In that manor in the Lublin countryside he showed two styles of behavior, two ways of courtship: the gay and the sad. Gustav, the "Warsaw fop," a gay playboy, courts his young lady in the Napoleonic manner. After all, he has been brought up by his Uncle Radost who, in his time, was a gay fellow too, and well remembers the way love-making was done in the days of the Duchy of Warsaw.

What we can see, in fact, is the picture of the period; we

see men of flesh and blood, and everything becomes most amusing. For we cannot take seriously the "maidens' vows," or the love of Gustav who, after a night spent dancing at the Golden Parrot, manages to make Angela fall in love with him between breakfast and tea, by means of very simple "magnetism."

"He saved Poland from general melancholy," wrote a discerning critic about Fredro in the year of his death. But Goszczyński took the view that there was no reason why old feudal Poland should be saved from melancholy. He, too, was right, and that, perhaps, is why he could not see how audacious the ending of *Man and Wife* was. He wanted Fredro to be shocked and indignant, and could not understand that a writer who was not shocked and indignant need not be a cold and indifferent observer. He wanted big words and morals and could not find them in Fredro's masterpieces because they were not there.

There are only four characters in the play: the husband, the wife, the lover, and the maid. Only four characters and yet the play is a complete picture of an aristocratic marriage in the post-Napoleonic years. The husband is unfaithful to the wife with her charming maid, the wife is unfaithful to the husband with his closest friend, the maid leads them all up the garden path: she takes away her mistress' lover and then deserts him for the mistress' husband. All this is done without a single coarse word being spoken, during a twenty-four hour period, with due observance of the classical unities and all the elegance of eighteenth-century libertinism.

Psychological insight is accompanied by an amazing concreteness of time, place, and milieu; by an unerring feeling for style and knowledge of a thousand little details; by audacity and a passion to understand things. This is true, above all, of the ending.

When the husband and the lover have been duped in turn, when the wife's infidelity and the maid's slyness have been revealed, we expect a drama, or a scene of repentance. Nothing like that happens. Everyone fears only one thing:

ridicule. As Stendhal put it, every high society has a dread of ridicule. The husband and the lover prefer silence to being laughed at. Nothing has changed, except that a new maid will be employed in place of the old one, who will certainly find an excellent new situation. The husband and the wife sit opposite each other by the fire and . . . yawn. Everything will begin again from the beginning.

Neither Mochnacki nor Goszczyński was able to appreciate the wise and fruitful realism of Fredro. Their judgment was certainly immature. But were they totally wrong? I do not know. If I had lived in those times, I would certainly have written far more critically, far more violently about Fredro. I would have been wrong. But from my point of view I would have been right.

Let us not compare ourselves to the great dead. I am not Mochnacki. And let us not deceive ourselves, friends, that there is a Fredro among us today!

(1954)

WYSPIANSKI WITH A VERY POLISH FINALE

In 1957 Wyspiański's *The Liberation*, was a success—thanks to the right city, the right theatre, the right director; above all thanks to the right time. Time in this case has proved to be an extraordinary and unexpected director. I am quite sure that a year, even six months earlier *The Liberation* would have been puffed up, artificial and shallow. But suddenly it became a live and succulent *Liberation*—topical though not made to be so, contemporary though historical, modern though fin-de-siècle, very Krakóvian but not provincial, clear and precise though very much in Wyspiański's manner, traditional and yet anti-traditional.

Konrad enters the empty stage. There is nothing more theatrical than an empty stage. But here the empty stage of the theatre is the designated place of action and the entire building becomes the set. Konrad, too, is in his place; dressed in a black, flowing romantic coat and underneath, a black, tight, existentialist pullover. He has just left a university seminar, stuffed with Marxism, and gone to wash it all off in the cellar Under the Rams. In Kraków even a cellar is bound up with tradition. One cannot put out one's tongue without putting it out at ancient walls and tradition. One cannot jeer at life without jeering at literature, because in Kraków life is more entangled with literature than in any other city. Everything here, in a very natural way, becomes

theatre at once. Every gesture, therefore, every move of the
hand, every protest becomes, just as naturally, anti-theatre.

The conference of literary scholars, organized in honor of
Wyspiański on the fiftieth anniversary of his death, took
place in the great hall of the Jagiellonian University. Where
else could it have taken place? The hall is new, pretends to be
Gothic and has huge canvases by Matejko on the walls.
It has grandeur and very poor acoustics; it invites rhetoric,
false and pathetic gestures—there is something of a national
theatre about that hall. Even today everything is theatrical
in Kraków. In Wyspiański's time the total impossibility of
distinguishing literature from life must have been much
more stifling. Everything was the national stage, and on
that stage Wyspiański placed his anti-theatre. But his anti-
theatre, bitter and jeering, was absorbed by Kraków, became pathetic and, in its turn, a new national stage.

Warsaw defies all literary tradition. The memory of writers
does not become legend; rather it is preserved in biting
anecdotes. Even the literary street names are out of place in
Warsaw: they either ring false, or are too good to be true.
There is a Winnie the Pooh Street in Warsaw, on which
the National Bank of Poland has its headquarters. Just imagine the Bank of England being situated in London on
Mickey Mouse Lane, or Alice in Wonderland Street.

Wyspiański's theatre has grown into Kraków to such an
extent that one cannot even tell whether the famous real
life "wedding" between a well-known poet and a peasant girl
happened first and Wyspiański's Wedding was written later,
or the other way 'round. Even the landscape looks like stage
sets here.

No wonder then that the actor Zaczyk appears on the
empty stage of the Juliusz Słowacki theatre in a romantic
coat and an existentialist pullover. He is Konrad, and the
workers free him from invisible chains. In any other city,
in any other theatre, the scene would be pathetic, symbolic,
and in all probability unbearable. Here it looks quite natural.
After all, they all wear somewhat funny clothes in this city,

and have beards, real or false. This is true even at the University, not to mention in literary or theatrical circles! They are disguised as statesmen and scholars, as Marxists and Catholics, as revolutionaries of 1905 and as positivists of 1957. Wyspiański's genius consisted in placing the national drama in the theatre's dressing room: there he saw first Kraków, then all Poland.

A theatrical dressing room is not only grotesque but has something lyrical and pathetic about it. Lady Macbeth is holding a bloodstained handkerchief in her hand, but you can offer her a cigarette and make a date to meet her in the café. There is a kind of perverse fascination about meeting Lady Macbeth in a café. Her shadow will follow her from the stage to the café.

Wyspiański was particularly sensitive to that mixture of fiction and reality so frequently evoked by the theatre's backstage, to the artistic shock that occurs from an unexpected collision of real people and characters in a play. He shared with other innovators at the beginning of the century the sensitivity to the perverse beauty of theatre within the theatre and to the poetry of the "wings." But his sui generis "Pirandellism" was Shakespearean, Polish and Krakóvian, all at the same time; it was very serious, too. Dressing rooms were not only backstage; Kraków was a theatre dressing room for all of Poland. That was why Wyspiański's modernist anti-theatre became the new national drama. If everything was theatre, then anti-theatre of necessity became a struggle for the soul of the nation. Anti-theatre meant in this instance a national puppet show, a very special show that had to measure up to *Forefathers' Eve* and outgrow it, a show that imperceptibly became itself a new *Forefathers' Eve*. In this lay Wyspiański's greatness and his misfortune. A political puppet show, performed in the wings of a theatre in the shape of a national drama; a political puppet show turning into a national mystery play—in the whole of world drama there is nothing like it. There is madness and genius here, in equal proportions. But whatever one may say about it, it is above all theatre.

Time has blurred the literalness of the allusions and brushed away the dust of professorial commentaries from *The Liberation*. After fifty years or so the first act has become clearer and simpler, grown to the dimensions of a national grotesque.

The first act of *The Liberation* has always been produced half-ironically. But only now have Dąbrowski and Stopka, the director and the designer, given it the full flavor and clarity of a national puppet show. To my mind this is perhaps possible only in Kraków, on the original and authentic stage of *The Liberation*, where the actors do not have to learn traditional gestures but have them in their blood; it is enough for them to show themselves and the tradition in which they grew up, and they are funny—more than funny: they are authentic, beset by the same problems that Wyspiański had to deal with. A chorus of the Poles calls to the smoky stove, "Send us a miracle!" but the stove goes on emitting smoke. The stove goes on emitting smoke, and all are waiting; waiting for the romantic Godot. At last he comes. He does not speak, only motions everyone to rise. The stove goes on emitting smoke; the coming of Godot does not change anything.

The second act of *The Liberation* is a struggle with national stupefaction. It is a great scene of the national hangover which, all of a sudden, strikes us with its topicality. The late night conversations, the national drunkenness, the slow sobering-up. Konrad and his little antagonists called Masks throw all the national ideological clichés at each other: art and mission, nation and loneliness, greatness and love, action and duty, fate and history, until the moment comes when Konrad has had enough; when he dreams of one thing only: that he may live like a man in a country like any other; that Poland may stop being the Christ among nations, stop saving herself and the world; that foreigners may stop admiring how noble, unhappy, and proud Poles are; that things may be as they are elsewhere; that there may be censorship and order;

that thieves may be thrown out; that conversation may cease to revolve around the ultimate things; that there may be an end put to the maddening national stupefaction. And suddenly, in all this, there is a dazzling explosion of great poetry, the purest poetry written in Polish since Mickiewicz's *Lausanne Lyrics*. "I want, that on a summer's day, on a dry, hot summer's day . . ."

The late-night conversation is over; only a couple of Masks are hissing in their chairs. The hangover and the Polish Walpurgis Night are over. Konrad is sobering up. He will never again be an ideologue. And suddenly everything begins all over again. The national stupefaction returns like malaria. Konrad runs out and snatches a burning torch from Hestia's hand. Hestia is standing by a neo-classical tomb, dressed in a half-classical, half-modern dress, which looks as if it has been cut out of a bad drawing in an illustrated periodical of the early years of our century. She has style, because art-nouveau is an established style now; she is ridiculous, because art-nouveau is still ridiculous. The puppet show becomes a national mystery play. All symbols, all styles are now mixed up. A new madness begins. Shakespeare and *Forefathers' Eve*, theatre and anti-theatre, Polish peasants armed with scythes and the Greek Erinyes, Mickiewicz and Prospero—everything is muddled up. Konrad chases the Genius out and throws down the trapdoor the chalice with the romantic poetry of the tombs.

Wyspiański was undoubtedly a great precursor. One can find everything in him, from Pirandello to Giraudoux, García Lorca, Camus, Ionesco. He has theatre in the theatre, statues that talk, a split personality, anti-theatre, the drama of fate, the modernization of Greek myths, antiquity, Shakespeare and the puppet show. That syncretism was certainly part of Wyspiański's artistic novelty. But can a modern Wyspiański be shown today in isolation from fifty years' experience accumulated in the European theatre? Artistic means have become more sharp and subtle. Wyspiański was a precursor, but today we look at his theatre through all his conscious and subconscious heirs.

If *The Liberation* still remains intelligible to us, if we still partly find ourselves in it, if it has not ceased to be a national drama, the reason is that the stupefaction persists, that we are still poisoned by the fumes. Let us imagine how a French, Czech or Swiss bourgeois, or a Danish worker, or an Italian peasant girl would look at *The Liberation*. What would an Englishman, or a Dutchman, or a German understand of this play? The answer is, nothing; or at most they would see in it a document of Polish madness. Perhaps they are right. Unfortunately, it cannot be helped. We are on leave from a lunatic asylum. And that is why the Kraków production of *The Liberation* was, perhaps, the greatest theatre event of 1957. Bronisław Dąbrowski can be proud of himself; and so can Kraków. Wyspiański's ghost lives in that city. I do not want to live in Kraków, though that ghost sometimes haunts Warsaw too.

(1957)

MY LADY'S VISIT

In the last general election to the Sejm one of the candidates was a young and talented woman writer who had been born in the "Landowner Class," as it is customary to describe it on personnel forms. It is perhaps because of her origins that her novels about squires and peasants are bitterly authentic and seem to reflect vital human experiences. It is not, however, my intention to write about her novels. By some chance —or by some courageous and defiant design—she was a candidate from the same constituency where the now-divided estate of her parents was situated.

I do not know if the manor where she spent her childhood now has a Crops Protection Center, a tractor co-operative, or a village social club. I do not know if she spent a couple of nights there on her last visit. All I know is that her standing as candidate caused a great commotion in the district. The peasants had not read her books and must have been somewhat stunned when they heard the young lady from the manor encourage them to deliver their compulsory supplies to the state.

It does not matter whether this story is true. It might not have happened exactly the way I have described it. But one thing is certain: it is excellent material for a play, a specifically Polish play.

What kind of play could be written from this material? A comedy, of course. Not only because there was a happy ending and the peasants voted for the woman, but also because an ex-landowner trying to persuade her own peasants to establish a co-operative is a humorous figure.

Or she could be an ex-landowner who is an enemy and creeps into the family manor at night to let the potato bug out of the Crops Protection Center. I can see how that material could be used in a film: the brave boys from the state farm chase the potato bug through the fields and woods on thoroughbreds from the state stud farm.

There could be another variation: the ex-landowner is neither ally nor enemy, but simply the lady from the manor, with a degree in art history and a divorce from her husband. Or there can be the lady from the manor as a pure Platonic idea—without a life history, without a social background. She is and she is not. What happens then? We have Leon Kruczkowski's *The Visit*.

The first act is mainly about the potato bug. The Wielhorska estate, divided in 1945 among local peasants, has next to it a state farm and a Crops Protection Center situated in the palace. The old servant, who used to be a butler and is now a laboratory assistant, grinds in a mortar murderous nitrides to kill the bugs. The young girl assistant who is breeding the bug in a test tube is in love with the director of the Center, the son of a poor peasant. He is so busy trying to invent a biological means to fight the bug that he does not even notice her. There are also a peasant, an old man of the village, and an agronomist from the state farm. The old man is a relic of the past. The agronomist, whose name is Pszonka (a word rather similar to the Polish for potato bug) is talking through the window with the noble director of the Center. He starts some intrigue. From his first words we can see that he is an enemy.

It is May, 1952. The potato bugs in the test tube will hatch any moment now. We have just learned that the off-spring of twenty pairs of the bugs can destroy two or three acres of the potato crop. The picture of the village is now complete: everything is as it should be. But we still do not know what Kruczkowski needs it for. Then there is the young lady of the manor. For the last few days a mysterious stranger has been sitting in the evenings at the edge of the woods and looking in the direction of the manor. Just at the point when the potato bugs are hatching, a professor of art history visits the manor with his female assistant. On seeing her, the old servant who is now a laboratory assistant lets the jar of nitrides he is holding fall to the ground. We know now who the mysterious stranger is: Miss Wielhorska, availing herself of the absence of the director, has decided to spend a night secretly in the manor. The telephone rings: the Center announces to the district authorities the news that the bugs have hatched. This is the end of the first act.

The dramatic logic of the exposition is quite clear. The problem of the potato bug and the problem of the young lady of the manor have to meet. Either we will see the continuation of the familiar outline of a "productivity play," or Kruczkowski will do a volte-face and ridicule the insipid anecdote of the exposition.

Nothing like that happens. Kruczkowski treats the first act as only a framework, and the problem of the potato bug as an allegory. The second act is a new national drama, a great night when consciences are examined and grievances reckoned, when the ghosts of the landowning past appear before the ex-landowner daughter. There is something here of Wyspiański's *Wedding*, but it does not come off.

The first act is a productivity pseudo anecdote; the second, a national pseudo drama; the third, a popular pseudo vaudeville. In the morning, peasants throng in great numbers to the manor drawing room, now the club, where Miss Wielhorska spent the night. They come arranged in proper Leninist classifications: the poor, the average, the rich, the once-landless and the state farm workers, the party activists and the village authorities. They all say what they ought to say at such a moment.

Are they real people? No. Why not? The answer is simple. Can there be a conflict between a pure Platonic idea and

real people? There cannot. What can happen? Well, the pure
Platonic idea of an ex-landowner's daughter can see the class
divisions of the village. And, indeed, she does see them.

The Visit is a failure, no doubt about it. But could it have
been a successful play? Why did Kruczkowski fail in his grand
metaphor? The vital question is: Is there a national drama
in the visit paid by an ex-landowner to her family home?

Not long ago I was told a story whose authenticity I can
vouch for. In a small district town of Southern Poland, a
young hooligan got drunk, came out onto the street and began to shout: "When there is a change of regime, I shall
hang all Communists. They will all hang on the lampposts."
He was arrested and the case put before the prosecutor. The
prosecutor wrote on the act of indictment: "Immediate discharge. His threat was unreal. The regime is strong."

I rather liked what the prosecutor did. The regime is strong
indeed. The ex-landowner's visit to her family home can result in nothing. There is simply no drama. The case has been
settled by history.

(1954)

I remember the day when I was first invited to visit André Breton, one of the founders and the grand mogul of surrealism. In the hall hung a huge picture of a nude, larger than life-size, cut off just above the eyebrows. Breton introduced me to the photograph: "My wife—Monsieur Kott." Coffee was served at a round little table. Suddenly I felt something fall onto my knees. There were two female legs clad in stockings, with slippers on the feet and lace furbelows above; just like the real thing. "So that the guests do not get bored," explained the host politely. "I have two pairs of them. I press a button and they come down." In the window there was a painted cog and the inscription: DANGER DE LA MORT.

In those days surrealism meant to me a challenge thrown to the absurdity of the world and a confirmation of universal chaos. And a splendid game. We used to invent surrealist objects. I remember that at one competition the first prize was given to an iron with a nail driven into its base. It was an iron made pointless, a surrealist iron.

At that time I did not know Picasso's "Guernica," or Éluard's poems of the Spanish Civil War. The time was just after the Munich Pact. Every day a new strike was being proclaimed in the Red belt of the Paris suburbs. Demonstrators were marching through the boulevards. The Popular Front swept through everything like a storm. I used to attend meetings. The biggest rally was—I do not remember exactly—in the Val d'Hiv, or the big hall of the Mutualité. But I shall never forget the thousands of clenched fists. Even now, after nearly twenty years, I feel the bitter shame and bitter rage of those days. The speakers were La Passionaria and Langevin, Cachin and Herriot, young poets and old Sorbonne professors. After every speech all those present got up and sang, or rather roared: "Allons, enfants de la patrie, le jour de gloire est évité." Indeed, the days of glory were to be missed by France, for quite a long time.

I shall never forget the sight of that tribune. At its two ends stood two monstrously big chamber pots and in them were immersed two tricolor flags, so that only the staffs were sticking up. The national flag in a chamber pot! Only in France would such a thing be possible. It would be inconceivable in Poland under any system—in the days of the monarchy, before the war, or now.

I understood then for the first time that there were two kinds of surrealism; that surrealism can serve not only to poke fun at reality and to play with metaphysics; that it can be more than a cruel game; that it can defend the real world against crime and stupidity; that it can jeer and accuse. I realized that surrealism had shaped the modern imagination; that it could serve the purpose of moral indignation; that it could become a political weapon. "Morning star disperses monsters" is the title of one of Éluard's most beautiful poems.

I was reminded of those experiences of twenty years ago when I was watching a guest performance given in Warsaw by the student theatre "Bim-bom" from Gdańsk. It is a theatre of poetic and intellectual metaphor, using surprisingly fresh visual means. Bim-bom's "play at modernity" is not a disinterested one; it is soaked with politics. Surrealist metaphor and leaps of imagination serve moral indignation and moral revolution. This is the only reason Bim-bom is modern; it is not the metaphor or the sets they are using that are modern. It is the spring of 1956 that is new—the late and vehement spring. This spring must be matched by our imaginations, hearts and intellects. "Morning star disperses monsters."

Everything else has merely the semblance of modernity. A short time ago a few actors, friends of mine, came to see me and invited me to join their proposed venture of opening an experimental theatre. I asked about their intentions. They wanted to play Cocteau and Witkiewicz. I thought it rather sad. I had been thrilled by Cocteau's *La Machine infernale* twenty-five years ago. But even then I had realized that Cocteau had nothing of the impatient enthusiasm of Apollinaire, the mad hate of the surrealists, the sour irony of Giraudoux; that he was a smart compère in a big theatre-properties storehouse; that his Greek statues were made of sawdust, his angels of plaster; that his devils were simply scarecrows. Later Cocteau became a French Academician; he alone of all the avant-garde. No wonder—he never really belonged to it. With Witkiewicz, the matter is more complicated. I have recently read his *Farewell to Autumn*. I avidly read the book that was the 1925 equivalent of *Animal Farm*. Thirty years ago I admired the surrealist theatre. But a grown-up man cannot play post office with the enthusiasm of a child.

There were years when students attended meetings of the Marxist youth organization only for fear of being penalized if they did not. Then came a period when the work of youth organizations was to be "made attractive." Samba, jazz, cinema and social games were introduced. Tickets for a circus were bought. It was not politics that was boring, dead and killing, but fictitious politics.

This is the reason, too, why the most modern of all poems now published is the *Ode to Youth* by Mickiewicz, recently reprinted on the first page of the student paper *Po prostu*. It is the spring of 1956 that is modern. "Morning star disperses monsters." The new modernity of this spring is awesome. It is feared by monsters on either side. Monsters growl when they see how politics breaks into literary periodicals, how political poetry is being created, how politics pervades the theatre. Soon monsters will start defending the abstract. Have they not always been on the side of the abstract? After all, dogmas and scholasticism are abstract.

Still, "Morning star disperses monsters."

(1956)

SMOKY STOVE AND THE POLES

CHORUS OF THE POLES. We have been standing here for centuries,
And this stove has been emitting smoke.
In winter or in summer,
Smoky stove, smoky stove,
Ah, the geopolitical reasons
Are destroying us.

SMOKY STOVE. O, poor, poor stove am I,
For centuries this has been going on.

. . . .

In winter or in summer
I emit this awful smoke
And nothing, ah, nothing changes at all;
These Poles only play Chopin and pray,
Ah!

After a period of total silence, everybody now wants to be
modern and talks about it, writes about it, looks for it and
accuses everybody else of plagiarizing Western trends. And
somehow no one has noticed that one of the most authenti-
cally modern phenomena in our art was Konstanty Idlefons
Gałczyński's cycle of playlets, or rather, dramatized parodies
and fables, *The Green Goose*. A truly modern art not only
gets ahead of average taste but, with time, becomes clear and
mature, like good wine. The posthumous triumph of Gałczyński's theatre is one more confirmation of this law. *The
Green Goose* was always amusing, but now, all of a sudden, it

turns out that it was very wise. And this is one of the great surprises of recent times. Gałczyński achieved an amazing feat: he demonstrated how abstract humor, surrealist metaphor, and volatile flights of imagination can serve to defend common sense. In this Gałczyński is still disturbingly modern.

Before the war many of us had picked surrealist fruit from the tree of the knowledge of good and evil. The apple from that tree had a strange quality: whoever tasted it even once was left with an aversion to naturalism for the rest of his life. But we soon realized that in that apple there were also very large pips of nonsense. Gałczyński was one of the few European artists who were first to spit out the pip and go on enjoying the apple.

Great discoveries are always simple. We read *The Green Goose* so many times and yet never thought that they were brilliant scenarios for a puppet theatre. In the last couple of years Gałczyński has been a great success in our cabarets. His little plays have been produced in every possible way. But only the Groteska Theater in Kraków has now revealed the true Gałczyński by discovering two elements at once: the surrealist poetics of *The Green Goose* and a new kind of puppet show—a philosophical fable played by puppets. In other words, the Kraków theatre has discovered a modern puppet theatre for adults.

Only a puppet can be abstract and real, grotesque and lyrical, intellectual and poetic, all at the same time. I first realized this when, a few years ago, I adapted Voltaire's *Candide* for a puppet show. In that tale there is a scene where an old woman tells how during a famine one of her buttocks was cut off. Then she raises her skirt and shows the result. In the theatre the scene would be impossible or very vulgar. In a puppet theatre it has considerable charm. To give another example. Candide visits Cunegonde who has become the mistress of the Grand Inquisitor. The affectionate scene between the reunited lovers is interrupted by knocking on the door. Candide hides under the bed while the Grand Inquisitor gets into bed with Cunegonde. Candide takes out his sword and, piercing the mattresses from below, transfixes the Grand Inquisitor as if on a spit. This again is an impossible scene for the theatre and can be played only by puppets.

In the Parisian cabaret Fontaine des Quatres Saisons I saw recently one of the most interesting modern puppet theatres. I was thrilled by one item in particular. It was a striptease done by a puppet. The puppet ran onto the stage, danced, threw her slippers, stockings and dress off, then her brassière and panties. She went on dancing and . . . stripping. Then she shed her eyebrows and big eyelashes, her eyes, arms and legs, until finally only her trunk remained, whirling round faster and faster, like a spool—a hollow, empty spool. Striptease had been reduced to the absurd. There is a diabolic metaphor in that hollow spool.

Tradition and modernity meet in strange combinations. *Candide* too was a great *Green Goose* written in defense of common sense. Without the Voltairian tradition Jean Effel's splendid series of drawings about the creation of the world would probably never have come into existence. The Groteska Theatre in Kraków has made yet another discovery: looking for the visual shape of Gałczyński's comedy *If Adam Had Been a Pole*, the theatre found inspiration in Effel's drawings.

These intellectual relationships are very strange indeed: Voltaire and the poetics of surrealism; Gałczyński and Jean Effel. They are not, however, chance relationships. In Effel, as in Voltaire, a high-class abstract humor serves rationalist tradition and, as in Gałczyński, surrealist metaphor jeers at angelology and mysticism. It is a most effective weapon. One of my friends, six-year-old Marek S. from Zakopane, used to say his morning and evening prayers with great devotion. His mother gave him for Christmas Effel's book, *The Creation of the World*. A few weeks later the boy stopped saying his prayers. When his mother tried to make him pray, he declared with all seriousness: "God is humorous."

(1956)

"I'VE NO DRESSES, I PUT ON
WHAT I CAN FIND"

You cannot turn back a river with a stick. Exorcisms help only those who believe in the evil spirit. No one can force jazz enthusiasts to sing an aria from Moniuszko's *Halka* and dance the Krakóvienne. The jazz group called Studio 55 performed for a week in Warsaw to a full house, packed with fascinated youth every evening. I had not seen such an enthusiastic audience for years, whether in a theatre, or at authors' meetings, or at concerts. There was something of a mass hallucination about those performances.

When you listen to jazz for half an hour or more, it enters you bodily. You jump on your chair; your arms, legs, head move. But here jazz entered bodily several hundred absolute enthusiasts at once. They all seemed to have an absolute ear. Every sudden leap of rhythm, or the rising of a cadence, higher and higher, to the limits of sound, electrified them. They responded by shouting, stamping their feet and applauding frenetically. It was as if a storm were passing through the hall.

In newsreels one can often see spectators at a boxing match, a motorcycle race, or a cup final. Their heads move up and down, left and right, as if on strings. Great outbursts of shouting are heard from the stands every few minutes. The crowds clap or protest. It seems as if they will leave their benches and leap forward. But they remain sitting, though shaking in their seats. Something similar was taking place in this hall. A

boy sitting near the window tore his sweater off and began to
wave it over his head. The demon of rhythm entered those
boys and girls. As Mickiewicz wrote in *Forefather's Eve:*

> In my youth, in the middle of the highway,
> The winged bandit attacked me, stripped me bare.
> I've no dresses, I put on what I can find.

The winged bandit is jazz. At least for a considerable part
of our young people. Perhaps there is still a flavor of forbidden
fruit in this enthusiasm. But the theory of forbidden fruit
does not explain much. If jazz, born on Negro plantations
and in Negro saloons, has conquered two-thirds of the world,
it must fulfill some real needs of the inhabitant of modern
cities; it must somehow correspond with our time.

I have always regarded the theory of sublimation of in-
stincts as suspect. It smells of idealism. It is easy to observe,
however, that among alpinists the largest group has been intellectuals, writers, painters. Surely what they have looked
for in the mountains is not just solitude and scenery. Climbing
gives one a psychic shock. Every climber who has had to
hang on a rope and entrust himself to three fingers on a sling
knows this well. There is a need deeply connected with the
modern way of life for violent experiences and emotions, an
ever-growing need.

Alcoholics are cured by insulin shocks; the mentally ill
are treated with electric shocks. Doubtless jazz is a rhythmic
shock, a modern catharsis, a great discharge. Phenobarbital, too, soothes the nerves. And yet, there are ideologists of
jazz but none of phenobarbital. The psychotherapy theory
cannot explain the fascination of jazz.

I've no dresses, I put on what I can find.

It is very difficult to define what is modern. The mythology
of modernity is dangerous too. But the lack of things modern
kills like the lack of air. For most enthusiasts jazz is synony-
mous with the modernity they yearn for.

Modernity does not mean a negation of boredom. Such a
juxtaposition would be false. There is a very modern boredom.

But in our country—especially for the young—being modern means the opposite of being bored. This is signified even by modernity in dress: by hair styles à la Gérard Philipe, bright ties, wide colored skirts, black tight pullovers, and low-cut blouses.

I've no dresses, I put on what I can find.

The most accessible form of modernity in art is jazz; and that is how the young see it. Its brutal vehemence relates jazz to all modern art.

Exorcisms are no use. One must make a choice. You have either the pseudoclassic style, the Congress Hall of the Palace of Cuture, the Byzantine domes and Renaissance arcades, red plush, columns, gilded ornaments and canopies, pathos, the cult of appearances, rhetoric, sublimity and didacticism, or you have the discipline of rhythm and material, mockery, enthusiasm and artistic risk, passion and intellect. I have chosen.

Do I write all this in defense of jazz? No, I write in defense of the political theme of our art, so that it can begin to make an impact. For you cannot leave out things modern. If our time is associated with the old-fashioned, then our modernity is represented only by jazz and the three scooters one sees in the streets of Warsaw.

In the last program of the Students' Theatre of Satire there was a little scene worth remembering. Two girls come forward; one shows the other her uniform tunic of the Marxist youth organization and says, "I bought this a year ago, but I can't wear such a thing *now*." The other replies, "You have to alter it." She takes her own coat off and reveals the same kind of tunic, only with the sleeves cut off and an extensive décolletage baring her shoulders and half-showing her breasts.

I've no dresses, I put on what I can find.

What I am concerned about is simply that uniform tunics be made so that one does not have to alter them.

(1956)

HOW MUCH DOES
A NEW PAIR OF SHOES COST?

Dürrenmatt's *The Visit* is the kind of play that stays with us. While we watch the performance, we are more fascinated by its theatrical qualities than awed by the play as such. But when we have left the theatre, the play is not to be forgotten easily. It oppresses us inwardly, swells like an ulcer. It certainly hits a sore spot; it annoys and troubles us. That is true of audiences in the West as well as in our part of the world, though it is not easy to define the particular sore spot. We are almost at the point of naming it when it again evades analysis. Dürrenmatt's play is complex and ambiguous. There is something of a nightmare, of a grotesque, of a myth about it, as well as something of a German popular fairy tale. But the most important thing is that it annoys and disturbs one. Why does it have this effect?

Güllen is a small town somewhere in Central Europe. It was once rich and famous. Goethe slept in an inn here, here Brahms composed a quartet, and even now guidebooks give Güllen Cathedral two stars. There used to be foundries and other industries. Now there is misery and poverty. Güllen is just lingering on. International express trains go through Güllen as before, but they no longer stop. A local train stops in Güllen only twice a day. The unemployed come to the station and look at the trains. For years nothing has changed, nothing has happened.

But now, all of a sudden, the richest woman in the world,

the multimillionairess, Claire Zachanassian, is to come to Güllen. The mayor and teacher are preparing speeches, the local choir and the town band are practising, the unemployed painter is putting the finishing touches to the welcoming banner. He will not have time, though. For the first time in years, the international express train stops in Güllen: Claire has pulled the emergency brake. She steps onto the platform followed by her retinue: her husband, dressed for fishing, with a collection of fishing rods; her steward, then her tittering blind eunuchs. Servants carry her trunks, the cage with her leopard, and a big black coffin. A splendid litter—the gift of the French president, taken from the Louvre—is already waiting for her. The litter is carried by two gangsters, condemned to the electric chair at Sing Sing, but released at her request. One of them is carrying a guitar on his shoulders. Claire Zachanassian is human but relentless, ironic but genial. She is over sixty, has red hair and looks like a living mummy.

There is something of a bad dream about all this; also something of folk imagery, of sensational low-level journalism, and something of the atmosphere of Kafka. Dürrenmatt builds his theatre from a blend of all these styles and elements, a surprising, disturbing, and odd mixture. Above all, he blends the grotesque and terror in a new way. Already in the prologue there is an element of terror. The old lady—red-haired, dressed in black, made up of artificial limbs—is at the same time a modern Moira, the Greek goddess of destiny. That at least is how the teacher of Latin at the local grammar school sees her. But Moira of the twentieth century is the richest woman on earth, and her biography is only partly mythical.

Claire Zachanassian was brought up in Güllen where her father was a bricklayer. He even left a monument to himself in the station grounds: ladies' and gents' conveniences. Claire was beautiful and experienced her first love in Güllen. When she was pregnant, her lover left her and married into a local business. She ran away to Hamburg and lost the case for alimony because bribed witnesses swore she had slept with them. Her child died, she went into a brothel, then embarked on her career. Her first husband was a multimillionaire; among her subsequent husbands were princes, famous actors, even Nobel Prize winners. She can buy everything. She has come to Güllen to buy justice.

Her first lover is waiting at the station. Anton Schill, like everybody in Güllen, is poor. He has a bankrupt little shop, a wife and two children. He is sentimental, vulgar, and stupid. He is also old and weathered. But the people of Güllen believe that Claire has not forgotten him and that he will be able to get some of her millions to restore the prosperity of the ruined town. Claire Zachanassian, indeed, has not forgotten anything. Together with Schill she visits their old meeting places: a wood outside the town and a deserted barn. Leaves are rustling, birds are singing. But the author lets the people of Güllen imitate trees and birds. Surrealist pantomime accompanies the awesome meeting of the old lovers. Grotesque becomes more cruel because of that. And still the same irritating blending of styles. Poetic nightmare originated with Kafka and the surrealists, but Dürrenmatt endowed it with a theatrical expression of his own.

Claire Zachanassian has not forgotten anything. At a banquet given in her honor by the mayor she offers a billion—half of it for the town, half to be shared among its inhabitants. A billion for them to kill Anton Schill. She has come to Güllen to buy justice. After forty-five years. For her wrongs, for the death of her child, for the unjust sentence in her alimony case. The two false witnesses are present: they are the two tittering blind eunuchs. She searched for them all over the world, found them, let them be blinded and castrated. Now she takes them with her everywhere. The pair of eunuchs are grotesque and unreal. That is how the author wants them to be. Otherwise they would be unbearable.

The people of Güllen reject the offer of money. They are Europeans, they are humane. In their town Goethe spent a night and Brahms composed a quartet. They would rather remain poor. But Claire Zachanassian has plenty of time. She can wait.

Nothing has changed in Güllen. Except that in front of Schill's shop a coffin has been placed on which wreaths are put every day by the order of Claire Zachanassian. But no, something has changed. Everybody has new shoes. New, yellow shoes are on everyone's feet: the teacher's, the mayor's, the butcher's, even the police sergeant's. Even the priest—who in the Warsaw production was changed into a minister—has new shoes. More than that, he has bought a new bell for the church. Everybody is buying things—shoes, radios, television sets. On credit. Schill begins to be afraid. He smells blood in the air. But still, nothing has happened—yet. No one thinks about murder. It is just that they are buying everything, on credit.

Schill is afraid. He is the only one who knows that the town is preparing itself for a ceremonial murder. But when he speaks about it, nobody will listen; nobody will believe this, or admit it, even to himself. Schill wants to go away, to Australia. The entire town accompanies him to the station. Still no one touches him, no one stops him. On the contrary, they tell him to hurry so that he will not miss the train. But Schill does not have the strength to go away. He is numbed by his own fear. He sees a thousand eyes round him. He feels himself in a net. For the first time he begins to view himself with the eyes of others. This is a great scene from Kafka.

Now everything in Güllen is new. Even Schill has a splendid new shop, bought on credit. His wife has bought a new fur coat, his daughter amuses herself, his son has bought himself a new American car. They have all bought themselves cars. Schill had been a poor pushcart owner. He had done what every one in Güllen would have done in his place, no better, no worse. Who would not want to marry into a shop? Later he thought, as they all did, that his guilt was cancelled by time. Then he began to be afraid. Now he is not afraid any more. He realizes that they all have inwardly accepted his death; even his wife and children. He himself has resigned himself to his death. He has understood the mechanism of it. If such are the laws of life, life is not worth living. One cannot defend oneself either. But Schill will not commit suicide. He does not want to make the choice easy for them. They have to take his death upon themselves. Claire Zachanassian is buying justice for a billion. But they can buy a billion only for a murder.

They will buy. All of them: the mayor, the priest, the police sergeant, the teacher and the butcher. But they will buy their billion not for a murder. After all, Claire Zachanassian is buying justice. So Schill will be murdered in all the majesty of the law, in the name of morality and ideals; he will be murdered by everybody and by nobody. How could he not accept such a death?

The people of Güllen parade on the stage joyful and smiling. *The Visit* ends with an apotheosis that reminds one unmistakably of the finale of socialist realist plays. The people of Güllen sing and dance, wave flags, sing a hymn in honor of welfare and art, freedom and peace, justice and Claire Zachanassian.

If *The Visit* had been an ancient tragedy, Claire Zachanassian would appear in the doorway of Anton Schill's shop. In her eyes he would see Moira's sentence. In the air there would really be a smell of blood. The Erinyes would appear and hunt Schill down. A catharsis would occur, and we would feel relieved: justice, albeit a cruel one, has been done.

If *The Visit* had been written by Ibsen, Claire Zachanassian would return to Güllen as an old beggar woman. Schill would meet her every day, motionless and withered, at a street corner or in front of the church. She would never speak a word. But Schill would not be able to look her in the face. He would confess everything to his wife. His wife would leave him, taking the children with her. Schill would remain alone, with the wrong he had done years before. He would end with a suicide. We would feel relieved: the account has been settled.

In Dürrenmatt's *The Visit* the account is settled, too. But its price is a new pair of shoes for every inhabitant of Güllen.

Claire's billion has been involved in the moral order. This is much too much. Because of that, it is not a play about Anton Schill's crime and punishment, or about justice. Nor is it a domestic drama with a moral. There is terror in *The Visit*, and the terror makes it modern.

Before the war I used to go to a hairdresser in Warsaw's Chmielna Street. He was called Jozef, was a reactionary, told bawdy jokes and anecdotes about Jews. But one day I found him pale with indignation. The windows of another hairdresser opposite, who was a Jew, had been smashed by Polish fascists, the Piasecki group. "We are Catholics, we are Europeans," repeated my hairdresser. "This is shameful." I passed by that way a couple of years later during the German occupation. Jozef was then occupying the ex-Jewish establishment where the windows had been smashed. I was on the point of stepping inside for a haircut, but someone warned me just in time: Jozef was in the habit of blackmailing his old Jewish customers.

That, of course, is only one real-life experience one could read in Dürrenmatt's play. There is also something in it of the wartime atmosphere of Switzerland, the country situated on Hitler's doorstep, which was then trading and getting rich. What else could Switzerland do when paralyzed by terror? Certainly, too, there is in the play something of 1956, much of the climate of West Germany, of the feverish prosperity coming in the wake of destruction and death.

"Claire Zachanassian is not a personification of justice, or the Marshall Plan, still less of the Apocalypse" wrote the author in his postscript to the play. Perhaps he became concerned with all its modern, topical allusions when it sounded in German from the stage? Perhaps he was right. I have no wish to simplify the brilliant play, or to impose one definite meaning on its metaphors. To my mind the venom and the terror it contains are more universal than all the allusions one can think of. In *The Visit* there is a deep conviction that one can make people do anything—and quite cheaply, too—for the price of a pair of boots. They will agree to a collective murder, and when they have committed it, will convince themselves that they have done it in the name of justice and ideals. This is one modern aspect of *The Visit:* the evolution of ideology from practical actions, ideology at any price, not on somebody else's order, but of one's own accord, simply in order to live.

It so happened that a few days after the first night of *The Visit* I read Henri Alleg's shocking account of how he had been tortured by French parachutists in Algiers. I was reminded of scenes from *The Visit.* In Dürrenmatt's play there is certainly the underlying awareness that in the last thirty years country after country has been gripped by a wave of torture. Every time, people are tortured and killed in the name of justice and the highest ideals. And every time the people of Güllen accept it.

(1958)

DÜRRENMATT

Romulus breeds poultry and behaves like a clown. From the day he became emperor twenty years ago, he did not once go to Rome, or even leave his residence, which he turned into a poultry farm. He gave his hens the names of Roman emperors. Every morning he eats an egg laid by Marcus Aurelius. Domitian lays well too, but Romulus does not want to eat his eggs, because Domitian was a bad emperor. Meanwhile German troops are occupying the whole of Italy. Romulus does not want to have anything to do with matters of state. He breeds poultry, drinks wine, and reads Catullus in the evenings.

Romulus has a clear historic sense. He knows that the world, or at any rate his world, is coming to an end, that he is the last of the Roman emperors. The scenario of his reign was written beforehand. In it he was given the part of the last emperor. He cannot alter the scenario, or choose a different part for himself. He can only play his part differently. Dürrenmatt's "unhistorical historical comedy" is a play about the attitudes one can adopt toward history; it is as poignant a play as *The Visit*.

In his *Reflections on History* Witold Kula makes the interesting observation that representatives of declining classes are often accused of imprudent or irrational behavior. He goes on to consider whether representatives of declining classes can behave rationally at all, that is to say, whether one scenario dictated by history offers them any sensible solutions. Louis XVI certainly behaved imprudently. But it is very difficult to say how he could have behaved prudently at a time of revolution and in his particular situation. Did he have any good solution?

We often declare that we are living on a volcano. Let us for a moment regard this saying not metaphorically but literally. Let us imagine that we are really living on the gentle slopes of a cone-shaped mountain coming down to the sea. At the summit of the cone is a hole, which begins to emit first smoke, then flames, and finally streams of lava. The mountain is surrounded by sea, but there are no ships, or at best nothing more than a couple of half-rotten rowboats. What can one do in such a situation? Can one behave sensibly?

It seems that there are at least four attitudes worth considering. The first is to go on breeding poultry and refuse to have one's breakfast disturbed even by the most alarming news about the progress of the lava. Not to accept the fact that the volcano exists. Not to let oneself be driven into eschatology. To live as if nothing had happened. Such an attitude has something of buffoonery about it, but it is also stoical. It is the volcano alone that, in the last resort, will decide whether that attitude will seem clownish or stoical. If the streams of lava suddenly cease to flow, the adamant poultry breeder will seem a madman or a buffoon. After all, everyone else tried to save themselves or to save others, but he went on eating soft-boiled eggs. If, on the other hand, hot lava swamps everything and the poultry breeder dies during his breakfast, our view of him will be different: his attitude will seem to us stoical and sensible.

The second attitude is to recognize the eruption of the volcano as a historic necessity. The volcano then becomes a kind of deity to which one ought to pray. If one is to think with more precision, this situation involves two variants: to rationalize eschatology, or to give it the attributes of myth. If the first is adopted, then instead of saying their prayers, philosophers argue rationally the necessity of the volcano's eruption.

The third attitude is heroic or grotesque. One has to fight the volcano: build barricades against tongues of liquid fire, glue paper crosses onto windows, dig shelters. The island is to be saved at any price. Camus in *La Peste* seems to defend this kind of attitude. The plague is to be resisted irrespective of the chances of victory. The threat of plague is a permanent condition. The plague is eternal, only its intensity can vary. But in this case, too, it is the volcano—or the progress of the plague—that will, in the last resort, decide whether this attitude is heroic or grotesque. If the plague has been checked, the struggle at any price means a heroic attitude. If, on the other hand, the lava has engulfed the island and all have died, then the building of barricades from sacks of sand against the sea of fire must seem to us a not very sensible and rather grotesque attitude.

The fourth attitude is trivial: business as usual. The eruption of the volcano creates a demand for masks and anti-radiation suits. After all, one can sell even tombstones. Sometimes one can even do business with the volcano. The world-wide firm of Caesar Rupf, trading in pants, takes into account in its calculations even cosmic disasters. The fourth attitude—as our wartime experience proves—has been the most common of them all. But in the face of the end of the world, it too seems grotesque.

My comparison of history to a volcano has one drawback. A volcanic island can disappear from the face of the earth, but the world and its history remain. Only individual civilizations die; one world dies, another is born. The Apocalypse is subjective: it can have a national or a class character. History does not know the Apocalypse. Or to put it in a more modest way, up to now history has not known the Apocalypse. The prospect of an atomic death would be the end of history, at any rate of human history. For this reason it cannot be rationalized in historical categories. There is no sensible attitude in the face of the end of the world.

Dürrenmatt's play deals with such an end of the world only marginally. There is in it something of the atmosphere of atomic disaster, but it can be interpreted far more simply as dealing with the end of a definite world and the beginning of another, in other words as a historical play; except that it concerns not past but future history, is a kind of history-fiction. But because of that *Romulus the Great* gains in poignancy.

The last of the Roman emperors breeds poultry, but he only pretends to be a clown. In fact he hates Rome and wants to hasten the end. It is even not so much that he hates Rome as that he is disgusted by her. He is disgusted also by what is to follow: the Germans and all future history. He loathes the entire grand scenario, so he adopts the part of a clown, regarding it as the most effective and human. He pretends to be a clown, but also wants to be a judge, a judge of at least that part of the world to which he belonged. He wants to control fate and speed it up; to bring about Rome's downfall and then to die. His own death is for him a moral argument. But he does not succeed in this. The first situation discussed in my metaphor of the volcano has occurred. History is not a volcano, and disposes of worse traps. In the bad scenario given him by history, Romulus desperately wants to preserve a sensible, dignified and stoical attitude. But there are situations in which one can choose only between grotesque attitudes, for other attitudes have not been provided by the scenario. In demonstrating this Dürrenmatt has shown his sting.

The best scene in the play shows the stupid and grotesque Romans who want to repeat with Romulus the events of the Ides of March. They hide in wardrobes and under the bed in Romulus' bedroom. They are draped in black mantles, armed with daggers. All of them are present: the heroic prefect of cavalry and the cretinous minister of the interior; the heroic Emilianus who has just returned from German captivity and the half-witted minister of war, the emperor of the Eastern empire, who has asked for asylum, and Romulus' cook. They hide in wardrobes and under the bed to demand that Romulus account for the war that has been lost and the downfall of the empire. But they do not really know by now in the name of what they are acting. Alas, the Ides of March cannot be re-enacted in any situation. The scenario provides for only a grim grotesque. The Roman generals, the emperor of the Eastern empire, Romulus' family and his cook can only board a rotten raft and drown.

Romulus remains alone. He is eating an egg and waiting for death. He is the only one not to have escaped. But he only thinks he has been in control of his fate and that he will not lose face. He counts on being murdered by the Germans. But Odoacer has no wish to murder him. On the contrary, he first pays homage to him, then proposes that he should continue to be emperor, and finally pensions him off. Romulus accepts this, for he knows that suicide would not solve anything at this stage; he is mature enough to see this. The last emperor going into retirement after the fall of Rome is tragic in a way, in the grotesque way. There never was any other role in this scenario, as it happens.

In this play there is also a view from the other side—not from the end, but from the beginning of the new world. This is not very encouraging either. Odoacer—not unlike Romulus —breeds pedigreed cattle, only his results are better. He is a practical man and makes deals with history. He hates war but knows he is the leader of a people who live by war. So he wages war. He tries to do this as humanely as possible, but does not succeed: his generals and soldiers become more and more cruel. It is also too late to withdraw from war. This very Shavian Odoacer, too, has historic superconsciousness. He knows that all this will lead to the establishment of a German empire that will be even worse than the Roman was; and that in the end he will be murdered by his own nephew.

Odoacer makes deals with history, but history gets the better of him. He succeeds much better with cattle breeding. He is not able to alter the course of history. He realizes he did not get a very good part in this scenario either. After all, it is not a very good part to be murdered by one's nephew.

His nephew is the only character who is satisfied with his part. In the play he is a well-behaved boy, who constantly repeats: "Yes, dear uncle," "Of course, dear uncle," "At once, dear uncle." He has no doubts or scruples. He simply draws and puts back his sword. His name is Theodoric. One day they will call him Theodoric the Great. He will murder both Odoacer and Romulus.

(1959)

THE DEVIL'S LOGIC

At the beginning there is the belief in the devil's existence, or rather in his constant presence and omnipotence. If the devil exists, witches must exist too. Until then there was only metaphysics. But the appearance of witches involves the social mechanism. Witches appear when they are needed, just like miracles.

The devil's logic is irresistible. It also lies in the fact that the devil is a safeguard of good. The devil is outside, which means that everything inside is good. Children die, women are barren, a husband is unfaithful to his wife, there is a cattle plague. One can assume that the world is evil, or that people are evil, or that medicine is worthless. But if the world is good, and people are good, and medicine excellent, one has to assume that the devil exists.

The devil's logic is rational, and quite horrifying in its rationalism. One has only to assume the existence of the devil and everything fits. Evil that has no cause is irrational; it leads to doubt and to blasphemy. One blasphemes against God, or medicine. But if God is good and medicine is good, the devil must exist. One has either to doubt the existence of the devil, or not believe in medicine. But medicine is rational; medicine is a science; medicine cannot be wrong. Still, children are dying, so the devil must exist. A rational man cannot doubt medicine, so a rational man has to believe in the devil. This has been the infernal devil's logic, from *Faust* to Senator Joseph McCarthy. Without the existence of the devil, the world is neither fully logical nor able to be totally rationalized. And so simple people and clowns have always believed that logic was the devil's invention.

The devil's logic is precise and sophisticated. The main proof for the devil's existence is the people who do not believe in him. For, had the devil not possessed them, they would believe in him. Arthur Miller observed this devilish logic in the work of the House Committee on Un-American Activities and demonstrated it in the example of a witch hunt in a small Puritan community in the colony of Massachusetts at the end of the seventeenth century. The devil's logic is irresistible. If the devil exists, witches also exist. If one witch is found, a hundred witches will be found. The devil's logic consists in multiplying witches. A person accused of witchcraft can admit to having seen the devil or can deny his existence. If one confesses to having seen him, one is lost. If one denies it, one is also lost, being doubly a witch: possessed by the devil and not believing in him. The more obstinately the accused denies the charges, the more dangerous he must be. Such a person is trying to destroy the social order, which is based on the existence of the devil, and is an enemy to society.

In practical terms, a person accused of witchcraft has only one way out: to admit that he has seen the devil and to renounce him. But there is only one way in which one can renounce the devil: to confess with whom one has seen him. For the devil ex definitione never walks alone. A witch must find new witches. The first trial for witchcraft raises doubts, mistrust, often indignation. But every trial that follows is more credible and trustworthy. Every trial not only collects proofs for the next one, but is a proof in itself.

In his introduction to the collected edition of his plays Miller describes the motives that led him to write *The Crucible:* "It was not only the rise of 'McCarthyism' that moved me, but something which seemed much more weird and mysterious. It was the fact that a political, objective, knowledgeable campaign from the far Right was capable of creating not only a terror, but a new subjective reality, a veritable mystique which was gradually assuming even a holy resonance. I saw forming a kind of interior mechanism of confession and forgiveness of sins which until now had not been rightly categorized as sins."*

The devil's logic also implies that in a trial for witchcraft everyone must take part, as accused, prosecutor, or witness. There are not really witnesses in such a trial, because witnesses, too, are either the accusers or the accused. If they believe in the devil, they will be those who accuse; if they do not believe in the devil, they will be the accused. There is not really a division between the accused and the accusers. The accused, if they do not believe in the devil, sentence themselves; if they do, they sentence others. The accusers, because they believe in the devil, have to believe also in the possibility of being themselves tempted by the devil. The accusers are the potential accused. In a witchcraft trial everyone is suspect. Thus the devil's logic is impeccable. There is no escape from it, since to deny the existence of the devil is the proof of his existence. The devil's logic is the price of fear; not only fear of imprisonment and death, but fear that medicine can prove false.

I saw *The Crucible* for the first time more than two years ago as a graduation performance at the Kraków Theatre School. The ministers, judges, sheriff, and governor were all acted by young graduates. Boys find it more difficult than girls to play older persons. In fact, the actors remained boys dressed up as adults. They were an organized group of choir boys who received authority not only to expel their sinful colleagues from school, but also to expedite them to the next world. The tenor of that school performance was even more awesome than that of the "adult" Warsaw production.

(1959)

* Arthur Miller, *Collected Plays, with an Introduction*, New York: Viking, 1957; London: Cresset 1958, pp. 39, 40.

IDA KAMINSKA'S MOTHER COURAGE

Ida Kamińska is coming back from town. Maybe she has managed to sell something, maybe she has just got a piece of bread by begging. She finds her daughter murdered, in an empty field. A strange peasant family has stopped by the body; they talk to her and try to explain something. She does not hear them. She does not cry; she cried everything out long ago. She does not weep; she has had no tears left for a long time. She just twitches her bony fingers as if she were raking aside some earth. She kneels by her daughter, silently; all the words of despair have been spoken long ago. She starts singing a children's lullaby, ridiculous, pointless, and tragic, which must have stuck in her memory. She sings it in a hollow, lifeless voice. A Jewish mother is taking leave of her last child—hurriedly, in an empty space, in the presence of strangers. She does not even abandon herself to her despair; she is all dried up. She is absent and yet present. She goes to her wagon, looks for an old rag, and covers the body of her daughter. Nothing else can be done. She searches for some money with which to bury her; she knows she cannot stay there. She just looks when they take her away. Then she goes up the empty stage, takes a few steps, then comes back again. A movement of her hand toward heaven—a helpless, surprised, resigned gesture. So all must perish. The Jewish mother does not rebel any more. God is silent and people are silent. She puts on her harness and pulls her wagon. She knows she has to pull it and that she will not be able to go on pulling for long. The wagon is nearly empty, but it is still too heavy for an old woman. But what else can she do except pull the wagon?

Ida Kamińska has performed a great tragedy. It was not, however, the tragedy of a camp follower of the time of the Thirty Years' War, who had trusted the war and lived by it and who was eventually deceived by it. It was a tragedy performed on the basis of Brecht's text but quite different and far more modern. The Jewish theatre was half-empty on Monday when I saw the performance. Kamińska's silvery voice resounded in the theatre, losing itself in it and sinking as if in sand. There is something uncanny about actors playing to a deaf audience. Hardly anyone could understand Yiddish. Somewhere in the corner one spectator was interpreting in a whisper for his neighbor. Perhaps that was the reaon why the tragedy of *Mother Courage* performed to a hundred people in a language they could not understand, a language close and distant to them at the same time, was acquiring quite different meanings, was a different play altogether. Or rather, the tragedy of Mother Courage was not performed on the stage. The spectators make the theatre as much as actors do.

In my life I have had many meetings with Ida Kamińska. I had seen performances of the Jewish Theatre in a number of cities: in Lwów and in Łódź, in Kraków and Wrocław. I have seen that theatre in moments of great joy and in moments of great sorrow; at the very beginning when everything was getting off to a new start after the war, and later when the theatre had been threatened with being disbanded, and still later at its great first nights. The theatre had always been full. It had had its public: Polish and Jewish, old and new, noisy and bilingual; a public that had loved its Theatre. And only now, in 1957, I saw that Theatre, at its home in Warsaw, without its audience.

I saw a theatre that was suddenly alone. In the last twelve years many actors left Ida Kamińska, but new actors replaced them. That fragile old woman with a silvery voice, with a beauty untouched by time, with inexhaustible energy, kept finding new actors anywhere any time—in transports coming from the East and in small towns; among craftsmen, weavers or bookkeepers. She infected others with her passion and her magic art. In a few weeks she made actors of laymen, taught them speech, gesticulation, movement. Some went, others came, to pull the wagon with Ida Kamińska. Until, gradually, the audience began to decrease. There are smaller and smaller audiences, in Wrocław and Wałbrzych, in Łódź, Warsaw, and Kraków.

Mother Courage goes on dragging her wagon. She is not a camp follower who lives off war. She has had no illusions for a long time. Mother Courage in Ida Kamińska's interpretation has not even been deceived by war. She accepts the world with all its cruelty, but she knows very well that there is nothing else left, except to go on dragging the wagon—against the logic of the world, in spite of everything that has happened. In her performance Mother Courage is more Conradian than Brechtian. And as I was looking at Ida Kamińska when, for the last time, she put on her harness and dragged her wagon up the slope, I suddenly thought of that strange sentence in Conrad's *Lord Jim*, composed in three languages: "To follow the dream, and again to follow the dream—and so—ewig—usque ad finem. . . ."

Ida Kamińska is one of the greatest tragic actresses now living. But this time she did not have to learn her part. She was and is the Jewish Mother Courage. And for this I have the deepest respect for her.

(1957)

IRENA EICHLER'S MOTHER COURAGE

In Irena Eichler's conception of the part, from her very first gesture, there is something of the Warsaw woman smuggler under the wartime German occupation. Even in her very first "dea-rie" one can hear the Warsaw cadences. Above all, Eichler differs physically from Helene Weigel and Ida Kamińska. They were dry, stubborn, burned out. Eichler is younger than they; she is big and somehow—in spite of her physical stature—gentler. Ida Kamińska was more tragic than Helene Weigel by all the crematoria and concentration camps. Eichler is more noble.

Brecht's Mother Courage feeds on war and the refuse of war; she feeds on carrion. The war is her war. To the very end she did not, could not understand anything. War was ruining her, but she was ruining others too. Brecht wrote *Mother Courage* in 1939. *Mother Courage* was not only a tragedy; it was an accusation. For Eichler, the war is not her war. She does not live out of war; she lives in a world in which there is war. She knows everything from the start. She wants to survive with her children, that's all. She feeds on war, yes; but how else could she live; how feed her children? The war is beyond her. She has to survive. She has to keep her booth in spite of war.

Irena Eichler is very Polish, Warsovian. She has the bitter wisdom of the years of occupation behind her, and the fierce vitality of the Polish people, and even something of the superb down-to-earth humor typical of the Warsaw streets.

But all this forms only the basic outline of her conception of the part—a couple of gestures, an intonation here and there. There is nothing folkloristic about her acting, which is distinguished by distance and toning down of violent effects. In the great scene following the shooting of her son, Weigel stood motionless in the silent cry of her open mouth. Eichler does it with the silent look of her open eyes. I remember that silent look from the days of the occupation. Silent look, and then, at the end of the act, the dead voice, with a pause preceding and following it: "I haggled too long." Eichler's acting is now more and more economical and austere. She seems gradually to stiffen, as if she were dying from within. And all of a sudden, when the cook returns, the fat old woman is changed—for two, three, four minutes—into a very young, radiant, incredibly beautiful girl. Almost nothing has been changed in her make-up. She is still the same, and yet different. This is acting at its greatest.

(1963)

In the first scene, Łomnicki is hanging over a balustrade. He is all flabby, like a punctured balloon. He turns 'round; he is small, plain, soft—nothing much to look at with his triangular, powdered face and funny beetle brows. I know that face. It is the face of a clown with the red line of the mouth, the goggling eyes. The facial is unerring, and by no means a matter of chance. This is the mask of Marcel Marceau. Thus, at the beginning, there is only a rejected clown, an empty shell, an unemployed buffoon. But this puppet moves his arms and legs when someone pulls the string. Gradually the flabby balloon fills with air. Arturo Ui jerks, gets angry, rages. His movements are still mechanical, limited, clownish. But he has an entourage. Men in long coats, revolvers in their pockets, are standing around. The clown is for hire, and so are the murderers.

Łomnicki is still empty inside, as if he were not really there, as if he were still a mechanical toy. But the clown suddenly begins to realize that they are afraid of him; that his wriggling is terrifying, that he is somebody; that he can have power; that he has power. He rules because clowning fascinates others. The clown learns gestures for he has come to believe in the effectiveness of clowning. The clown calls an actor. The assassins for hire, sprawling in their chairs, assist in the great lesson of mimicry. It is not a disinterested lesson. The old actor teaches Arturo Ui great Shakespearean roles. Mark Antony speaks over the body of the murdered Caesar. The assassins for hire go on sprawling in their chairs.

Shakespeare at his cheapest becomes all of a sudden a modern theatre of Parteitage.

Łomnicki is transformed again. The jerky clown grows in stature and suddenly becomes Hitler. Even in the first scene he was never funny. But now he is frightening. He still has the face of a clown and ridiculous beetle brows. He has not ceased to be a clown, but he has also become Hitler; he has adopted Hitler's gestures and is setting the world on fire. It is one of the greatest scenes I have seen in the theatre—and one of the most terrifying. Łomnicki stops shouting: his voice has failed him. He toots silently, as it were. In silence he comes down the imaginary platform, is flabby again, the punctured balloon, just a clown again. But soon he tries once more: sits, walks, talks, becomes Hitler again, terrifies again.

With *Iphigenia in Aulis* and *Arturo Ui* Łomnicki has proved that he is an actor of unlimited technical resources. His acting is of the highest calibre and the most difficult kind. Just imagine an actor who begins playing his part as a flabby clown and develops it—without any change of make-up, without any external help—to the menace of Hitler rampaging on his platform. From the first to the last scene he is a clown; but not once does he make the audience laugh. And this is his greatest achievement. Hitler was not funny. Murderers are never funny, even when they are clowns.

Arturo Ui is a very strange play. It is certainly not Brecht at his best. The gangster story, if treated literally, seems flat, overwritten, even trivial. As a historical parable its simplifications and intrusive didactics are annoying; it seems naïve. There is not one dazzling sentence in it; it sounds forced. And yet it is a text that somehow abounds in theatrical potential. After all, there have been three theatrical successes, from this inferior text in the past two years. *Arturo Ui* produced by the Berliner Ensemble was a revelation. *Arturo Ui* produced by the Théâtre National Populair in Paris was a deeply disturbing play. *Arturo Ui* produced by the

Contemporary Theatre in Warsaw was the best production of
the season.

A few steps from the hotel in which I stayed on a little
Paris street, I found every morning a slogan painted in large
black letters on the wall: "OAS–Assassins." "OAS–Murderers," shouted the crowd during the big Paris demonstra-
tions. Brecht began to write *Arturo Ui* in 1940. This parable
of gangsters does not of course explain Nazism, nor can the
annexation of Austria be explained by a story of the rivalry
between two trusts of cauliflower dealers. And yet both the
slogan on the wall and the cry of the crowd shouting "Murderers" contain the simplest, most credible, most tangible truth
about the OAS and about the Nazis. "One must destroy
respect for murderers," Brecht wrote in his *Remarks on the
"Rise and Fall of Arturo Ui."* This is the true importance of
the play. Shakespeare in *Richard III* did the same thing:
destroyed respect for a crowned murderer. Woszczerowicz
played Richard III as a clown. Łomnicki achieved something
still more difficult for an actor: he demonstrated that a
flabby clown, having mastered the art of jerking and rampaging, can become Hitler. Art in our time can achieve nobility
only by demystifying.

(1963)

HOLOUBEK, OR THE ACTOR

He is not exceptionally good-looking. He has, however, marvelous eyes—very bright, sometimes blue, at other times green. There is nothing of a lover about him, either of the affectionate, soft and boyish "juvenile lead" type, or the scornful, bitter rebel type. Nor does he cut a "splendid figure of a man." Gustaw Holoubek is an amazingly modern actor, but by quite different standards.

One thing is certain: he is the greatest Polish actor of his generation. Many critics regard him simply as the greatest.

According to the traditional classification, actors are divided into warm and cool types; those who experience and those who imitate; those who lose themselves in the characters they create, and those who remain themselves throughout. According to these divisions, Holoubek would be a cold, imitating, and observing actor, as postulated by Diderot; and an actor who is detached from his part and can judge it, as demanded by Brecht. But all these definitions become meaningless when applied to a great personality.

Holoubek told me recently that he was happiest in his acting when he knew he was on the stage, when, acting in Sartre's *Le Diable et Le Bon Dieu*, he could, without ceasing to be Goetz, observe his partner's mistakes and himself with the eyes of the audience. At such moments, even if the theatre had caught fire, he could have mastered his panic and gone on being Sartre's Goetz, although in situations not written into his part. Would he then be himself, or still the character in the play? And what does it mean that an actor is, or is not, himself?

A critic does not choose the characters he writes about; at most he can choose among those that have been written by someone else. He cannot alter Hamlet's fate and make him stay with Ophelia. He would rather Othello did not murder Desdemona, but he cannot persuade the Moor that his action is not necessary now that he has come to believe in her unfaithfulness and to know that he could kill. The critic cannot change one word in Hamlet's soliloquy, or in Othello's last speech. Yet every true critic propounds a different Hamlet and a different Othello. Whom does he then write about, Shakespeare or himself? The question is naïve. He writes about Shakespeare, but he interprets Shakespeare through everything he knows and thinks about the world. Holoubek creates a character on the stage in the same way.

In every actor's performance there is what we might call a basic or starting position. It can be seen most clearly when the actor is on stage but does not speak. There are many actors, often quite prominent ones, who simply cease to exist when they are silent. Just as there are critics who do not exist unless they are quoting lines from the text. Such actors are merely mannequins in costume and make-up. They are not themselves, because they have nothing to say of themselves; they are not stage characters, for they have already said everything their characters had to say. Holoubek on the other hand is often most interesting in these textual gaps, because he has not lost himself in the part but from the outset has been a man who acts. To say he acts also means he comments.

One of the assumptions of the old theory of acting was the consistent construction of a character: its full development from the first speech to the last; a character was to be created and his transitions made credible and well motivated psychologically. It is easy to see that this theory of acting is in accord with the conception of the nineteenth-century novel where fate and character are related. There are scenes where Holoubek, acting Goetz, shows him from within, almost identifies himself with him. There are scenes where he looks at Goetz from the outside; he is then marking the action and commenting. This is not, I suppose, a consistent construction of a part, or of a character. But this is how a modern novelist writes. He knows he cannot know everything, even about a character he has himself created. He does not wish to be consistent. He simply solves a problem he has set himself.

Holoubek has told me that he acts as if he were solving a problem in front of the person dearest to him in the world. He acts to the audience. He plays out a situation that has been imposed on him, in which he has found himself, but that he did not choose. But, in fact, we all of us find ourselves in situations that have been imposed on us and that we did not choose. We play them, and we do it as if we were on stage, in front of an audience. We try to keep a distance in relation to ourselves; we are distrustful, we do not want to be naïve. We want to be aware of what is happening to the end. And we do not want to be identified with the part we are playing. We do not want to be defined once and for all, because we are ourselves; that is to say, we are different from all the parts we have played and will play. That is why we are recognizable.

This is the way in which Holoubek is absolutely recognizable. And only in this sense is he himself on the stage, even though he is playing not himself, but characters written by others. And it is in this sense that he is the most modern actor I have ever seen. In the theatre the word "overacting" means artificiality, excess. Holoubek's acting is absolutely natural; beside him, all other, often very good, actors seem to be "overacting." To be natural means to have discovered the modern area of sensibility; to have discovered, not imitated it; to have discovered, and to impose it. This is the fascination in the performance of a great actor. I am fascinated by Holoubek.

(1959)

OEDIPUS IN PROSE

When Odysseus has killed the suitors, the old nurse Eurycleia goes to Penelope's bedroom, wakes her up and tells her that her husband has come back and is waiting for her downstairs. Penelope does not, will not believe her. "My dear nurse, the gods have made you daft. It's as easy for them to rob the wisest of their wits as to make stupid people wise. And now they have addled your brains, which used to be so sound. How dare you make sport of my distress by waking me when I had closed my eyes for a comfortable nap?"* Then she goes down and in the beggar sitting on a stool in soiled clothes, she recognizes Odysseus at once. She does not, however, approach her husband but sits opposite him by the other wall. She still does not, will not, is afraid to believe. She fears that once again she will be deceived, as she has been many times before. She fears that if she is deceived again, she will take it so hard that she may not survive. Or perhaps she is simply afraid of that moment for which she has waited twenty years. "For a long while Penelope, overwhelmed by wonder, sat there without a word. But her eyes were busy, at one moment resting full on his face, and the next falling on the ragged clothes that made him seem a stranger once again."*

* Homer, *The Odyssey*, trans. by E. V. Rieu (Penguin, 1945), Book XXIII.

I have read *The Odyssey* many times in verse translations and never noticed that scene: it was not there, it evaporated between the rhymes, could not be contained in the alexandrine. Odysseus and his adventures were a myth, a legendary and unreal story. *The Odyssey* in a recent prose translation is not made to appear modern, but it does not need commentaries. One can read it without believing in Greek gods. One can read it and confront it with all our experiences and literature from Homer to Mann and Proust. *The Odyssey* goes successfully through both these tests. Or rather, one can say that *The Odyssey* can be read in a prose translation without the condescension one applies to some old classics.

Sophocles' *Oedipus,* translated into prose, emerges triumphant, like *The Odyssey,* from this double confrontation and double test. At the moment I am concerned only with the principle of translation and its consequences. *Oedipus* in prose ceases to be a sacral and liturgical text, ceases to be the story of a myth. On the other hand, prose makes *Oedipus* concrete, turns the story into a real one, that is to say, into a story that happened, or could happen. Prose makes *Oedipus* earthy, both metaphorically and literally.

The events happen in a real city. The city is not a big one and is situated near the mountains. From a small square, steps lead up to the royal palace. A temple stands in the square. There is a plague in the city: children are born dead and cattle die. Oedipus descends the stairs. He saved the city from a plague once and as a reward became its king. Now they want him to save it for the second time. Laius, predecessor to Oedipus on the throne of Thebes, was murdered, and his murderers have not been found. The people ascribe the plague to the anger of the gods. Oedipus sends his brother-in-law to consult the Delphic oracle. Oedipus is prepared to take the risk.

People ascribe the plague to the anger of the gods. People ascribe. *Oedipus* is a story that takes place among people; only among people. There are no gods in *Oedipus,* at least in the literal sense. There is no machine. That term of the old poetics signified the influence of gods or demons. Machine meant deus ex machina. I am not concerned only with the lack of stage gods in *Oedipus*. In *Oedipus* translated into prose there are no gods at all; there are only people who try to believe and not to believe.

Laius and Jocasta had been forewarned by the Oracle that their son would murder his own father and marry his own mother. Laius and Jocasta believed the Oracle, and when their son was born they ordered that he be left in the forest with his feet and hands bound as prey to wild beasts. Had they really believed the gods? If they had, why should they kill the child? After all, gods are infallible. The Oracle had to come true in any case, no matter what they did. If they had not believed the gods, it would be one more reason not to have the child killed. But Laius and Jocasta believed and did not believe at the same time. They wanted to behave prudently; they wanted to be safe.

Oedipus is saved by a shepherd. He is brought up by a foreign king whose son he thinks he is until one day, in the course of a quarrel, someone tells him he is a bastard. Oedipus consults the Oracle to find out the truth. The Oracle renews the warning: he will kill his own father and marry his own mother. If Oedipus had fully believed, or not believed the gods, he would have remained where he was. But Oedipus, too, both believed and did not believe; he wanted to be safe and prudent, so he left the city. These events precede the proper action of the tragedy. But even they—when translated into prose—have a striking moral poignancy and psychological ambiguity that does not require any "modernization"; it is modern enough as it is.

What does it mean to believe, or not believe, the gods? Gods speak through soothsayers. Their will and the events that are to happen are expounded by priests, who divine from the entrails of victims, or from the flight and cries of birds. Soothsayers are not always willing to talk, or they talk when it is too late. This rouses suspicions. The flight and cries of birds are not very clear either. Soothsayers and birds can get things wrong. It is prudent to consult the Oracle, but one cannot trust it blindly either. An oracle provides information, but information only of probable, not certain, facts. This is how Oedipus looks at the Oracle until he is ultimately shattered by events. This is how even the chorus looks at the Oracle in the first part of the tragedy. This is very much how Odysseus sees oracles; he regards priestly divinations as no more than a meteorological forecast. He lets birds loose: if they fly to the left, he delays his departure by a day or two. Then he lets birds loose again and sets out on his journey without paying any attention to the divinations.

Oedipus translated into prose, like *The Odyssey* rendered in prose, deals with a world not so very remote from our own. What, then, is *Oedipus* when it ceases to be monumental, when it ceases to be a matter between gods and men? To my mind, *Oedipus* is what it has always been: one of the greatest plays that has ever been written about human suffering. "When, having discovered the cause of all our misfortunes, I wanted to know their reason, I realized that there was one quite sufficient, consisting in the natural misery of our condition, weak and mortal, and so unfortunate that nothing can move us when we contemplate it closely."

When we contemplate it closely . . . Pascal as a writer was one of the closest to the atmosphere of *Oedipus*. In his *Pensées* we find the same shock at the misery of human existence, the same desperate attempt to seek salvation in theodicy; the groan of Oedipus who blinded himself so as never to look at the world and himself again. The figure of Oedipus is more than a close reflection on human misery: it is its demonstration. For the demonstration to take place, the Oedipus story has to be shown and performed in all its material concreteness, in all its psychological wealth. This can be achieved only by rendering it into modern prose. The story of Oedipus cannot be told satisfactorily in even a most beautiful oratorio sung in Latin, or a ballet in masks, or with a chorus singing Gregorian chants, or by means of a pitiful reconstruction of a Greek theatre. The story of Oedipus has first to become credible; only then can we debate whether gods exist.

Oedipus is a play about traps set by the world; about snares that go so far beyond ordinary experience that they seem irrational and meaningless. Oedipus is a play about the cruelty of chance against which even the best gifts of nature and the intellect, or the most cautious safeguards cannot protect one. In the case of Conrad's Jim, fate turned out to be not much less cruel than in the case of Oedipus. And there is no reason why one should regard one of these characters as more monumental than the other. They both are examples of human fate. Jim jumped from a sinking ship, leaving the Muslim pilgrims behind. He should not have jumped. Everything in his nature and upbringing led us to believe that he would not jump, that he of all people would not break down in a critical moment. He had for years foreseen such a moment and prepared himself for it. And yet he jumped, escaped from a sinking ship. Why did he do it? He did not know himself. Conrad's Lord Jim is not only a story about a merchant navy officer who failed in what had been expected of him. Lord Jim is also a considered reflection on that story. For this reason, perhaps, the story is not developed directly, but narrated by Marlow, who, as a fictitious narrator, performs the function of the chorus in a tragedy. He contemplates closely, as Pascal would have it, the fragility of, and contradictions inherent in, the moral order.

Conrad created the character of Lord Jim. Sophocles inherited the story of Oedipus. It had been before him, and was after him, a frequent theme of epics and tragedies, from Aeschylus to Seneca, from Voltaire to André Gide. In the many versions and transformations of the theme only the basis of the plot—the cruelty of the world and the traps of fate—remained unchanged. But the meaning of the tragedy underwent violent and extreme changes. The tragedy was either a confirmation or a negation of theodicy; a confirmation or negation of the moral order. Of the great tragic trio of antiquity, Aeschylus was the one who believed most strongly in the gods. He even attributed human justice to them. Laius was punished by the gods in his offspring because he had slept with men. This was how the misfortunes of the Labdacidae began. Euripides jeered at the divine order and saw in the old mythological stories only images of dark passions and still darker chance.

There is no "pure" *Oedipus* of Sophocles, just as there is no "pure" *Hamlet* of Shakespeare. Both plays and their protagonists are not only overgrown with stage tradition, but lead extratheatrical lives in literature, psychology, and modern philosophy. I had the impression that the primary assumption of the recent Warsaw production was not an attempt to make *Oedipus* modern, but to demonstrate that it is modern. The actor playing Oedipus did not have to repeat Goetz's gesture from Sartre's play: the challenge thrown at the empty Heavens; he had to know, however, when ultimately leaving Thebes, whether heaven was empty or not. Holoubek knew; he execrated himself and the world; the skies above him were empty.

"The world of tragedy," wrote Malraux, "invariably means the ancient world: man, crowd, elements, woman, destiny. It can be reduced to two acting persons: the protagonist and the meaning given by him to life." Malraux's formula seems too monumental and classicist to me, but its last sentence is enthralling. In tragedy there are always two great protagonists: the hero and the threatened world of values; the hero and the chorus. But in Sophocles' tragedy Oedipus' ultimate reasons and the Chorus' ultimate reasons are not identical. The world collapsed for Oedipus when he learned the truth, but for the Chorus the moral order remained unchanged. A prose translation gives even more poignancy to the inner contradictions tearing this tragedy apart; or rather it shows two tragedies present in the Sophoclean *Oedipus Rex:* the tragedy of piety represented by the Chorus and the tragedy of experiencing the truth, which befalls Oedipus.

In the Warsaw production only Oedipus was given his motives. Yet it is not only Oedipus who is modern, but also the

Chorus. In Sophocles' play the conflict pertains to the existence, or non-existence, of an objective world of values. The
Chorus wants to make us recognize that order, to call dark
elements and blind chance *fate*, to accept that "what is to be
will be." The Chorus demands that we believe in theodicy.
The absolute has for Sophocles the names of Greek gods. But
in the eighteenth, nineteenth, and twentieth centuries, the
same theodicy, the same absolute, inhuman, and merciless
order, was called respectively Reason, Nature, and History.
The Chorus prefers cruel gods to the non-existence of gods.
It is at this price that the Chorus offers us purification—
catharsis. I do not accept such a purification; Oedipus did
not accept it either when, having torn his eyes out, he set
out on his lonely way from Thebes. But I do want to hear
the voice of the Chorus persuading me to accept this purification. There was no such voice in the Chorus of the Warsaw performance.

From the very first line, when Oedipus descends the steps of
his royal palace, to the last, when Creon tells him: "Stop
behaving as if you were still king, Oedipus!" the action logi-
cally follows the course of an investigation. This may be
why the dramatic structure of *Oedipus* is so impeccable. I
would not hesitate to use even another comparison: it is the
logic of a detective story. Oedipus and the Chorus interrogate
witnesses: they want to know "who done it." In this great
investigation, the prosecutor becomes the accused and Creon,
the chief accused, the prosecutor. Oedipus and the Chorus
want to get at the truth. Toward the end of the tragedy,
Oedipus and the Chorus are men of principle; they debate the
question of the existence, or non-existence, of the absolute,
of the existence, or non-existence, of an eternal order. This
would, perhaps, point to a solution of the problem of a
tragic chorus on the intellectual level of the play.

All the other characters in the tragedy represent the world.
All of them are people of compromise. Even Jocasta. Even
Creon. They know the truth, or at least part of it. They know
more than the Chorus, more than Oedipus. They do not want

to talk; and not only because they are afraid. They consider the truth dangerous, and so it is better not to reveal the whole of it. They think that a compromise is possible, that one can live in a world of half-truth.

Goethe's *Iphigenia* is classicist and rational: truth, goodness, and reason triumph in it. There is in that play "la belle nature," nature made noble. For this reason, its performance can and should be based on an absolute purity of style. Sophocles is far more brutal; his characters are not made of marble, but of big blocks of rough stone. Gogolewski as Creon seemed to me too elegant. Creon, when speaking his last, harsh words to the blind Oedipus, ought to sound not unlike Fortinbras over Hamlet's body, or Octavius over the body of Antony. The great ones have disappeared from the earth and only the Creons remain.

As Oedipus, Holoubek demonstrated the dazzling range of his acting, from the most subtle to the very broad—a scale previously unknown on the Polish stage—and his mastery over all styles. On occasion, however, that absolute craftsmanship could be noticed, as if some traces of the effort he put into the part were visible.

This is not important. In three or four scenes, Holoubek reached the utmost limits of what the modern actor's art can become. I am thinking of the scene of orgiastic dance when the Messenger from Corinth has told him of Polybus' having died a natural death; I am thinking of the scene where he takes leave of his daughters, fragile, airy, all constructed upon inner suppressed weeping; I am thinking of the immensely moving cry: "Cloud, oh cloud . . ." uttered at the top of the stairs, when for the first time he appears as a blind man with empty eye sockets.

But there is one scene in which all the limits of the art of acting have been surpassed, a scene performed "on the other side" as it were—outside stagecraft, outside theatre. It is the scene where Oedipus slumps down on the sacrificial stone. He says: "World, oh world . . ." He knows everything now. In these two words there is leave-taking, reproach, Pascal's awareness of human misery.

Baird's music, based on the human voice treated as raw material, oratorial and devoid of melody, seemed to me not unlike laments in a Jewish cemetery on Yom Kippur.

Oedipus, fleeing from Thebes down the empty road with the hesitant step of a blind man, becomes, in that last scene, the Wandering Jew. It may be that every tragedy reaching beyond the measure of human endurance has for us the face of the burnt-down Ghetto. The care for the purity of style I leave to the aesthetes.

(1961)

AN UNEXPECTED RACINE

"There is a young girl here, slender, with a very attractive figure. I always observed her at a distance of five or six steps and regarded her as very beautiful. Her complexion seemed to me pleasing and dazzling, her eyes big and exquisitely black, her bosom and everything else that they quite freely lay bare in this country, white to perfection. I thought of her with affection and was near to infatuation, but I used to see her only in church, for—as I have already told you—I am even more of a recluse than my cousin advised me to be. At last, however, I resolved to find out if I had not been mistaken in my view of her, and I took advantage of the first possible occasion. I went up to her and addressed her. But as soon as I opened my mouth and regarded her closely, I could not speak a word. On her face I saw spots as if she had just recovered from some disease, and my thoughts were distracted at once. Truth to tell, I must have met her on one of those disagreeable and obnoxious days for women, the cause of which is their very nature. . . . Ultimately I was most glad of that meeting, which cured me of a certain disquiet. I am now teaching myself to live somewhat more prudently and not let myself be distracted in all directions. I am beginning my novitiate . . ."

Who wrote that letter, perhaps a bit old-fashioned in its style, but so modern in its psychological insight? Was it Benjamin Constant in his *Cahier rouge?* Or Proust's hero after his first meeting with Albertine? No! This was Racine writing to his friend when, at the age of twenty-three, he left his Jansenist tutors and for the first time went to Provence.

That letter shocked me. It did not correspond at all to the image of Racine I had formed from earlier reading. His tragedies had seemed to me too pure, noble and monumental. I was tired of his high-flown dramatic writing, irritated by his stilted heroes. My view of Racine was like young Stendhal's. He seemed to me a court writer, cold and artificial, unbearable with his rhetoric, deafening with his tirades. Until I saw Irena Eichler's Phèdre. Then I began to read Racine again; but now I read him differently.

Watching Eichler, I suddenly heard the words of Jean Baptiste Clamence's monologue. And I realized that a letter very similar to the one I have just quoted could have been written by the hero of Camus' *The Fall.*

Jean Baptiste Clamence was always prone to psychological analysis. He delighted in himself, to a degree; and had moral scruples, to a degree, until the moment when crossing a bridge on the Seine one night he heard the cry of a drowning girl and ran away. From that moment onward it was not just scruples, and nothing remained of the disinterested delight in analysis; everything now became tragic.

The meaning of existence was undermined. He crossed the border.

When Phèdre appears on the stage for the first time, she has already crossed the border—the same one. The world has ceased to exist for her. She is alone with her sin and can only slowly poison herself with it until she dies. The world has departed. It is amazing to what an extent Racine's world is empty. There are no objects in it, no landscape, no nature. Twice in *Phèdre* the word "forest" is uttered. But forest is only a place name; one cannot hear leaves rustling, or smell their fragrance. There is only a palace with a statue of Venus; there are names of Greek deities and heroes. The palace and the names are only imposing sounds. Phèdre's tragedy begins in an absolute void. Her crime is almost incomprehensible to the world. What has she done? Has she committed a sinful action? No. She has sinned only in her mind, only in desire. She has heard her own cry and suddenly realized that it is the cry of a drowning woman, that she is already among the dead. In vain does the world tempt her with a chance of happiness, with the offer of a moral compromise. From now on Phèdre knows she is lost. She can only struggle and wriggle helplessly in a bell glass from which the air has been pumped out—in a void.

On the surface *Phèdre* can be seen as a late nineteenth-century moral and psychological drama. A mature woman suddenly falls in love with her young stepson. She is ashamed of and shocked by her feeling and regards it as indecent. She suppresses her love until she learns that her husband is dead. She is now free to reveal her feelings. But to the youth her love is repulsive; he is in love with a young girl. The words have been uttered, though, and hang over the characters. Are there any heroes to speak of? There is only a bourgeois wife, a banker who has dallied somewhere in his travels, a more or less worthy youth, and a seamstress he got to know while ordering some shirts. The play could be a comedy, could be a farce, even if it ended with a pistol shot, or with a bottle of vitriol.

In Racine's *Phèdre* the story is only a pretext. Phèdre examines her conscience in a world that is morally unacceptable; in which love exists, but every love is a sin; in which the need for happiness exists, but happiness is impossible; in which God exists, but God is blind, deaf and vindictive. It is not Phèdre who is tragic, but Racine's world. All human conflicts are insoluble under the terrible pressure of moral imperatives. Phèdre can only choose death.

The smile never leaves Eichler's face. It is a Mona Lisa smile, mocking, puzzling, almost out of this world. She talks to her confidante, to Hippolyte, to her husband. No, this is an illusion. Eichler's entire performance is a monologue: she talks only to herself and to the gods. It is a confession as merciless, shocking and passionate as the monologue of Jean

Baptiste Clamence—and just as modern. Eichler speaks verse magnificently, but the thoughts, passions, the horror of the word flow, as it were, under the verse, under that magnificent rhetoric. It is as if words, all words, were just a surface, because the true tragedy is being performed somewhere more deeply, without words.

Irena Eichler knows that the part of Phèdre is a confession and a monologue; that Phèdre is alone from the first to the last moment; that the entire drama is performed within her alone. When she is dying, she strokes the earth with a slow and affectionate gesture. Earth has betrayed her, but death reconciles her with it.

(1959)

IVONA COMES OF AGE

Gombrowicz's *Ivona* published in 1938, is not unlike those cruel, perverse little plays written by schoolboys in the class-room behind other pupils' backs. They are usually grotesque and a kind of caricature, directed against teachers, mocking younger brothers and elder sisters, trying to ridicule literature and history; in essence they are a kind of showdown with the entire world, for at that time of life the world consists only of teachers and parents, brothers and sisters, history and litera-ture lessons. It has happened once or twice that such little plays were written by boys of genius. Such was the case with Alfred Jarry's *Ubu Roi*. It was to be a school skit, a satire on stupid schoolmasters and history classes. It was enough, how-ever, to dress schoolmasters as kings and make them per-form a classic historical anecdote for a preposterous situa-tion, the grotesque discrepancy between man and the part he is to perform *and* the situation in which he is involved, to grow to monstrous dimensions.

Gombrowicz's *Ivona* was written by a conscious writer, but something of a schoolboy's vindictiveness, of a schoolboy's obsessions and jokes, remain in it. Not only in *Ivona* but in all of Gombrowicz's writings, schoolboy obsessions reappear. Af-ter all, two terms invented by Gombrowicz, which have passed into common speech and at the same time become almost philosophical concepts: "to be fitted with a bum" or "mug"—

were taken from schoolboy idiom. School remained for Gombrowicz the purest mechanism of social life.

We have all of us had, from time to time, a dream about taking our final examinations. In the dream we are terribly afraid, even though we may not have been afraid when we were actually taking them. We feel ridiculous because we have not ceased to be adults even in that dream. The situation is "fitting us with a mug" we do not want to have, but we are helpless. The "mug" and the "bum" are stronger than we are. It so happened that I had to pass a couple of exams as an adult. My examiners were my colleagues, yet it was a nerve-racking experience: I turned into a schoolboy again. That mechanism was one of the discoveries made in *Ferdydurke*.

Life often imitates literature: Gombrowicz would probably be amazed to hear that one of the youngest theatre critics in our country put on shorts and went to school pretending to be a schoolboy. The "Ferdydurkism" of this story, however, is much more venomous in fact; it appeared later that the critic had been sent to school by the Minister of Education himself to write an article for a literary periodical.

Perhaps Gombrowicz would not have been surprised, after all. He himself willingly practised "Ferdydurkism" in life. He adored those situations in which something shameful was suddenly revealed, in which conventions were disturbed and a trial of strength followed to prove who would dominate whom. Domination was his favorite word. He practiced social provocation as a psychological experiment. In the 1930s, whenever I sat down at his café table, his opening words invariably were: "Mr. Kott, you are being admitted to our company today, although you are of base origin."

In those days Gombrowicz was often in the company of Stefan Otwinowski, the writer, and Andrzej Pleśniewicz, a young, very promising and erudite historian, who was later killed in the war. Gombrowicz began the conversation by saying: "When I visited Andrzej yesterday . . ." Pleśniewicz tried to deny this, but that was exactly what Gombrowicz was waiting for: "What do you mean, I didn't visit you?

Didn't you offer me bad tea and stale doughnuts . . . ?" Pleśniewicz again tried to deny this, but Gombrowicz would not relent: "You went out for a while to see your old aunt, and taking advantage of your absence I opened a fat notebook lying on your bed . . ." Pleśniewicz was desperate by now, "I have no aunt and no notebook." But Gombrowicz continued, "Do not try to deny it, Andrzej; it was a green notebook, with a paperweight on it. I opened it and under yesterday's date I read: 'I have met Stefan Otwinowski; he is a fool and a hack.'" Then he waited calmly to see what would happen.

There is a lot of that Gombrowiczian psychomania in *Ivona*. Ivona herself is anemic, passive, obstinately silent. But she exists. Her very presence, her very existence is a constant challenge. It compels everybody to take care of her. It provokes them to jeer at or pity her, in any event to adopt an attitude toward her. All conventional feelings, gestures, situations become incongruous in the face of her refusal to play an active part. The very presence of Ivona humiliates everybody. They cease to be self-contained, they are compelled to play ever more stupid parts, to get involved in ever more preposterous situations. They have to look at themselves with her eyes, and then things shameful, indecent and stupid are revealed and exposed in every one of them.

Everybody has been fitted with a bum by Ivona, everybody feels a monstrous mug growing on him. Only Ivona's death can rid them of this nightmare. To kill Ivona one has again to fit oneself with a mug, leave conventional stereotypes behind, and create the situation of murder. But that situation, too, is incongruous, does not fit any convention, is inwardly humiliating. In order to kill Ivona one has to disguise oneself as Hamlet or Lady Macbeth; one has to become pathetic. One of Gombrowicz's most brilliant inventions is a scene in which the Queen tousles her hair and daubs her face with ink in order to encourage herself to poison Ivona. She enters a Shakespearean role, leaps into a ready-made cliché—a literary and a schoolboy cliché at the same time.

There are more such psychological discoveries in *Ivona*. The play is derived from the spirit of *Ubu Roi*, but its philosophical problems are far more mature and up-to-date. *Ivona* waited twenty years for its first production and has now come of age. It has not dated, it has merely become more clear. We are becoming more and more sensitive now to exactly this type of intellectual grotesque and perverse wisdom.

(1957)

A VERY POLISH CARD INDEX

In Różewicz' *The Card Index* there is first a card index of ideas, means, ways, gimmicks and tricks borrowed from the new theatre and anti-theatre—from Beckett, Ionesco, Thornton Wilder, Gombrowicz. The Wagging Policeman and the Fat Man are very much like Pozzo and Lucky from *Godot*. Action is going on simultaneously with all the times mixed up, the characters coming and going. The entire principle of structure reminds one of Wilder's *The Long Christmas Dinner*. The gibberish is taken from Ionesco; the examination, Teacher and the mutual "fitting with bums," from Gombrowicz. The letters taken out of a wastepaper basket and the enchanting poetry of advertisements is borrowed from the heroic period of the surrealists. The good Uncle, washing his feet in a real basin, and the digestive troubles of the Fat Lady are Beckett again. And so on, and so on.

But all these ideas, tricks and gimmicks served all those authors some purpose; there was a method and a philosophy in them. Beckett changed man into a monstrous torso and put him in a rubbish bin. Ionesco turned man into a thing, a machine that is out of order. In *The Long Christmas Dinner* grandparents, parents, grandchildren are sitting together, then the grandchildren are grandparents; once again someone eats a piece of Christmas cake, the conversation is about some cousins and an aunt who was poisoned by mushrooms, and another hundred years has passed.

Różewicz has done a very curious thing—having borrowed all these things, he has changed them into something else: the universal into the particular; cruelty into sentimentality; elements modern, semimodern, quarter modern, sur-modern, into Polish traditional drama, so close, so dear, so familiar.

The hero is lying in bed, the bed is standing in the middle of the street, behind the bed is a wooden fence with posters. The fence has been standing since the end of the war at the corner of Marszałkowska and Aleje Jerozolimskie streets. The hero is called Heniek and Wiktor, Zbysio and Piotruś, he could also be called Franek, Stasiek, and Janek. He has all the Polish names, but only Polish. He is four, eight, sixteen, and thirty-five years old, but he was twenty years old when the war ended and he left the camp. Then he applauded at political meetings, worked a little, engaged in the ideological struggle a little. Now he is tired and lying in bed.

The hero is lying down and experiencing his tragic situation. As is commonly known, a tragic situation experienced lying down is the highest kind of tragic situation. Tragic situations are divided into those that are experienced lying down, those experienced sitting, and those experienced standing up. The standing up tragic situation is idealistic; the sitting, phenomenological; the lying down, materialistic.

The hero's tragic situation experienced lying down seems to me, above all else, very Polish. The hero is lying down; he is tired and empty. They all try to persuade him to do something. But he will not budge; he is just lying down and worrying. They try to persuade him to feel love, compassion, trust, to have an affair, a talk over a cup of coffee; to take an examination, support an ideology, go on an excursion to Częstochowa. But he will not budge. They try to persuade him to go to a conference, to take part, to struggle for peace, not to keep his hands under the blanket, to pick his nose, to save the world. But he will not budge. Finally he gets up, finds a rope, approaches the wardrobe, gets inside . . . but he does not hang himself; he gets out of the wardrobe and goes back to bed.

The hero is called Piotruś, Jurek, Wacek, Tadek. There is only one name lacking: Konrad. Because that is what he really is: Wyspiański's Konrad, even though the masks talking to him are different. To create his effects, Wyspiański needed the Primate, the conservative Stańczyks, the Muse, an 1863 Insurgent, the peasant Scythemen, the Harpies and Erinyes. All that Różewicz requires is the Fat Man and the Gentleman with a Part, a couple of women and girls, fat and thin, a German girl, and a journalist. Wyspiański attacked Mickiewicz, accusing his poetry of exerting a deadly influence on the nation; Różewicz laughs at Wyspiański. Wyspiański needed Wawel Castle as background; Różewicz puts an ordinary iron bed at the corner of Jerozolimskie and Marszałkowska streets.

I am serious. Różewicz has, indeed, written a traditional national drama. Konrad and society, Konrad and Poland, Konrad and the world. Konrad is still waiting for the Great Idea. Konrad is still tormented by Erinyes. All right. But why is this new Konrad so emotional? If he is lying in bed and worrying, this should lead to something—either to a justification or an accusation. Maybe there is nothing around him except puppets and trunks, alienations, frustrations, big jeering faces, radio monologues and dialogues, records playing. But this should have been demonstrated, instead of having the Policeman, the Journalist, the good uncle from Częstochowa and the German girl come for a cup of coffee. Moreover, the hero should not have left the wardrobe once he disappeared inside!

But perhaps the new Konrad was wrong to be lying down and worrying. Perhaps he should have got up, dressed, fought for peace, passed his high school examination, gone for a walk with a girl and not been quite so late in attending the conference. Perhaps he is not quite so noble, unhappy, tragic. Perhaps he is not the spokesman of his generation. Perhaps he just imagines all this. Perhaps he is comfortable with his complexes and merely looking for excuses; perhaps he is just good-for-nothing and lazy. Perhaps he has not been doomed to his tragic choice in the absurd and empty cosmos.

Różewicz's hero is nice and full of charm. He is naïve and noble. Above all, he is lyrical. Beckett's, Ionesco's, Wilder's characters are not noble, or lyrical. Różewicz's hero is very Polish, very authentic. Why should we reproach him for that?

It is only on the surface that *The Card Index* has borrowed from the plays of others. Everything essential is Różewicz's own: the lyrical hero, the shock caused by war, the bitter, frightening and affectionate childishness, even the style of writing, the way phrases are constructed. *The Card Index* is a really well written play, and that is why it can be performed satisfactorily. Różewicz's language has its own inner dramatic quality, its own sphere of sensibility, its own obsessions.

The bed is standing in the middle of the street; behind the bed there is a fence; behind the fence, Chagall's sad horse. There are also two big wardrobes, and that is all. Jan Kosiński designed the right kind of scenery for *The Card Index*. The hero is Poland, in all the postwar years. The hero is five, twenty-five and forty years old. We accept the convention of *The Card Index* at once, from the very first line, without any resistance. The convention seems obvious, as if it were the only one, the natural form for the theatre. A "well-made play" with three acts, prologue, epilogue, floor and ceiling, logical sequence of events, and laborious development of a plot, seems odd and old-fashioned beside *The Card Index*, like a tablecloth hand-embroidered with a pattern of shepherdesses and stags. Every epoch has its "natural" way of writing, its "natural" theatre. Różewicz is right. His are not only gimmicks and ideas adopted from Beckett, Ionesco, and many others; his is a modern alphabet. Using that alphabet, one can write very different things, including, as Różewicz has shown, highly emotional Polish national drama.

(1960)

MROZEK'S FAMILY

Let no one leave here, until we find an idea. Eddie, do not
let anybody out.

TANGO

I

"Revolution and expansion—this is our slogan. Destroy old
forms, down with convention, long live dynamics! Live in
creating, move and strive beyond all limits, beyond form,
beyond form!" These words come from Stomil, one of the
characters in Mrożek's *Tango*, a terrifying modern grandfather. But in the chronology game we are to play, real
biographies do not matter; only the identification marks of
generations are important. Stomil represents not only the
Polish older generation of "modern" ladies and gentlemen—
"Do we submit to superstitions, or conventions which hamper humanity? Do we not wage a continuous fight against the
old era? Are we not free? All these bonds, these crusted fetters
of religion, morality, society, art. Above all art, Stomil, above
all art!"—he also represents the whole generation of European
formists, dadaists, surrealists: Tzara (1896), Breton (1896),
Éluard (1895), Cocteau (1892), Artaud (1895).

I myself attended a short course in surrealism in 1938. I
remember the games of "the exquisite corpse" at Breton's

and competitions for "de-sensed objects." A year ago these objects were shown at a surrealist exhibition as museum pieces —a carefully bandaged violin fastened with a huge safety pin; a plate with an immobilized fork protruding from it. Once these objects were frightening, now they seem good and simple, even touching. They are as childish as were the provocative actions in the sphere of morals in those days: "You possessed me in front of Mummy and Daddy on the first night of *Tannhäuser*, in the first row of the stalls, as a sign of protest. What a scandal that was. Ah, the times when it still made an impression!"

In *Tango*, as always in Mrożek, the terms of reference are not just Polish, but European. He is concerned with the way of life, the "style" of a generation, that of la belle époque. All of life's joys were treasured, but whatever emancipation there was was for a very private use only. Conventions were there to be respected and evaded. That is why Uncle Eugene easily comes to be on Arthur's side. Arthur says, "This house is beset by inertia, entropy and anarchy." We can recognize Arthur's year of birth by "entropy," a word used in place of "the fourth dimension" and the "theory of relativity." Arthur is no more than twenty-five years old; he was born in 1940. He has no political memories. October is to him only a month with very bad weather. Ala is only seven years younger than Arthur, but differences of generation, seen up close, are strongly marked for young people with only a few years' gap between them; only later does it become clear that they belong to the same generation. In Mrożek's family, Arthur is the last of the ideologists. He looks for resistance because he wants to repair the world, to set it right. Ala does not really understand what it means to "set it right." To her everything seems natural: herself, her bed, the political system. She has no conflicts and her attitude to love is antiseptic, which is said to be a characteristic of young Scandinavian girls. Mrożek has an excellent ear. All the differences between the mentalities of these half-generations are contained in the following dialogue:

ALA. Stomil pinched me twice today.

ARTHUR. The scoundrel.

ALA. He is your father.

ARTHUR. I am glad you have drawn my attention to the fact.

ALA. Well you use such old-fashioned expressions about your father. No one talks like that about his father these days.

ARTHUR. How do they talk then?

ALA. One does not pay any attention to one's father at all.

Here one could end the chronology game. It once seemed that family comedy meant merely wife, husband, lover, children in conflict with their parents, or a bride from a wrong social class, that this convention could produce nothing new, that it was good for nothing except drawing-room comedy. Whenever farce or the tragigrotesque of the absurd tried to drop the family, it found itself beyond time, beyond real time at any rate. In family comedy there were grandparents, parents and children; time was not abstract, it consisted of concrete biographies. Another Polish playwright, Mrożek's direct predecessor Witkiewicz, was one of the first to put the absurd family comedy in the context of historical time, historical costumes, historical gestures, but with one difference: Witkiewicz had the end of the world in mind. His was a grand family burlesque with an eschatological ending. Mrożek's eschatology is different. The grandmother in *Tango*, lying on her catafalque, is taken from the poetics of the absurd; the corpses are taken from Witkiewicz and from Ionesco; but the variations of time are real. Mrożek is a realist, saying his obsequies over Polish absurdities.

II

"It's just no use trying; the thing is hopeless. You are monstrously tolerant." (*Tango*)

Two weeks after the publication of Mrożek's *Tango* in the

Warsaw monthly *Dialog*, I met the wife of my friend, a prominent astrophysicist. "Isn't Mrożek wonderful?" we greeted each other. And then, as usual, we began to discuss our daughters. "How is yours?" asked my friend's wife. "Impossible. And yours?" "Impossible," said my friend's wife and added, "But it's really our homes that are impossible. They are not homes fit for children." "Mrożek," said I. "Mrożek," said the wife of my friend.

Our daughter comes and says, "Mother, I am a Marxist." We reply, "Very well, dear child, very well. Your father was a Marxist, your mother was a Marxist. It is nice you are following in your parents' footsteps."

Our daughter comes and says, "Mother, I think I have become a Dzilasist." We reply, "A Dzilasist? Couldn't you have thought of something else? But, all things considered, it's an interesting Marxist deviation. Very well, be a Dzilasist, if you want to."

Our daughter comes and says, "Mother, I've become an Anarchist." We reply, "An Anarchist? Very interesting. No one has been an Anarchist for a long time. This is a credit to your intellectual independence."

Our daughter comes and says, "Mother, I am a practicing Catholic." We reply, "Your father doesn't believe, your mother doesn't believe, but freedom of conscience is the most important thing. This is your affair. All things considered, Catholicism is a very beautiful religion."

Our daughter comes and says, "Mother, I've got a lover." We reply, "A lover? At your age? You're only sixteen. But some doctors say that one has to begin early. The most important thing, my child, is not to tell a lie."

Our daughter comes and says, "Mother, I am pure and will remain pure." We reply, "Some doctors say it is very healthy. The most important thing is to be at peace with oneself."

Our daughter comes and says, "Mother, I have two lovers." We reply, "Two lovers? At your age? This is naughty. But perhaps it's the accepted thing nowadays. Some doctors are in favor of a change. It is most important for you to have absolute trust in your parents. They never forbid you anything."

III

The theatre of the absurd has had its representatives in Poland for quite some time. There was Witkiewicz between the wars; there is Gombrowicz, who embarked on his literary career before World War II. Witkiewicz came too early; Gombrowicz has lived abroad (in Buenos Aires, Berlin, Paris). Mrożek was the first to come at the right time, not too early and not too late, according to both Polish and European clocks.

The drawing room, the revolver, the villain, and the corpses in *Tango* are all inherited from Witkiewicz; the language and the basic philosophical and psychological juxtapositions from Gombrowicz. Ala takes after Miss Youthful in Gombrowicz's novel *Ferdydurke*; Stomil's fly is unbuttoned, also after the fashion of Gombrowicz. The conviction that the artist is the litmus of his time is a Witkiewicz concept. "Artists are the plague. They were the first to corrode our time," Stomil says, a belief that has been shared by many outstanding statesmen (Truman and Eisenhower, for instance). The struggle of form with nothingness, of convention with sloppiness, is Gombrowiczian, as is the "absolute impossibility" into which Arthur falls; just as Uncle Eugene is "fitted with a bum" in the Gombrowicz manner and almost sent back to school in his shorts.

Arthur says, "Nothing is serious, or means anything at all in itself. Everything is null. We will drown in this nullity, unless we give things a character. We must create some meanings if there are none in nature." This is Gombrowicz almost literally. The Gombrowiczian system of discoveries began with a grotesque image of inadequate prewar Poland; later all his "mugs," "bums," "juniorities," and "nullities" became only language, a universal but abstract language. All those mugs and bums found themselves in a void. Mrożek restored to them their reality, and, even more, their new historical literalness.

Mrożek's buffo tone is unambiguous. His serious tone is far more difficult to interpret. I personally think that Mrożek also sees his world in terms of a cataclysm, but his catastrophic tendency is different from that of Witkiewicz. As always in Mrożek, it is ambiguous and ironical.

(1964)

II: Journal of a Traveling Spectator

IN THE CHINESE THEATRE

Ophelia

The Chinese Ophelia was fifteen years old and lived during the Ming dynasty. She could have been the contemporary of, or just a little older than, the other, more famous Ophelia. Both tragedies were performed at the same time; one at the Globe in London, the other in the vestibule of one of the countless Buddhist temples in Peking.

The Chinese Ophelia today is in fact sixteen and looks twelve. She is a slender swarthy girl with pink cheeks and long pigtails tied with red ribbons. She is dressed, as all the actors are, in a navy blue drill blouse and badly cut pants of the same color. She is a sixth-year student at the classical opera actors' school. In a moment she will be appearing before us on the stage. We sip bitter green tea and smile at each other, for a smile is more eloquent than the interpreter, who started learning Russian only two years ago. The Chinese Ophelia is really called Fou.

Fou means happiness. Her tiny fingers draw the black signs of one of the most beautiful hieroglyphs. In the country where calligraphy is an art, inscriptions hang like pictures in every chamber of the imperial palace. They are painted in black or red ink on big silk scrolls. Writing is a picture, or an idea of a picture. The Fou sign hangs by the imperial throne. It consists of four elements signifying man, earth, clothing, and food.

Ophelia's entry is preceded by a clatter from the orchestra. The hou-chin—a kind of Chinese violin with two strings ending in a resonator shaped like a small drum—plays the same monotonous phrase at a higher and higher pitch. The hou-chin is producing a shrill, wailing sound, which is suddenly accompanied by a high squeal from the shou, a little pot with a mouthpiece on which stands a small tower of pipes, long and short. The little la-pa trumpet answers in a high drawling tone. At last these wailing sounds are drowned by the ever faster and stronger bangs of the big metal plates called lob. Ophelia enters.

I would never recognize her. Her face is red, divided with a thick white, shadowlike line. Her eyes have thick black rings around them, her brows are like the pointed arches of Chinese roofs. On her head is a diadem of feathers, pearls, silver and colored balls. Her earrings hang down to her shoulders. She is dressed in rich, patterned, gaily colored silks, under which a silver sandal on a buskin occasionally shows. Her hands are hidden in wide sleeves and fluttering white kerchiefs.

Ophelia's stepfather is the evil mandarin. His face is painted yellow, except for a big white oval around his nose. Yellow means hypocrisy; the white spot signifies cruelty. On his head he has a black velvet cap with big flaps indicating he is a minister. He has imprisoned Ophelia's husband and wants to make her the emperor's concubine. Ophelia's old nurse has overheard the mandarin's conversation with the court procurer. She is dumb, so she runs to her mistress and tells her everything in gestures; her miming is accompanied by a wailing flute and the vibrating four-stringed banjo with which Chinese musicians achieve the effect of percussion.

Ophelia weeps. Standing with her back to the audience, she raises her arms; her shoulders are trembling. Her cry is also a dance, a dance in which only the shoulders and arms move. Ophelia turns slowly around. Her face is still impassive. The traditional make-up, with thickly pasted-on colors, changes the face into a mask. The mask is always the same. Only the mouth and the eyes are left to perform. No, not the eyes; just the look, expressing tears, though there are no tears.

Only now do the hands emerge from the wide sleeves. They are painted white. They begin to perform. Every finger is subjected to the rigors of an art whose rules were first set down over five hundred years ago. Nothing has been left to chance. But the discipline of the gesture can be as effective as the discipline of the alexandrine, as exact as mathematics, and as moving as the flutter of a bird. Two middle fingers, raised upward, the little finger bent to the side, have performed their dramatic phrase. In a moment the hands will disappear again in the folds of the sleeve. They are like actors who appear to speak their lines. The orchestra makes its sounds again: hou-chin wails, shou squeals. Ophelia sings with a constricted throat.

There is only one thing that can save her. In a little mime the old nurse tells her mistress that she should pretend to be mad. Big drums called kou, little drums called cha, and brass plates called lo are banging. Ophelia is called by her stepfather for questioning. The mandarin's flapping ears move under his black cap. His movements are those of a fox. Even if his face were not painted yellow, his movements would betray him.

Ophelia bursts out laughing. She laughs gaily, as young girls do. But the laughter goes on until it becomes terrifying. It is no longer a girl's laughter; it is a mad laughter. Suddenly it breaks, at the highest pitch, and only the drums bang their monotonous rhythm, louder and louder, faster and faster.

Ophelia puts her hands forward; she sees a bird, which we can see too. She chases it, wanting to catch it, but then she draws back, stands still, and escapes. The bird has changed into a snake. She runs up to her stepfather. She is shy; she is bold; she is ashamed. She is a virgin; she is a lover; she is a young bride on her wedding night.

We are watching the dumb nurse. Terrified, she flutters her hands. She no longer knows if the girl is pretending to be mad or has really gone mad. The mandarin draws back with revulsion. He has understood: she takes him for her husband.

This tense drama is quite unlike our theatre. Every gesture is moving, but never natural. It does not cease to be hieratic, even when it is most ambiguous. It expresses but does not imitate a real situation. It is always metaphor, convention, art.

Someone who has never seen classical Chinese opera may find it difficult to understand its formalism. Like classical ballet, it is based on discipline and metaphor. Every movement demands full control over one's body; every movement means something. Ophelia chases the mandarin by running fast on her knees. She is applauded, for a fast run on one's knees is technically very difficult. But the applause is not only for young Fou's technical accomplishment. A run on one's knees is also the expression of the lowest abasement and the deepest despair. When its metaphor is not understood, the Chinese theatre is merely the most beautiful of ballets.

Romeo and Juliet

In classical opera everything, except human emotion, is conventional. Feelings are genuine, violent, and elementary: love and hate, anger and jealousy, courage and cowardice, loyalty and betrayal.

A boy takes leave of a girl. She loves him. He does not know this and does not even know that he loves her. Their leave-taking is long and ceremonious. Confucian formalism lies even heavier on the theatre than on life; it is a social convention, a ceremonial that cannot be broken, a discipline of gesture.

The girl goes out and the boy looks after her. She has left the stage, but we can still see her going down the road, disappearing behind the first bend of the road, appearing again higher up, disappearing again, and coming in view again on a slope. The stage is empty; the boy is standing between the curtains. Everything is in his gesture and look. He stops looking, goes on his way, still on the empty stage. Then he pauses; he does not want to leave the spot where he has parted from her. He turns his head in the direction where the girl has disappeared. We know now that he does not see her any more, that he is looking at the empty road.

The short leave-taking scene lasts a number of minutes. It is full of emotion, though not one word is spoken. It depicts the moment when love is being born. Stendhal called it crystallization. But hundreds of years are needed to build theatre culture up to a point where crystallization can be contained in a look and a gesture.

I saw that scene a number of times, in Peking and Hangchow, in Chungking and Canton. I was more moved by it than by anything I have seen in the theatre so far. But only after many nights—invariably spent at the Chinese opera—did I learn to distinguish an individual actor's mastery from a gesture transmitted by generations.

The scene is part of one of the most popular operas in China today, *Liang Shan-po and Chou Ing-taj*. The boy is called Liang, the girl Chou. The story of their love comes from a very old Chinese tale. The opera was composed, or rather recomposed, in our times. The pathos, austerity, and simplicity of the old tragedy have remained intact, but a strange coating of sentimentality—probably dating from the first years of our century—has been superimposed. The opera is beautiful nonetheless.

Chou Ing-taj was a mandarin's daughter in the time of the Tang dynasty, almost fifteen hundred years ago, or perhaps in the time of the Sung dynasty, which was contemporary with Genghis Khan, or even in the time of the Yuan dynasty when Marco Polo arrived in China in 1275—Marco Polo

whose odd stone statue I saw in the Green Cloud temple in
Peking. He stands there in the company of five hundred stone
lohans. Lohans are the disciples of Buddha, something like
our Apostles. How the crafty Venetian became a Buddhist
saint is quite another story.

The brave, affectionate and noble mandarin's daughter
could also have lived in the time of the Ming dynasty: it is
most difficult to find out any date in China. For a modern
young Chinese, even one with a university education, the
historic past is divided into three periods: liberation; the
Kuomintang and the Japanese occupation; and feudal times.
The many ages of the feudal period are just one long period.

After a month in China I learned how to distinguish
roughly between the buildings, temples, and monuments of
the Ching, Ming, and Yuan dynasties. To my Chinese comrades all of them had been very long ago, in feudal times.
We Poles have a vivid historical consciousness; at least the
last three hundred years are full of meaning to us, present in
our experience. To a young Chinese, however, the feudal past
is one and indivisible. Of course, the history of China is four
thousand years old and not easy to learn. But that is not the
difficulty. For the present younger generation in China, history really began only five years ago. Living history at least.

At one of the exhibitions we were shown a color diagram of
the different epochs in Chinese history. A long black line
marked the period of the decline of feudalism. I looked at
the dates: the period began with the Sung dynasty and ended
with the Kuomintang; it covered a thousand years.

I also remember a spacious and sunny maternity center,
at Canton or Chungking. The visit began with the customary
lecture given by a young girl. Suddenly I heard the words,
"Our women now give birth in the socialist manner; in the
past they gave birth in the feudal manner." I asked the
interpreter to repeat the sentence. After a while he repeated
the same words. I could not help asking what it meant to give
birth in the feudal manner. The girl, surprised at my being
so naïve, said, "In the feudal times women gave birth in

filth, without hot water or any protection. To give birth in a socialist way means to do so under the care of a midwife and a doctor."

Chou Ing-taj lived in feudal times. She wanted to be educated, but girls were not allowed to attend school. She managed to get her father's permission and went to school, disguised as a boy. She wore long black robes and something like a medieval biretta with a square buckle. She was accompanied by her loyal maid who, also disguised as a boy, carried two small coffers on a bamboo stick.

In many Chinese operas we find maids and servants out of Molière. They are sometimes arrogant, invariably crafty and gay; often they represent courage, loyalty, and the popular feeling for justice. They are on the side of young lovers and help them in their troubles—when they can, that is, for most operas end tragically.

Liang Shan-po is also on his way to school, and his faithful servant carries his bags. The rest is quite simple. The girl falls in love with her young companion but does not divulge that she is a woman. She has promised her father never to reveal this, and she has to keep the promise. Three years later, the old mandarin calls his daughter home. Liang sees her off. They come back by the same road. The girl wants to tell him about her love, tell him that she is a woman. But how can she; how can she tell the secret and not tell it? They cross a footbridge hanging high over a mountain stream. There is no bridge, of course; the stage is empty as usual. Only occasionally is a fragment of the Chinese landscape marked on the backdrop. Liang is the first to step on the non-existent bridge. He does not look back after his companion, for he does not know she is a woman. Chou Ing-taj pretends to have lost her balance, begins to totter and cries out. Liang turns back, gives her his hand, and helps her to cross. The bridge in this scene is not real, but the girl's love is.

In the course of the scene, the actors also conjure up a well into which they look; two pigeons, which the girl shows to the boy; two fishes splashing side by side; and even an entire Buddhist temple where a marriage ceremony is going on. But the boy still does not understand, and only in the great leave-taking scene with which I began is he suddenly enveloped by the flames of love.

When Liang visits the girl at her home, it is too late. The old mandarin is preparing to marry her off to a rich man. The girl has to obey her father's will, and Liang dies for love. All she can do is persuade her father to let her visit her beloved's tomb on her wedding day. She is dressed in white, the color of mourning. She breaks away from her litter, which is actually only a silk veil carried over her head by two extras. Now we have genuine romantic thunder, plebeian and anti-feudal. The tomb opens and engulfs the loyal Chou Ing-taj. In the last scene, the tragic lovers, turned into butterflies and happy forever, dance in the sunshine.

A Little History

The Chinese theatre is older than any preserved texts or descriptions. Like every theatre of antiquity, it originated in ritual and religious dances, was connected with the cult of ancestors and heroes and with the ceremonious celebrations of the new year, the feast of spring, and the feast of autumn. We know that during the Han dynasty, from 200 B.C. to the early years of our era, the emperors used to bring actors and clowns to the court. The oldest fragments of plays known to us are from the northern Tsi dynasties (550–577). There is a story about a knight who saved the emperor, and a great hunters' drama about a young man who avenged his father who had been killed by a tiger. That splendid pantomime is performed to this day, and I saw it in Peking. The tiger was enchanting. To the same period belongs the first comedy about a drunkard; it is rather like the medieval farces about the sly treacherous wife and her lazy brute of a husband.

With the Sui and T'ang dynasties (590–906), whose rulers reunited China after a long period of division, the dramatized knightly epic began; something like the *Song of Roland* performed in the theatre. Around 750, Emperor Hsuan-tsung, an excellent ruler though excessively addicted to pageantry, established the first drama school of the Disciples of the Plum Orchard. The school was patronized with the greatest of enthusiasm by the emperor's beloved concubine, the famous Yang-Kuei-fei, who was said to be the most beautiful of women. She was very fond of the little nuts called litchi, whose stone tastes like a fragrant raisin. Yang-Kuei-fei arranged for a special imperial post to bring her fresh nuts every day from the south. This was the sole duty of those messengers, although they used the chance to plunder the emperor's subjects. The concubine's greediness was punished when feudal lords from the south rebelled and demanded Yang's beautiful head. The story was told in a number of later plays. The emperor lost his crown but gained immortality and became the god of actors.

In the great period of Chinese civilization during the Sung dynasty (960–1279), the theatre also flourished. Two great centers were created: in Peking and in the new capital Hangchow. We know almost a thousand titles of plays from that period, but not many texts have been preserved. Among those that have are satirical comedies whose targets are evil mandarins and inflation. Plebeian heroes appeared more and more frequently, and a new figure was born in the theatre—the young, valiant girl who saves the prince and the state in the manner of Joan of Arc, though without recourse to religion. Four large flags grow out of her shoulders, each representing an army of ten thousand men. The Chinese Joan fights with a sword against spears, and she always wins. To this day she remains the favorite heroine of Chinese audiences.

In Hangchow, near the big green lakes where the landscape is so sweet and artificial it is almost unreal, as if it had been painted by generations of Chinese masters of ink drawing, I saw the tomb of a hero of the Sung dynasty. He was Jue Fei, a general who victoriously resisted foreign invaders but died through the treachery of his own ministers who had been bribed. There is a temple dedicated to him, and he used to be worshiped like a Greek hero. Not only he but his father and mother, his four wives, his twelve sons and their wives, his brothers and all their wives have temples of their own. Altogether there are several dozen magnificent monuments devoted to their memory. The Confucian cult of ancestors is a cult of the family. But in addition to the monuments to the entire family of the heroic general, in the corner by the wall, beside a magnificent tomb, stand four pitiful statuettes. They are those of the minister who betrayed the general, his wife, and the two judges who condemned him. Next to them is a plaque with a worn inscription: PASSER-BY, PISS ON US. Jue Fei lived over eight hundred years ago, so it is no wonder that the statuettes of the traitors are in a miserable condition. The story of Jue Fei is a favorite theme of Chinese dramatists. It became a popular legend, and in this form returned on the stage.

In the eleventh and twelfth centuries China had the highest culture in the world. It was then that a learned mathematician, Shao Yung, wrote his famous sentence: "I am happy because I am human and not an animal; because I am Chinese and not a barbarian; and because I live in Lojang, the most beautiful city in the world." The great period of cultural development ended with the invasion by the Mongols who conquered China in the middle of the thirteenth century.

An old Chinese proverb says, "All rivers melt away in the Chinese sea." But before the Mongols melted away in the Chinese sea, they seriously disrupted the traditional feudal institutions. In their initial fervor they abolished the civil service system of examinations and banished from court the old noblemen and learned mandarins, many of whom had practiced literature and philosophy. Now they could not write for a sophisticated court elite any more, because the elite had ceased to exist. In order to reach a wider circle of readers they had to give up the old Confucian Chinese idiom, which was no longer intelligible to people, and write in a colloquial, living language. From then on plays were written in the new idiom.

This was one of the reasons why the theatre flourished. During the reign of the Yuan dynasty (1280–1368), called the golden age of Chinese drama, drama divided into three main types: moral, social, and mythological.

Moral drama was the most strongly influenced by Confucianism. The plays were moralistic and didactic, and the problem of concubines was the most important theme. Polygamy had existed throughout Chinese history and—together with other relics of feudalism—presented the authorities of the People's Republic with a grave problem. Some suggested that it should be abolished at one stroke, by a revolutionary decree. But one cannot change customs, or turn back the flood, by decree. Where would the old women go once they were turned out of the family community? The new marriage law prohibited polygamy in the future but recognized the validity of existing unions. The regulation of rivers and the full emancipation of the Chinese woman are both matters of a generation. The revolution in China not only struggles against a somewhat underdeveloped capitalism, but has to overcome huge rivers of feudalism, still threatening the nation with floods.

In the old China, the first wife was chosen for the son by his father. But husbands freely chose their concubines. These were mostly very young peasant girls whom they bought from the parents. The first wife had a privileged position, but her children and those born of concubines had equal rights. Some historians maintain that this is the reason the ruling feudal classes managed for centuries to avoid degeneracy. But the laws of social hatred are stronger than blood relations.

In a museum in Kunming I saw a terrifying exhibition of peasant misery. In showcases on one side one could see dresses, jewelry, and dishes that had belonged to landlords—magnificent fur coats, silk robes embroidered with golden threads, heavy silver bracelets, and earrings with pearls the size of peas. On the other side were poor peasants' clothes made of leaves and rags, a wooden plow and a primitive hoe, examples of the weeds and berries they had eaten to delay death from starvation. In a glass case, too, was a contract for the sale of a daughter, attested by finger and toe prints.

The moral drama of the Yuan dynasty did not attack the traditional institutions directly, but its sympathy was fully on the side of the underdog. Sometimes in the plays it is an unhappy pair of lovers who cannot be united; sometimes the heroine is a loyal and wronged wife. The most famous of those plays is about a singing girl. "The singing girl" and "the girl who always laughs" are Chinese names for prostitutes.

A certain rich merchant introduces a singing girl into his home as a concubine. He orders her to make the prescribed four bows to the first wife, who has a right to expect this and should—according to the rules of the detailed ceremonial—acknowledge only the fourth bow. But the first wife does not respond and, after a great quarrel, dies of grief.

The singing girl decides to get rid of the merchant. With the aid of her lover she sets the house on fire, steals his money, and throws the merchant into a canal. The criminal couple also plan to strangle the merchant's seven-year-old son and his nurse. Fortunately they are interrupted by a passer-by who buys the boy for a piece of silver. In the second act it turns out that the merchant managed to save himself and is now working as a swineherd. The starving nurse has become a singing girl. She meets the ex-merchant by chance, takes him with her, and supports him.

The third act takes place thirteen years later. The boy, bought for a piece of silver, has been carefully brought up by his guardian and is now a judge. He comes to his native town on business and stays at an inn. He asks for a singing girl to be brought to him, and to his amazement recognizes his nurse. After some dramatic and affectionate scenes he meets his father. Soon a pair of bandits is brought before him for trial. They are, of course, his father's concubine and her criminal lover. The judge condemns them to death and remains with his father who marries the loyal nurse.

This bloody drama contains what seems to us an amusing mixture of romantic melodrama and the naïve optimism of Dickens. But let us not forget that it is also an opera, in which even the most drastic situations are performed in a conventional and stylized manner.

A comedy about a miser, which is closer to Plautus than to Molière, belongs to the same type of morality play. It also abounds in purely oriental motives. I remember a scene in which the Chinese miser, who wants to save the expense of condiments for his rice, goes to a bazaar and handles the roast ducks that are for sale there. Then he returns home and eats his rice, licking his own fingers with delight.

The hero of the social plays is usually an industrious and learned young man who leaves his native town and goes to the capital to pass his examinations. The traditional institution of great state examinations existed for hundreds of years. The successful candidate, who had learned by heart all the Confucian books and mastered the most beautiful systems of calligraphy and the most difficult signs of the alphabet, became a high court official. At one time the French Encyclopédistes were most impressed with this democratic way of recruiting ministers and contrasted the Chinese kingdom of reason to European despotism. These competitions of learned candidates were abolished in the first decades of the Yuan dynasty, but later restored and survived until the last dynasty.

The plays dealing with examinations provided the dramatist with an opportunity to portray the court and all kinds of family conflicts. Thus the learned young man either is hopelessly in love with a girl from a higher class, or leaves his poor wife and poor parents behind at home. He places first in the examinations and becomes a dignitary. What a source of conflicts there! The young lovers can now be united, or the newly nominated mandarin forgets his wife and parents and marries, for instance, the prime minister's daughter. All the principles of Confucian morality are interpreted in detail in these plays; good is rewarded and evil punished.

The most interesting, however, are the mythological plays, a strange mixture of sharp realistic observation and the beliefs and myths of Buddhism and Taoism. There is one satiric comedy, from the time of the Yuans about the reincarnation of You Hsin, which is like a medieval Chinese version of Voltaire's *Candide* and Gogol's *Government Inspector* combined.

You Hsin, a corrupt judge, does not fear the emperor's deputy. He takes the view that nothing can change destiny and no one ever dies before his time. When the emperor's emissary arrives in town, the other bribetakers are terrified, but You Hsin receives the news calmly, goes to see the local shaman and asks for his horoscope. He learns that he will die in two hours. He returns home, mocks the imperial inspector, warns his young wife not to marry again, and dies.

In the next act, You Hsin stands accused before the judge of the underworld. For his meanness, extortion and bribetaking he is condemned to count coins immersed in a huge caldron of boiling oil. It is a very unpleasant occupation. Fortunately for him, the shaman arrives from earth to save him. For the price of a double vow of purity and poverty and the promise to convert to Taoism, You Hsin obtains the right to return to earth.

In the third act we are back on earth. Unfortunately, You Hsin's wife has already cremated his body. You Hsin has no choice: he must return to earth in the body of a butcher who has just died. The butcher was lame and very ugly. You Hsin will now be lame. In his first incarnation, the commentator adds, he had a crooked conscience; in the second, he will have crooked legs.

You Hsin returns to his young wife in the butcher's body, followed by the butcher's old wife. The two women engage in a violent quarrel: to whom does the husband belong; which is more important, the soul or the body?

In the fourth act, in a sharp satiric trial scene, You Hsin

declares that for the sake of peace he is ready to live with both women. The shaman arrives unexpectedly and reminds him of his vow of purity. Such is the sad end of the corrupt judge.

In the time of the Yuans, Chinese drama flourished. In the era of the Ming dynasty (1368–1644) plays grew longer and longer. A four-act drama with a prologue and epilogue was expanded into stories in dialogue which night have from thirty to eighty acts. Basic themes remained unchanged, but additional episodes and plots were grafted onto them. Almost the entire life of the hero was shown on the stage. The border between a novel and a play became blurred.

During the Ming dynasty, theatre returned to the imperial court, but retained its popular character. By that time it was deeply rooted in the life of the nation. Every province, every town had its own troupe. Comedians performed at weddings and family festivals; performances were an inevitable part of every feast and celebration. Actors wandered around villages and performed in the vestibules of temples. Theatre became inextricably linked with the customs of everyday life. It was splendid ballet and magnificent opera at the imperial court; but at the same time it was a popular simple entertainment all over China.

The basic form of Chinese opera was shaped during the Ming dynasty. It underwent many changes later, of course. Aristocratic and plebeian tendencies struggled for ascendancy. The rigorous and hypocritical Is dynasty removed women from the stage. Music was radically transformed; the old Chinese instruments—the flute and the two-sided fiddle—gave way to pipes and strident percussion instruments. But the character of the performance did not change. It became fixed and survived almost unchanged to our time.

(1954)

OBRAZTZOV AND THE PUPPETS

The lion is young and playful. The tamer is old and ugly. The lion regards his tamer with utmost indignation and is disgusted when the tamer puts his head between the lion's jaws. The tamer's hair is filthy; it is no pleasure to hold a head like that on one's tongue. The lion loathes the tamer. But what can he do? The tamer is stronger and holds a long whip in his hand, so the lion has to obey. He opens and closes his mouth to order. But in the end he gets bored. Even a trained lion can lose his patience. He opens his mouth somewhat wider than usual and simply swallows the tamer. Everybody enjoys it immensely; people laugh and clap their hands. And rightly. This is not a circus but a puppet theatre.

Obraztzov has discovered a great secret of the puppet theatre. In the circus the audience's sympathy is with the tamer; a lion gobbling a man up would evoke terror and fear. In a puppet theatre it is the lion who evokes sympathy and the audience applauds the tamer's tragic end with full moral satisfaction. The same rules and the same moral laws apply to the puppet theatre and the fairy tale. Obraztzov has discovered the domain of realistic fantasy for the puppet theatre.

"An actor is, first of all, himself and only then the hero of a play," Obraztzov told me at supper in Leningrad. A puppet is the image of man, man in general, man as man. One cannot represent a matchbox by means of a matchbox; one can only show the matchbox. This is the difference between the word *show* and the word *represent*. By means of a matchbox one can represent a man, a horse, or a motor car. All one has to do is fasten to it some circles, sticks, or a little ball. An actor shows man, a puppet represents man.

It is not man that actors present on the stage but different kinds of men. Puppets enable the more general human qualities to be expressed. Molière's Harpago is an excellent portrait of a miser. But the raven in La Fontaine's fables is pure pride, and the fox pure craftiness. For this reason fable and fairy tale are the puppet theatre's natural domain. Man can be expressed only by something that is not a man. A puppet expresses what is most human, what is common to all men.

"And this is why," Obraztzov went on, "I do not like to work with puppets whose faces are too expressive, too characteristic. They are dead and will not live on the stage. They cannot change and are limited to a few gestures, to a single facial expression. Disney's Mickey Mouse, on the other hand, can perform any character, and he is different every time."

Obraztzov calls his method of representing man through puppets "the art of improbability" and finds his supreme models in Swift, La Fontaine, Krylov. I would instead call his art a theatrical philosophical tale. By means of puppets, Obraztzov shows the real world: patterns of feelings, gestures, situations, suffering and passion, wrongs, dreams, even politics. This is what Voltaire used to do. After all, what are Candide or Dr. Pangloss but puppets endowed by the great writer with a few unchanging gestures and a great deal of common sense? Yet the picture of the eighteenth-century world shown in Candide's travels is true and tells us more about dying feudalism than many a historical dissertation. I would like to see *Candide* in a puppet theatre.

Obraztzov is the greatest wizard now living. In Leningrad I attended his own performance where he manipulated the puppets himself. He hid behind a low screen, which was made into a miniature stage, put little puppets on the fingers of both hands, and offered us magic. Two little kittens sang and lived a romance both moving and tragic; a sad drunkard got tipsy and drank vodka out of a bottle not much smaller than himself; a Spanish Carmen danced with a toreador who then betrayed her.

Obraztzov demonstrated all the technical possibilities of a one-man puppet theatre: one puppet; two puppets playing together; a puppet and a man in a mask and costume; three puppets, one placed on the puppetmaster's head, the other two on his hands; the head puppet alone. Imagine a humorous puppet of a sentimental woman singer with an elaborate hairdo and her hands crossed on her chest. They are the hands of Obraztzov himself, disproportionately big compared to the face, which makes her look even funnier. The hands perform the complete story of a sentimental love song: meeting and desire, desertion and disillusion, bitterness and despair. They tremble, flutter, are bent and wrung.

But the greatest wonder was reserved for the last part of the evening. Obraztzov showed us a puppet theatre without puppets. He put little wooden balls on his index fingers, and his hands became puppets. An ordinary human hand with a wooden ball on its index finger personifies all human feelings; not symbols of feelings or vague moods, but movements, gestures, and human characters depicted in a visionary caricature with the mark of genius. Obraztzov's hand transformed itself into the figure of a decadent Russian intellectual, straight out of a novel by Dostoevsky. The hand disintegrated morally, took bribes, got drunk, excited passions, repented. We all know the gesture of despair when one puts one's head in one's hands. His hand put the head on the knees, embraced it. The hand had a head, a face, knees, hands, legs, chest. Obraztzov's hand with a little wooden ball on the index finger was transformed into the most real Smerdyakov I have ever seen in my life.

These were the utmost, the furthest limits of the theatre. A theatre without décor, actor, or puppet—a theatre that is only a hand, a hand emerging from behind a screen to personify a living man endowed with facial expression though he has no face; gesticulating, though he has no hands; dancing, though he has no arms or legs. The five fingers express passions. It was one of the greatest artistic experiences of my life.

Obraztzov was an actor in Stanislavsky's theatre. In 1920 he began, as he himself puts it, to play with puppets; first for his own enjoyment, then professionally. Supported by a handful of enthusiasts, he created the Soviet puppet theatre. In czarist Russia there had not been a single professional puppet theatre, and the tradition of folk puppetry was slowly dying out. Today there are over a hundred professional puppet theatres and nearly three times as many amateur groups, all indebted to Obraztzov.

Obraztzov is actor and producer, theoretician and organizer, even maker of many of his puppets. Above all, he is a great artist. Since 1930 he has been in charge of the State Central Puppet Theatre which he founded in Moscow. Unlike the marionettes of the Italian Dei Piccoli theatre, his puppets are manipulated from below by a system of wires and are mounted on sticks. They are of different sizes; often the same puppets are made in several sizes so that they can perform on different levels and give the illusion of perspective. There are fantastic puppets—for instance a variety of devils in Gogol's *Christmas Night*; realistic ones—figures of the actors and the child in the same play; caricatures—the figures of singers, dancers, and musicians in *The Concert*.

I cannot really describe the unbelievable technical perfection of these amazing performances: the pianist moves his fingers as he plays, the dancers perform their steps, the cellist moves his bow in time to the music. But the great charm of Obraztzov's theatre is not only the skill of its technical execution. It is, above all, a theatre of dazzling wit and invention. Sometimes it is a specifically puppet joke— the big bosom of an operatic singer inflates like a balloon. Sometimes the joke arises out of a particular situation—in

Christmas Night an imp attaches his torn-off tail to his be-hind, hoping that they will grow together again. There are also superb moral and political jokes—a Cossack deputation kow-tows before the little barking fox terriers who accompany the czaritsa at the imperial court.

(1947)

RAIKIN

It is enough for him to move his hand across his face; his nose thickens and droops or tilts naïvely, his mouth widens in a smile to his ears or is contorted in a grimace; his eyes become round and shiny, or watery and sad, or narrow and sly. It is enough for him to smooth or rough up his hair, to stick on a mustache, put on a hat, or pull a cap over his eyes, and he is a dentist, professor, personnel manager or his victim, director, messenger boy, hooligan, student in love, a timid applicant, an awesome superior, anything you like. He can be any of us.

The old lady—one of those who before the war used to guide visiting foreigners—has hardly disappeared behind the door when, in another door, a Hindu appears, arriving at the Intourist office in Leningrad. He has gone and at the same moment an English journalist enters through a third door.

He withdraws his head behind the curtain for the twinkling of an eye, and a new character stands before us. Sometimes he puts on a mask or uses a prop. But this is not necessary. He does not even need his face; his legs are enough; a few steps and a character, situation, psychology has been sketched—just by the way he walks.

Raikin is one of the last representatives in Europe of the art with which acting began and that for many centuries was the only popular theatre. It is the great tradition of mimes, clowns, and transformists or quick-change artists.

This art requires absolute control over the body, precision of movement, an unfailing memory of a thousand gestures, faces, intonations. Raikin as an imitator is a genius. An actor creates a character out of several dozen, or several hundred, lines of dialogue, and out of a thousand situations that enable him to perform his drama. In the genre represented by Raikin, minutes are counted in seconds—a minute means an act; within a minute a whole play has to be performed. In the course of a couple of seconds, the actor has to sketch out a character, make it credible and convincing, evoke the feeling of sympathy or raise laughter. It is art in its original, literal and pure sense, like conjuring, virtuosity and acrobatics.

It is an art bordering on witchcraft. Raikin reminds me of the other great wizard, Obraztzov, who can enact a love story with two little balls fixed on his index fingers. Raikin's art is even simpler. He acts with himself, so there is no room for metaphor in his art. In the art of a mime and a quick-change artist, text plays the part of a prop; it is just a scenario, nothing more, because the character is always created by Raikin himself.

He creates a hundred characters, but never ceases to be himself. Raikin presents a character as a conjuror presents his trick. Then he bows and stands there before us—a smiling gentleman with shining black eyes, a bit self-conscious, probably sad. In the great art of imitating shown by Raikin there is nothing of the cruel jeer and almost no bitterness. Rather there is sentiment, gentle humor, a little irony and much goodness; even understanding. It is a very human art.

Raikin and his group perform their scenes against the background of abominable sets and appalling music, which remind one of a provincial theatre at the turn of the century. But at one point those awful landscapes with a blue pond in a haze or a painted monument ceased to bother me. I suddenly visualized nineteenth-century Warsaw with its garden theatres—Swiss Valley, or the Saski Gardens. Somehow all these characters belong to that period: the fireman shyly courting a girl on a Sunday, the old professor recalling his youth, the whipping boy in a tailor's establishment, the Don Juan who has been hooked by a shrew, or the husband writing a learned work while minding the baby. This type of humor, of moral satire, of make-up all belong to those years; as does the collection of human sins here presented. Raikin's theatre is a blend of provincialism, the nineteenth century, and genius.

(1957)

KNOW'ST THOU THE LAND . . .

A comedy written by a Neapolitan about Neapolitans should open with the drinking of coffee. Life in Naples begins with coffee. Nowhere else does coffee have such flavor, not even in the narrow, gold-and-blue streets around St. Mark's Square in Venice. Coffee in Naples is served in tiny cups; there are not more than three sips of it, but with those three sips the day begins and the heart beats. Neapolitan coffee has a unique bitter taste which remains on the tongue for a long time. The best blend is called Vesuviana, which is also the name of the electric railway that leads to Pompeii and Sorrento. Indeed, there is something of hot lava about that coffee.

But smoky Vesuvius appears only on the oh-so-blue postcards as a background to the pair of lovers kissing under an orange tree, or to a girl, made up to look like Lollobrigida, modeling a new bathing suit. In real life it is not easy to see Vesuvius from Naples. What one can see very well are two huge furnaces emitting tall columns of fire, day and night.

"Know'st thou the land where lemons ripen . . . ?" I know it. The real Naples is a big industrial city of nearly a million inhabitants. Work here has always been hard to get. The inhabitants of the north say that Neapolitans are lazy and prefer lying on warm stones to doing honest work. But here in the south people know very well that there is not enough work and macaroni to go around for everybody. In this world there is only enough sun, water, and love for all.

At five A.M. old peasants carrying cases full of tomatoes, grapes or lemons get off the Vesuviana railway, preceded by a crowd of youths in white tee-shirts and rolled-up trousers. They go to work, or to look for work. The countryside here is still semifeudal in its structure. Large estates and vineyards, climbing up green and brown hills, lie next to little fields of soil burned down to ash.

The village misery closely surrounds the city. In the stony little squares beside a Renaissance fountain or a chipped Greek statue, a market for farm workers is going on, just as it did a hundred, or five hundred, years ago. The frontier between the white and the black city, between riches and misery throughout Italy, is marked most clearly in Naples. If you walk from the sea up the Via Roma, on the right, sunny squares go down to the center, full of plumes and statues of kings; there are chairs and tables under colorful marquees; green parrots squawk in their big cages. Everywhere is marble, steps, space.

On the left from the Via Roma, streets go up, so narrow that with outstretched arms one can touch the walls on either side. They are dark even in daytime, they are stuffy even at night. Old dilapidated houses are four or five stories high; the streets are simply corridors between walls. A strange net of ropes with drying laundry reaches from the ground level up to the rooftops. White sheets, yellow, blue, red clothes and rags hang everywhere. It looks as if the whole of Naples did a gigantic washing every day. The place smells of onions, garlic, fried fish.

The streets are black and thronged with people. I have seen such streets only in Canton. Everybody shouts, gesticulates wildly, swears, curses and laughs. Half-naked begging children crawl at one's feet. Street vendors push their carts with red fish cut open, starfish moving on tin plates, and little golden calamari. In the doorways mothers give breasts to their babies. In the little shops opening onto the street one can see street barbers and dentists. On street corners candles are burning in front of statues of saints and the Madonna. There seem to be no miraculous pictures in Italy, just marble Madonnas. Some have had their noses chipped off, though. They are those who did not answer prayers during the plague.

Naples—the city of millionaires. Everybody wants to sell everything here, including himself. Most people, however, sell shoelaces, belts, sunglasses, large whispering sea shells, and American contraband; or lemon juice diluted with water and cold remnants of not very freshly brewed coffee; or, most of all, Neapolitan pizza, which takes the place of bread.

Naples—the city of millionaires . . . What are the millionaires to live on if they are not to die of starvation? They live as they can, off the tourists. On the way out of the railway station you are nearly torn to pieces by taxi drivers; toothless old women explain something to you in a most complicated manner; intermediaries take you to hotels where you will never get a room; boys and girls throw quick appraising glances at you, from top to bottom, and then look you questioningly in the eye; theirs is a velvet and meaningful look. The waiter adds to your bill a bottle of wine you have not drunk, and then swears by all that is holy, spreading his arms in a helpless gesture, "It cannot be otherwise, signore." You can haggle to your heart's content, you can pay five hundred lire instead of two thousand, and still you will have paid twice as much as the worth of what you are buying. "It cannot be otherwise, signore." Cheating is the law here; it is as natural as the sun, air and hunger. But it is always accompanied by a smile asking for forgiveness and admitting the guilt.

There are fine museums in Naples and in them some of the most beautiful Greek and Roman sculpture. But why look for antiquity in the museums? I was there in September while the festa di Napoli was on. Carts and trucks, covered with flowers, splendidly decorated, displayed mythological scenes in the Corso. Four-year-old girls dressed as marquises and Colombines in rustling tissue gowns were dancing in the streets. Complete in their fancy dress, even with beauty spots, they solemnly curtsied before the street photographer, who exploded his magnesium, as in the good old days.

But it was the crowd that I found the most delightful and moving. I had been to Paris on July fourteenth but here, for the first time, I saw a city's entire population amusing itself. On the embankments, groups of boys and girls were running, segregated, as is usual in the south. Every boy and every girl was carrying a twig with a bouquet of tissue paper at the end. The twigs became entangled with one another, tickled the eyes, lips, breasts. A large paper pot fell from behind on a couple of lovers who carelessly stood by the wall. The shrill sound of whistles was deafening. A group of boys came running fast as the wind and beating everybody, left and right, with fish bladders. I did not know Greece, but for the first time I had an idea of the Dionysia.

Naples is unforgettable—unlike any other city, innocent and sensual; pious and blasphemous; ancient and modern; deceitful and boiling over with simple human friendliness. Forgive me for writing about the city and not about its plays. But without Naples there would be no comedies of Eduardo de Filippo. He is actually more Neapolitan than Italian. He is of that unique city; full of the spirit of the fair, full of acute observation; friendly and melodramatic.

The scene where someone pretends to be dead, or the scene when the jealous husband crawls under the table, are the classic tricks of the theatres in the fairs and they were familiar to the old commedia dell'arte. The alleged corpse is a father who wants to cheat his impatient heirs, or a lover who wants to know the real feelings of his fickle mistress. De Filippo has modernized the scene and given it realistic motivation by transferring it to the period of the last war. It is a Neapolitan tram driver who pretends to be dead during a police raid so that he can hide a load of groceries in his bed.

In de Filippo's comedies, people, gestures, the little and

the big dramas of everyday life are true. The climate of their city gives them brilliance. Perhaps this is all that is needed to write a comedy. *Naples, the City of Millionaires,* is a play about simple human feelings. There is a certain amount of melodrama in it, but one must not be afraid of that. There is bourgeois melodrama as well as popular melodrama. Eduardo de Filippo's is a popular play in which goodness triumphs. Let us not reproach the author. Perhaps this time the beautiful Maria Rosaria will stop walking with Americans and Amadeo will stop stealing car tires. In real life it happens otherwise, but the Neapolitan playwright knows this as well as we do.

It is worth going to see *Naples.* But before you go to the theatre, have a cup of good coffee.

(1955)

THE RETURN OF THE HARLEQUIN

For the first time in my life I saw a comedy written for voices and gestures, for ballet, circus and mime, for action and improvisation. Every actor in that enchanting performance was an instrument, but an instrument of a strange kind; he had not only a definite register of tones, but also a register of gestures. Commedia dell'arte is a concerto for actor-instruments. In that concerto there is brass, woodwind, and percussion: the old men, the lovers, and the Harlequin. Or rather, a movement for marionettes, a movement for china figurines, and a movement for Harlequin.

Pantalone and Dottore are a couple of narrow-minded, quarrelsome, ridiculous old men. Pantalone is thin and wears a mask with a huge black nose, like a beak. Dottore is fat and constantly murmurs lines from a fat book he is holding. Dottore speaks with a bass voice, Pantalone with a treble voice. Dottore stretches his hooked finger toward Pantalone's chest: they are quarreling, shouting, talking faster and faster, until Dottore, with his bass, is droning: Boo, Boo! Imagine now a viola da gamba and a French horn who are rich Venetian merchants, arrange marriages for their children and play a morality scene in an inn; imagine a French horn and a viola da gamba that dance, sing, and play.

The beautiful Beatrice of Turin appears for the first time in female attire in the third act. Pantalone struts and swells. His beak is raised up, he bristles, shifts from foot to foot. Pantalone has now become an old cock. He has a cock's legs,

claws on his feet; he flutters his wings. He is a cock, but he
has not ceased to be a quarrelsome Venetian merchant.
He is a mask, a bird, a marionette.

Now he has descended from the wooden rostrum of a stage
put up in the market place, has taken off his mask. He is
only an old man. He is walking slowly, wiping his forehead
with a large handkerchief. Suddenly he jumps back onto the
wooden stage. He shakes the actors, mixes them up, asks
them to sing; he is now a conductor.

Clarissa is funny and beautiful. She has very thin, very
long arms and legs. She has a porcelain voice and porcelain
gestures. Now she faints rhythmically, swaying on her little
spider's legs. They raise her up and again she falls into her
posture of a Sèvres or Meissen figurine.

Harlequin is small and stocky. His dress and mask are
the most authentic. A black mask with openings for eyes
and mouth gives his face the look of a cat or a fox. It is a
mask strikingly similar in its shape to the masks of the
Chinese opera. Harlequin belongs to a different world than
the old men, the lovers and Brighella. They have a limited
repertory of gestures. Harlequin has every possible gesture.
He doubles and trebles himself, changes and transforms himself. He is a poor starved servant and a great conjuror. He is
all intelligence, elemental, a demon of movement. He puts
two flowers in his mouth and, for a dozen seconds, is a beautiful woman. He is neither a clown nor a marionette. It is he
who pulls the strings of all the other characters in the comedy. He sets the mechanism of this little world in motion. But
at the same time he parodies and mocks it. For he is the
only one who knows all the moves.

The return to such a conception of Harlequin seems to
me to be the greatest achievement of the Piccolo Teatro of
Milan. I cannot tell when exactly Harlequin of the commedia dell'arte became the sad rococo Pierrot; when he lost
his plebeian, goatish and devilish qualities. Gilles of the
eighteenth-century theatre was still the old popular Harlequin. But Pierrot in the Watteau painting is only a sad,
disillusioned boy, lost at a court masquerade.

The grimace on his mouth lasted all through the nineteenth century; the dumb participant of courtly minuets passed onto the cushions of bourgeois drawing rooms. From the days of symbolism onward he again disturbed painters' imaginations. The twentieth century dressed him up as a clown, discovered Harlequin still had a whitened face and a sad grimace. He was an ironic poet; sometimes he moved, sometimes he jeered. He was expelled from real life; he was dead. He was stuffed with sawdust, was a puppet. A puppet can be given any posture, even the most disturbing one. The Italian theatre restored Harlequin to life by discovering in him the original character of the theatre, perhaps even the very principle of the theatre.

Every theatrical reconstruction—of which we have seen so many—was stillborn. At the best of times, it was a theatre museum set in motion. The Milanese production of *Harlequin, Servant of Two Masters*, is, in its costumes, masks, gestures, musical and ballet score, a faithful and close reconstruction of the old commedia dell'arte. And yet, it is a refreshing performance, as refreshing as a cold shower. Theatre at last, true theatre at last, theatre we had dreamed of.

Certainly there is in it a perfection of actors' technique. To achieve this dazzling purity of gesture and the freedom of apparent improvisation, months of rehearsal and years of training were needed. It is not the technique that enchants us in this performance, however, but its authenticity. It radiates the joy of life.

Every gesture, every situation is stylized, finished and complete. And yet, we have the impression that everything is taking place for the first time, that it has just been invented and we are the only ones ever to see it. This return to commedia dell'arte is at the same time an enchanting revelation of the very nature of theatre. Harlequin's return is his triumph.

(1958)

Spoleto, 22 June

At the inaugural luncheon yesterday I met an avant-garde poet and playwright—author of some comedies—by the name of F. They call him: dottore. This word "dottore" sounds to me as if it had been taken out of a comedy, a comedia dell'arte; I don't know why. F. is employed at a South American embassy in Rome; he is something of a journalist and runs after celebrities. His comedies have not been published, but with the second brandy he manages to tell me that they are being translated into many languages. He is translating them himself, trying his strength in languages he does not know. He translated his last comedy, with the help of a friend, into Kurdish. He says that in Kurdish his comedy is particularly interesting. In Italian the comedy is less than a page long; in Kurdish it is still shorter, for Kurdish is said to be a very concise language.

I am called maestro here. Most amusing that. G. is right. It is situations that make us. The Spoleto Festival is a ballet, a commedia dell'arte where parts have been distributed in advance. The setting is magnificent. The town itself is the set. In the theatre the order is reversed. The main stage is the auditorium. The boxes are open like little stage models with the fourth wall removed; little boxes in which twice daily, in the afternoon and in the evening, the principal commedia dell'arte of Spoleto takes place. In these Italian gilded theatres the auditorium is like a box of chocolates. Female chocolates are in colorful wrappers, male chocolates in gray and navy blue dinner jackets. All the chocolates keep turning round, licking their lips, tasting, or at least rustling their black and colored wrappers.

Dottore F. was in his box with a very young Italian ballerina, who was sitting straight like a marionette. With her hair done up very high she looked like a dwarf out of a picture by Goya. The little ballerina is fourteen and a half. Dottore F. says that primavera foreshadows summer. The parts have been distributed, but they are few; some are from Viennese operetta, others from commedia dell'arte. No wonder then that I have to play two parts in town; that of maestro in my trattoria and that of a poor student in the festival committee. For in the festival comedy *dei Due Mondi* there are also studenti.

Boys wander about the streets and cast glances. Only the Englishmen are fair, some of them looking like young archangels. They sit in the boxes of the Italian theatre dressed in black, navy blue, even red dinner jackets, composed, distant, absent. In the daytime they look very sporting in light unbuttoned shirts, with sweaters thrown over their shoulders, Italian style.

There are also smiling, mostly very tall, English and Canadian women, who belong to the summit of the social Olympus here. Smartly dressed, they speak excellent Italian, French, and English. My wife calls such girls "alibians." They are always impeccably brought up. What astonishes me, however, is that one of the principal alibians of the Festival is pregnant. But perhaps this is the very summit of alibianism.

Real girls come, or rather are brought, here only at weekends, in cars the size of battleships. They are taken at once to Pentagramma, the most exquisite restaurant in Spoleto, and stuffed with rice salad. It is a kind of risotto, boiled rice with little pieces of meat and vegetables, rather like chicken feed. In our country chickens and ducks are fed in a like manner shortly before they are due for slaughter.

Spoleto, 24 June

Yesterday I saw for the first time in my life a satellite in flight. It was as if a star suddenly started to move. At the first glance it seems motionless. And then the sudden shock: it begins to move. The satellite in flight could be observed for a good couple of minutes.

It is not a pleasant sight. It disturbs ingrained habits far too much. It is as if an established order were collapsing. When one looked at the stars they were always fixed. The sky changes very slowly, never while you are watching it. It changes from night to night, or rather from month to month. There is enough disturbance as it is with the phases of the moon. I feel as if the basic security of the skies were being threatened.

It was just after twelve. The heat could still be felt slightly. Piazza della Libertà was still crowded at that time while the festival was on. Men were standing in groups and pointing toward the satellite. But no one got up from the tables huddled together along the side of the square adjoining the ruins of the Roman amphitheatre. Hot espresso was sipped, spoons banged against ice-cream bowls, glasses in which a black coffee bean could be seen in the transparent sambuco were raised against the light. Perhaps the satellite often passed over Spoleto at this hour. Or they were too lazy to get up to look. To them it was a normal occurrence. Perhaps my feelings, my fear, were medieval.

26 June

Two evenings spent with Negroes of the *Gospel Time* choir. The fattest, kindest, most likable of them was called

Anna Washington. In no time she showed me a photograph of her daughters. The eldest was twenty, the youngest four. In her familiarity she reminded me of an old, fat, Jewish mamma.

I cannot resist the impression that these Negroes are Jews. Maybe that was the reason their show moved me so. A group of Negro men and women dressed in short, colored cottas praise the Lord with their marvelous deep voices. They throw their hands about, shout, jump, slap their hands, try to convince one another that God has been born, for them, and that he is next to them, in the stable. They keep repeating the same words, like God or gospel, or good tidings. They repeat them a hundred, a thousand times, as if they still could not believe in them. With their splendid voices they sell their good tidings; like the proprietors of little stores with haberdashery and second-hand goods in Bielańska and Tłomackie in Warsaw before the war, who used to drag the passers-by into their tiny shops and repeat ten, a hundred times over in fine guttural voices, "This is the most beautiful piece of silk cloth in the world."

Negro spirituals are songs. But in this marvelous ensemble suddenly hands and feet, belly, the entire body begins to sing. The joy at good tidings is physical, shakes the whole body. This physical mysticism gradually spreads to the auditorium, until everybody claps enthusiastically.

The next day

In our cultural sphere to nod one's head at prayer seems strange. One can put it in a sophisticated way and say that we have lost the Dionysian element in religion. Or one can simply say that we do not dance prayer. Vehement rhythms do not lead us to religious ecstasy. These Negroes singing, shouting, clapping their good tidings keep reminding me of the Jews.

Nearly two months ago I strolled early in the evening, as

was my custom, round Saint-Paul and the rue des Rosiers.
The streets were almost empty at that time. Suddenly, a fat
old man in a hat approached me and asked if I had already
said my prayer for the dead. I said I had not. "Would you
like to say your Kaddish?" he asked. I said I would.

He talked in guttural French, but he asked me something in
Hebrew and Yiddish. Once more he reassured himself: "You
are a Jew?" He took me a couple of streets farther on to a
small private synagogue. In the lobby a group of women was
standing. Inside on the left there was a long table, at which
men in round hats and long coats were sitting. They were
eating and drinking. In the middle of a fairly small room two
huge candlesticks were burning in front of tablets with the
Commandments. On the right stood another candlestick, a
small one. In front of it a lean-faced young man waggled back
and forth, slowly at first then faster and faster, almost to
frenzy, shouting something, the same words over and over
again, it seemed to me.

I stood in front of the burning candlesticks and thought
about my father and mother; and about my father's parents,
and about my mother's parents. That was my prayer for the
dead. On my left the men in hats were eating and drinking
at their solemn Friday supper. On my right, the young Jew
stopped rocking and stood motionless in front of his little
candlestick. In what other town will another stranger ask me
if I have said my Kaddish?

Spoleto, 28 June

Last night I went to *La Traviata*; or rather to the first three
acts of it. I found the third act hard to bear. The performance
is said to be musically poor; the chorus and the conductor
are disappointing. I do not know much about it and do not
care, really. I was interested in Visconti's production. He
went the whole hog, to the very limits of nineteenth-century
descriptive realism. He was fascinated by fragments, details,

particulars. He wanted everything to be real, lifelike. He wanted tables and settees to be in the right period style, the dress coats to have an authentic nineteenth-century cut; he even wanted the trinkets to be authentic. After supper—with real wine, of course—guests threw their napkins on the table or on the floor. With obvious relish Visconti instructed his actors to tread on them. In the second act, there was an iron flue on the stage which led across to a small stove. Not an expressionist flue, not ugly and monstrous as in American neo-realism, not a symbolic flue, not a metaphorical flue— an aesthetic flue ashamed of itself, but an ordinary flue, a genuine flue, a simple pipe leading to a burning iron stove. I can imagine how Visconti enjoyed having that flue on the stage.

Everything here was excessive. One settee, two settees, three settees. I thought that someone would lie down on them, that they would serve a purpose, play their part. Nothing like that. No one sat on them. They were just there.

Visconti wanted *La Traviata* to be an opera, an unashamedly nineteenth-century opera. Visconti did not require intelligence from his artistes. In the style he adopted no gestures could offend. Let the tenor be just a tenor, very much a tenor. Let the coloratura soprano press her hands against her ample breasts. Visconti decided to achieve the purity of genre by bringing bad taste to absolute perfection. This he achieved. While rehearsing he must often have dreamed of Stanislavsky. I am afraid, however, that those dreams were nightmares.

Spoleto, 7 July

Last night I went for the second time to *Gospel Time*. It is not music to be listened to; one eats it. Jazz enters one's body, gets inside one. The same happens with some of the songs from *Gospel Time*. God is praised here with music we know from night clubs. The rhythm, which was to us an

erotic sign and symbol, tells us now of the birth of Jesus.
That is why we are shocked. In this rhythm we have never
prayed and only sometimes, very infrequently, dreamed.
Spirituals are akin to blues, which preceded jazz. There is fear,
longing, despair, yearning in them. We do not always understand their message.

To us jazz is the language of alcohol, eroticism, abandon,
brutality. And suddenly in this language the story of Mary
and Joseph is being told. Hence our astonishment. There
are no distinct languages to express pain and exaltation,
rapture and fear, blasphemy and joy, prayer and eroticism.
Just as there are no distinct kinds of music. Spirituals reveal
a common dark sphere in which rapture and longing, fear
and desire are all mixed together. In jazz, as in love, vulgar,
loathsome, indecent words become expressions of promise,
seduction, endearment. They can even become prayer. The
Infant Christ can be praised through rock 'n' roll.

8 July

I became friends with K. and L., a couple of young stage
designers. They were shocked by my attacks on Visconti.
I told them he was killing the theatre, leading it into a blind
alley. Visconti can do anything, they replied. No one else
can achieve absolute purity of style. In vain I tried to persuade them that purity of style is lethal; that theatre is by
definition, by principle, and in its very essence, impure; that
our epoch, our sensitivity, even our thoughts are impure.

They talked to me rapturously about the film Visconti
made of Lampedusa's *Leopard*. They also told me that Visconti is to a certain extent like the narrator of the novel:
an aristocrat who so despises our own time that he invokes
all other periods—past and future—to avoid the present.
Therefore Visconti is at the same time a patrician, a libertine
out of his time, and a near-communist intellectual.

9 *July*

A wonderful afternoon spent at the performance of Sicilian marionettes, the Opera dei Pupi from Palermo. Unfortunately the *History of Roland* is not performed any more, but I saw the adventures of the dauntless Corradino. In Sicily the institution of storytellers who for a couple of lire tell unending romances of chivalry in the evenings has survived to this day. The marionette version of *Corradino* tells of a late medieval romance, one of those that, like the famous story of Alexander, toward the end of the sixteenth century became popular folklore literature. The synopsis is given on the poster at the entry to the theatre: CORRADINO DISTRUGGE L'INCANTO DEL MAGO ROSSO, UCCIDENDO IL GUARDIANO E MOLTI ANIMALI E LIBERA ORCANO SUO PADRE DELLA PRIGIONE.

The marionettes, two feet to two feet eight inches tall, are made of wood, held by a stick and operated by at least three strings. Corradino is clad from head to toe in Renaissance armor, has a shield and a sword, which he takes out of the scabbard and puts in again, and a plumed helmet with a visor, which he lowers for combat. His face is the most beautiful thing about him: gorgeously painted red cheeks and large black eyes.

Corradino fights the dragon and an eagle, a whole lot of devils, an evil knight and an evil sorcerer. Each duel lasts a long time and gives a chance for a masterly display. The marionettes attack each other with great impact; the dragon in the shape of a monstrous lizard and a huge bird with a sharp beak jump at our valiant knight and attempt to overturn him, or attack him from above and try to bite his head off. At last they perish under the blows of his sword. The little knight raises his visor: his fixed black eyes go on looking joyously at the audience; his flushed cheeks go on shining beautifully.

This theatre has survived unchanged for centuries. It has

the beauty and literalness of the primitive, the passion for
violent effects and the rigid division into bad and good
characters. Everything is serious here: the sorcerer's den is
guarded by devils, bundles of real straw are burned in hell,
and a real fire rages furiously on the stage. As in all great
primitives, literalness exists here side by side with magnificent displays of imagination: devils are half as big as the
evil sorcerer; round the hero's head a little demon hovers
rustling, like a magnified, vicious dragonfly from the pictures
of Bosch; and sometimes the demon flies at his face or creeps
up his legs. Duels are accompanied by furious stamping of feet
and ear-splitting metallic percussion. The rose-cheeked knight
with his little sword keeps hacking at the dragon's neck until
its head falls and rolls away like a ball in a bowling alley.
Even more terrible things happen. In the *History of Roland*
a crusader chops another knight's head off, or rather splits
his skull through vertically until half of it falls with a bump
onto the stage. In vain does a beautiful siren try to seduce
Corradino; she emerges from the water, has round breasts
and not one but two splendidly divided fish tails, which
makes her disturbingly fascinating. Corradino is almost over-
powered by her charms but suddenly raises his hands to his
ears and departs with his ship. At the end of the play he
liberates his father from the sorcerer's cruel captivity. His
father, Orcano, wears the same kind of armor, has the same
shining black eyes and jolly red cheeks and can be distinguished from his son only by his black beard.

The stage of the Opera dei Pupi is small, and from time to
time one can see above it the hand of an actor guiding the
marionettes on a stick. The hand seems so big that it almost
frightens one by its monstrous size. There is something revolting and shocking, surprising and nightmarish about that
hand. We have simply got used to the dimensions of the
marionettes, we have come to believe in them and their
world. We are shocked by the unexpected appearance of a
hand that does not belong to it and does not conform to it

in its proportions. The hand is three times as big as it should be. It is a surrealist hand in the unambiguous world of the Opera dei Pupi.

14 July

Robbins always begins with an authentic gesture. Boy takes girl by the hand, impetuously pulls her to him, then pushes her away, pulls her again, pushes her away, holds her at arm's length. He now makes her shake like a piece of wood. Brutality gives way to affection. Both of them are now entranced with the same rhythm that has already entered their bodies. Rhythm becomes fascination, sex becomes a quiver maintained at arm's length, though passed on through their joined hands. Robbins' ballets are modern not only in their rhythm and arrangements but above all in their truthful gestures.

I went to see the *Little Dance*, Robbins' small ballet set to music by Brubeck, three times. I saw it twice on the little stage of the Teatrino delle sette and then in Caio Melisso. It is danced by three girls and two boys, all dressed in black tights up to their waists and in bright colored tunics. The girls look plain, have none of the ready-made beauty of ballet dancers; it is only when they start dancing that they become fascinating.

I regard this little ballet as a masterpiece. It is abstract, non-representational, or at any rate, devoid of "literary" contents. It is dense, intense, from the opening to the closing sequence. There is in it a gradually increasing fascination with gesture and with the demon of movement, a seduction with gesture and movement; there is joy, simple eroticism, a conquering and compelling force.

After the performance, late at night, I saw in the little café in the Piazza della Libertà one of the boys teaching a very young dark girl the same rhythm to the music of the juke box; the quick, short movements of arms bent at the elbows looked like a boxer's fight with a dummy. Gradually the rhythm embraces the muscles of the abdomen, arms and legs. Now they were both dancing. The dark girl was entranced by the rhythm.

In the *Little Dance* I saw Patricia Dunn, a Korean who lives in the United States. When I looked at her in the dressing room she was not beautiful. She has nothing of the fragility of the Southern Chinese, or of the gentle sweetness of the Japanese. She is big, with strongly shaped legs and a tired face. When she dances, suddenly a smile begins to play on her face; it transforms her in a flash. She is a great dancer.

Robbins' ballets are not very musical, at least in the traditional sense. Music in his ballets is initiation and echo. In Warsaw I had seen a Robbins' ballet without music, in absolute silence. The music was within the dancing bodies. In these ballets everything is abstract—except the body. The body is always concrete; it means the bodies of boys and girls. There is no pure dance for Robbins, only a boy or girl who is dancing.

On the day before one of the boys dancing in *Little Dance* had twisted his foot. Robbins did not want to cancel the last performance and undertook to stand in for the boy. I saw him at rehearsal on the empty stage early in the evening at Caio Melisso. Dark and swarthy, looking somewhat Spanish with his small trimmed beard, he had seemed older than I when I saw him in the café. He looked younger while dancing. Hidden in the box, I was, perhaps, the only spectator at the rehearsal. He was to dance with young people, perhaps with the youngest of his pupils. He was certainly a better dancer, but he had to dance like them—without effort, without fatigue; with the same joy. He practiced for a long time on the empty stage; not the movements and rhythms, which he knew by heart for he had arranged them, but to dance without fatigue and without effort. He was practicing not the dance, but youth itself. He was restoring his own youth, with anxiety, with fear, with effort. I could see the strain on his face; and I saw how gradually the strain disappeared. I admired Robbins. In the evening I admired him even more. He was the youngest of them all.

The English Ballet Rambert searches for modern forms with equal eagerness; not in movement and gesture, however, but in the world around them. Projected on the screen are hands outstretched in prayer, faces set in an expression of terror, mutilated bodies; while on the stage an old-fashioned leading trio and corps de ballet of sleek dancers whirl around, bounce, then lie down flat. This is to signify atomic fear. The story is impossible for a novel, even for film. And they want ballet to relate, warn, agitate, just like that. A friend of mine called this sort of thing ballet for reading.

Of course, great ballet always belongs to its age. More than that, it is the age. I realized this when I first saw *Swan Lake* at the Moscow Bolshoi. That great classical ballet, untouched by time, has remained imperial, or rather, czarist. The little ballet dancers, all of the same height, stood motionless, with glued-on smiles, stiff, erect like guardsmen. They stood stiffly on two toes of one leg, throwing the other leg high up as if on parade. Then suddenly, abattement, the pirouettes began. The corps de ballet went about their movements like guards reviewed by the czar. That classical ballet sur les pointes was abstract like a military drill, liturgical like a parade, hierarchical like a court ball; faceless and ready for the call like aides-de-camp. Classical ballet has something of a changing of the guard, of a court ceremonial. Pushkin was the first to realize this. It does not exist without the czar.

Spoleto, 15 July

The romanesque church of San Paolo is situated extra muros but very near to the town. I went there by way of medieval aqueducts, down wooded hillsides, along vineyards and occasional little fields of oats. The portico is almost intact; in blocks of stone are carved splendid mythological beasts, one on top of the other, as in almost all the small churches of Umbria. But the interior of the church is empty, as if eaten away by ants. I went round the church. At the back I found dwellings, actually inhabited. People have dug out little holes in the huge mass of stone. Washing is being dried everywhere, the little balconies are full of flowers. I am constantly made aware in this part of the world how much the people feel at home in churches, in historical relics, in the past. They have been stealing stones off historic monuments for ages, just as Polish peasants would steal wood from the forest to prop up their cottages. This is the reason everything is on top of everything else. When walking in the Roman town one treads on it simply and without any fuss. The arch of Drusus is half grown into a mercer's shop. The concept of the purity of style does not make sense here. Everything is built of the same kind of stone. The Roman town is only a couple of yards below; I can see it when leaning over a bit from my chair in the small ice-cream parlor. Italian ice cream, orgies of gluttony, return to childhood. Gelati con panna, one ice cream, another ice cream, ice cream for the third time. I haggle about them with myself as I have to do in Poland with my small son.

Rome, 16 July

On Saturday and Sunday I had breakfast on board a small boat moored by the bridge of San Angelo. A cool breeze was blowing from the Tiber. It was a very modest trattoria. The proprietress was praising the salad, calling it belissima. No one would describe salad like that in France. Angels, white-hot in the sun, stood a stone's throw away. We were eating that "most beautiful" salad, made of tomatoes, cucumbers, onions and fish cut into very small pieces. We were also given black beans and very cold wine. It was one of those moments of simple happiness and simple joys that Stendhal wrote were impossible in France.

Of the physical joys only eroticism has remained in Paris.

But there even simple eroticism seems vulgar. It requires complications, refinement, awareness. Here in Italy it is too hot for that. Only the simplest gestures are possible. And the simplest food. I constantly find this simplicity here, even in gestures. In the little square nearby a young woman has unbuttoned her blouse and gives suck to her three-months-old baby. She is leaning on the pink marble of the fountain, covering her eyes with her right hand. She makes no attempt to cover her dark breast and the still darker, almost black, swelling nipple.

Before the war Paris was a town in which one could live without money. Everyone around had very little or no money. The greatest pleasure was to wander about the streets. Paris has remained the city for wandering about, and one can still do that free. But to have no money is now not just an inconvenience, or a temporary nuisance; it is a source of shame, a mark of failure or laziness, or even a deficiency of character. To have no money is a proof that one is raté, that one has wasted one's life, that one does not have—and never had—any talent or intelligence. Intelligent people have money. Having money has become compulsory in Paris. Maybe this is why everybody says that life in Paris is impossible.

17 July

About the pope. He was not exceedingly wise, says Ch., and he was not, as they write about him now, completely devoid of diplomacy. He was above all a good priest, in the sense in which one talks about a good country parish priest. He was also a good man. A very humane man. And suddenly, to the immense astonishment of simple people, believers and non-believers alike, Jews, Protestants, socialists, to the horror of the Roman curia, all realized that the chair of Peter was occupied by an old man who was good, sensible, tolerant, and friendly toward all. That was why the whole world looked in amazement at John XXIII, a pope who was a good priest and a good man.

18 July

Compared with French intellectuals, Ch. strikes me as
Polish in his style—expansive, uncalculating, much better than
everything he does, the critic of a theatre that does not yet
exist. There is no theatre in Italy, he said. The theatre was
destroyed by Mussolini. Through a system of stipends he
transformed artists into messenger boys. After the war, everybody that had any life in them threw themselves into film.
Film meant money, success, direct contact with the present.
Schools did not produce actors, or went about it in the wrong
way. Nobody wrote for the theatre. The theatre seemed superfluous.

I try to reply that most the same factors worked against the
theatre in every other country, and yet the theatre survived.
Ch. smiles. Perhaps the Italians are too lazy. Or it may be
that the street is too much of a theatre. We are sitting in Via
Veneto, the time is one A.M. It is the only really living theatre
in Rome. Everyone here is an actor and a spectator in turn. I
am reminded of G. again. There is something exciting about
this mutual exhibition of arses, one's own or those one
sleeps with. The ice cream here is not good, though.

19 July

I told Moravia about the success of his books in Poland,
even at my own home. My daughter decided to read Woman
of Rome at the age of fourteen. Italian girls are quite mature
at fourteen, Moravia said. Only mothers, grandmothers and
priests do not want to see the woman in a fourteen-year-old
girl. Shakespeare's Juliet was thirteen. Shakespeare did not
invent Juliet. Lolita is the kind of novel that could only
be written in the north; by a puritan.

A marriage with the real Lolita does not alter anything. It

would still be against nature; it would be even more revolting. It would mean breaking a taboo. In Italy there is no Lolita problem because mammas and aunts take thirteen-year-old pregnant Juliets to the marriage altar. They feel not only relief but exaltation. The parish priest has given his dispensation. Nothing has been done against nature.

Rome, 20 July

On Saturday night I went with an Italian from the Vatican publishing house to a rather expensive restaurant in Via Appia, called San Calisto. Chicken is served roasted there, or rather smoked in a bunch of burning dry leaves. It was late. The burning leaves were crackling, sparks went up high. The chickens served here are big and fat, and are smoked in pairs on vast iron spits. I can still see the huge birds with low hanging heads driven onto them and raised high in a halo of sparks. Chickens must have been roasted here in a similar fashion as long as three thousand years ago. Their skin is crisp, they smell strongly of burning, like the potatoes smoked in juniper in our country.

The following day

There is something of a drawing room about Italian piazzas, especially as regards their proportions. They are for people to meet and converse. A square is large enough to enable one to escape mamma's eye for a while, avoid an intruder or a bore, let an embracing couple disappear behind a fountain, or hide for an instant under the arcades. But it is not so large that one cannot make a date, or not notice a friend or debtor. Its proportions are on the human scale. One can walk round, see friends and be seen by them. Italian squares inherited social functions from antiquity. They are the city's salon.

But the Capitol is unique in the world. It combines all the beauties of sculpture and painting; sweetness and wisdom.

Rome, 22 July

I was told yesterday that the magnificent chickens in the restaurant on Via Appia are smoked with leaves. The smoke of the dry leaves of juniper gives the same bitter taste, but Latin chickens are smoked in dry laurel leaves. Such is the end only of the select few, of course, because only in the most expensive restaurant in Rome are chickens served that way. Chickens in laurel; chickens—laureates.

23 July

The day before yesterday I spent the whole afternoon and evening with the Ionescos. The Ionesco trio—Eugène, his wife and eighteen-year-old Marie-France—is an absolute, wonderful and magnificent Ionesco theatre. The wife is practical, industrious, provident. Marie-France is intellectual, metaphysical, lost and affectionate, following her father. Eugène amuses all those round him, and even more himself, by changing his plans all the time. Tomorrow he is going to Orvieto and on to Pincio, to Switzerland and to Ireland. The day after tomorrow he wants to be in Poland, in Mexico and in Israel. No, he wants to be in Mexico tomorrow, and in Orvieto the day after. He has hardly ordered spaghetti before he calls the waiter back to ask for tortellini in brodo. Marie-France has ordered prosciutto on melon. Eugène calls the waiter and also wants to have ham. Absent-minded and yet totally aware; frivolous and prudent; bustling and thrifty; childishly conceited and fully convinced that in the world only the Ionesco theatre exists—and perhaps Shakespeare as well, but only out of sympathy for myself—and enjoying his childish conceit more than anyone else, Ionesco is the most

Ionescian of all Ionesco characters. With sudden flashes of genius, like a perfect appliance, faultlessly geared to every absurdity in language or in a situation. "Where are you?" he asked me in the morning on the telephone. "Here, at my place," I replied. "You can't be here, you are *there*, I am *here*."

"Eugène," says his wife, "you will not go tomorrow to Africa, or to Sweden, or to Mexico, because I have an appointment with my dressmaker and you have to take me there." "And you promised to see the Sistine Chapel frescoes with me," says Marie-France. Well, this is Monsieur Bérenger in Rome.

24 July

In a new language one usually discovers literal meanings, forgotten affinities, genealogies. In Italian *sinistra* means only left; to me it also means sinister, but the association remains purely linguistic. I have only now discovered that *gauche* in French also means unsuccessful, awkward. This sounds even more strongly in the word *gaucherie*. Poor French political left!

In Polish the sinister aspect of left has been obliterated and very few of its traces remain in the living language, expressions like *rabić na lewo*—do something "on the left," i.e. illegally. *Lewy* (left) means false. In the word *prawy* (right) old meanings have been preserved more distinctly.

I am always amused when a situation arises that restores concrete meaning to a metaphor and makes it literal; when a now-metaphorical expression means again what it used to mean. It is like a coin on which we can see again the outlines that had worn off. One says, "Avoir ses entrées par la petite porte." Before I left Italy I had had difficulties about the renewal of my visa. A high official of the prefettura intervened in my case. When telephone calls proved ineffective, he lost his temper and asked me to follow him. We went down the corridor, then up very narrow stairs, so narrow that we had to walk one behind the other. The stairs ended with a very small door through which one entered directly the prefetto's office; more than that, one landed, if not on his head, then at least on his desk. This is what "Avoir ses entrées par la petite porte" means.

"All roads lead to Rome." In Italy all roads really lead to Rome. All kilometre-posts indicate the distance to Rome.

I was equally thrilled once when I saw a naked man in the nettles. One morning in Kazimierz-on-the-Vistula, a gentleman in the nude suddenly jumped straight from the window of my woman neighbor into a huge patch of overgrown nettles which spread right by the verandah. I saw a metaphor, in all its beauty.

25 July

A talk with Z. about the Spanish Civil War. Here one is far more aware of that war than in Poland. Conversations lasting late into the night dealing with essential matters, with politics, continue to revert to the Spanish question. The only Poles who took part in the Spanish Civil War were the Communists. They returned to Poland in a very roundabout way. The experiences that befell them after the Spanish War were far more of a shock and inevitably pushed the memories of Spain into the more distant recesses of their minds.

The Spanish War was a civil war for the Italians too. To a far greater extent than in Poland it meant a fundamental choice, a vital decision that faced the twenty- and thirty-year-olds. From that choice there was no escape. That was why not only Communists went from Italy to Madrid but anti-fascists of many different kinds: syndicalists, anarchists, left-wing socialists. They all knew what fascism was. Madrid was for them the first experience of Stalinism. Z. told me about his friend who had been murdered in Barcelona as an internal enemy; he was an anarchosyndicalist.

I remember how shocked I was reading Malraux's *Man's Hope*. He knew that the Apocalypse had no tomorrow. At that time he wanted to transform the Apocalypse into an organization. My Italian friends still talk about Spain with acute bitterness, as if it all happened yesterday. Spain hurts them like a scar after a badly healed wound. They lost in a double sense. Once, because the fascists were stronger; again, because it turned out that the role of archangels of the revolution was played by secret-police officers.

Evening

Rome, I told Chiaromonte, is the last open city, a true città aperta. The pope resides in Rome, he replied. Every power creates its own hypocrisy. But in Rome there are two powers. And two hypocrisies.

I thought then that Paris was the only city where there is a total separation of Bed and State. Perhaps that is why the Poles like coming to Paris so much; and the English too.

I remember my feeling of terror driving through London at night for the first time. All the ugliest objects were illuminated: Broadcasting House, the television tower, banks, hotels in the Strand. London is an avowedly anti-tourist city. Perhaps because London is so dead serious. Like everything else in England, London is unostentatious.

In Paris even before the war some public buildings were illuminated, but not excessively and not very frequently. On feast days one went to the Concorde and Rond-Point to look at illuminated fountains. Versailles was illuminated three, at most four times a year. A great city, until recently considered one of the world's capitals, cannot with impunity regard itself as a tourist object. Recently I saw by the Seine, not far from Notre Dame, clumps of trees lit in such a way as to give an emerald effect. In this nightly illumination of Paris to make it look like an immense Christmas tree, there is a painful resignation, abdication. Paris, imperceptibly, has become

provincial in relation to New York, Moscow, London. Even
the very beauty of Paris has changed suddenly into a nineteenth-century, old-fashioned beauty. When I came to Paris
from Poland in the autumn of 1938, I was dazed by lights
and movement. The Champs Élysées, the Grands Boulevards, even the Eiffel Tower seemed to me the essence of
modernity. Paris was to me the most modern of cities.

And suddenly Paris became first historic, then a period city.
A period piece, like furniture and bric-a-brac from la belle
époque, like oil and fiacre lamps which one now buys in
antique shops. One does not walk around Paris any more; one
tours and sees the sights, as one does in Rome or Florence.
The smartest thing to do is take a nineteenth-century horse-
drawn cab and drive from the Opéra to the Madeleine and
then through the Concorde and the Champs Élysées to the
Étoile. In London one goes to see the Tower and St. Paul's,
just as one goes to see Notre Dame, but no one would think
of driving in a hansom cab from Hyde Park Corner through
Oxford Street to Piccadilly Circus.

The beauty of Paris really is for that matter a nineteenth-
century one, just as the beauty of Rome is that of the
Baroque. At six P.M. the sky and the clouds over the Villa
Borghese and over the Pincio are golden. The air over the
Seine, in the morning and at dusk, is material; the light has
its density and its weight, as if it consisted of separate little
dots.

Cities are perceived through painting and through literature.
The Paris easiest to perceive, the Paris that first revealed itself before the war to a newcomer from Central Europe, was
the city of Balzac and the Impressionists: the banks of the
Seine, the bookstalls and the Luxembourg Gardens, Boul-
'Mich and Saint-Germain, the Odéon and the Palais Royal.
There was also Montmartre, but there one went for Utrillo
and long night walks. None of the people one knew lived
there. With Montparnasse things were different. I went
around Montparnasse with Marcoussis as if around a newly
established cemetery. Montparnasse was dying, but to him it

still seemed alive. In an old woman sitting beside us on the
terrace of La Rotonde, her face covered with rouge, he still
saw Kisling's young model with large almond eyes. The fat
mulatto who passed us, her huge posterior swaying, to him
still slept with Hemingway. Two old ladies cackling near us
and looking like balding hens in their ridiculous remnants of
hats were Marie Laurencin's lesbians. I was bored by all this;
I was too young to take delight in this evocation of ghosts; all
I could see around me were old, ugly women.

By that time I knew Proust, of course, but only up to *Albertine*. I read the last volumes much later, toward the end of
the war. I was still reading Proust like Balzac: like a new human comedy, or a school of vivisection. I was made sensitive,
of course, to the easiest of the Proustian effects; I got to know
the taste of the madeleine melting in my mouth, the taste in
which one recalls the memories of childhood. I was, however,
blind to all that meant in awareness of the passing of time. I
knew nothing of time and its destructive influence. I was
naïve enough to imagine the Proustian hell like the biblical
Sodom and Gomorrah. I was not afraid of old age, for I did
not know what it meant. The women Marcoussis pointed
out to me on the terrace of La Rotonde were old. But they
were strangers. At that time I did not yet know any woman
who had become old, that is to say, who had first been young,
then old. They were either young or old. They always had one
face only. I knew only two kinds of time: the present and the
past. Past meant the history one read about in books. One's
own past was so thin that it almost did not exist. It was only
much, much later that I discovered the Proust who is terrified by the passing and dying of everything.

My wife took me once to the Parc Monceau. That had
been Proust's Paris. Marcel had played there with Gilberte.
Odette de Crécy had lived in Passy. I took a horse cab and
went through the Champs Élysées to the Bois de Boulogne.
At the Rond-Point, too, Marcel had played with Gilberte. I
found that difficult to visualize. There were no horse cabs in
Paris. One did not go down the Élysées in a shining two-horse

carriage with a liveried bowler-hatted coachman. Now horse
carriages are again in vogue. Perhaps that is why I now find it
easy to imagine Swann in a gray top hat; I have seen just such
a top hat in the window of a men's clothes shop at the
corner of Boulevard Saint-Germain and rue de l'Ancienne
Comédie. I used to pass by that shop every day for a while
when I had breakfast in the Restaurant Prokope and Odette
in a little round, white or pink, hat made of feathers and lace,
with a broad veil draped all round (such hats were worn that
spring in Paris) when they ride in a carriage at eleven A.M.
through the Rond-Point and turn up to the Étoile.

There was a time, in 1938, when I followed Balzac's traces
in Paris. Later I looked for traces of Apollinaire. I found them
not in the deserted and desolate Closerie des Lilas, but in an
amusement park near the Place de la République and in a
square beyond the Porte d'Italie where a big circus had
pitched its tents. But that is another story. This spring Paris
assumed for me a nineteenth-century look. The Parises of
Balzac, Proust, Apollinaire, they have all got mixed up. They
were all there.

Pescocostanzo, 28 July

In the evening at Pescocostanzo, flocks of sheep are brought
down from the hills. As in our country, the sheep are accompanied by big, gentle white sheepdogs. The only difference is
that our shepherds take with them to the mountains a big
linen umbrella. As in our country, the main work is done by
horses. The horses are heavy, big and good-looking. Peasants
ride them slowly, with large bundles of brushwood strapped
on their sides. Many of the men wear dark hats on their
heads. They have a dignified, almost a Renaissance, look.

The countryside here reminds me of Poland, in that it
abounds in animals. The soil is cultivated by man and horse.
After a year spent in France and England I observe in myself
an aesthetic reaction to a wagon carrying hay, as an element of

the landscape. I am almost tempted to take a photograph of a peasant riding a horse, as a folkloristic curiosity. In Poland I would not dream of it.

Never before did I realize that folklore means a view from outside, from an alien circle. One cannot consider *oneself* as a part of folklore; or rather one cannot do so with impunity. Like those people who one morning put feathers in their hair and become Indians on a reservation. Folklore made conscious immediately becomes a stall with ready-made souvenirs, a circus, or a masquerade. Like those people who put on colored pants or a bodice embroidered with beads and go to a harvest festival in Warsaw. I have seen the participants in the harvest masquerade buy cheap cretonne the next day, and the younger ones ransack shops for nylon underwear.

The shepherd with a big linen parasol in a black wide-brimmed hat, bringing down a flock of sheep in the evening, looks beautiful to me. An evening in Pescocostanzo, with cattle being driven home for milking, with carts full of hay coming in, with women majestically carrying troughs of flour, or pitchers full of water on their heads, seems to me peaceful, harmonious, in accordance with nature.

In Chatburn, sixty-five miles from Manchester, where I had stayed a week with friends, a neighbor used to clean and dismantle his tractor at the end of the day's work. In the stillness of the evening, the tractor produced horrible sounds in the process. It was quite out of character in the gentle autumn dusk.

The aesthetic experience of seeing a herd of cows being driven in for milking in the evening has its limits. They may simply be the limits imposed by civilization or by geography. There have to be cows and the scene is bucolic. If the shepherd wears brightly colored pants and a peasant girl wears an embroidered bodice, the scene is both bucolic and quaint. But if there are buffaloes instead of cows, the scene is exotic. And what if there are no buffaloes either?

I went to China almost exactly ten years ago. I well remember the evening we arrived by air at a big city in the southern

provinces. It must have been Chungking. We came from
Yunnan Province, land of eternal spring where rice is planted
and harvested three times a year. From Yunnan it was not
far to the Himalayas. Not far in Chinese distances, that is; a
thousand miles or more. Yes, it must have been Chungking.

The city was situated on a hill, or rather on a range of
hills, along a very broad sandy road. We were told that the
city had half a million, or a million, or two million inhabitants.
In China it is very difficult to find out how big the population of a city is, since it is counted with that of the province.
One could not even see where the city ended. Beyond
stone walls houses continued by the road as before. But at a
little distance from the road and higher up, on the slopes of the
hills, stood clay hovels which looked like big swallow's nests,
one by the other, one above the other. Every hill, every
available space was full of these nests. There was no end to
them. They were hanging by every road, they were above,
under, next to it.

Roads, wide and narrow, and paths too, were full of people,
swarmed with people. "Swarmed" was, indeed, the right expression. There was something disturbing about that city;
we all felt this but no one could say why.

All those people around us—children, old people, women
and men—were carrying something on their heads or on bamboo poles. A couple carrying a load on a bamboo pole
walked like paralytics or people suffering from epilepsy. They
did not walk but ran, hopping under their load to counteract
the vibrations of the pole. It took a long time to get used to
this sight. The objects carried in this city on people's heads or
on bamboo poles were strange and difficult to define. Sometimes they were sacks, but more often stones or large cubes of
pressed grass. Sometimes they were torn leaves of plants unknown to us, or sugar canes. Often they were rags, or parts of
objects, like gnawed remnants of things that had once had
some practical use. Nearly all the grown-up women and even
the fairly grown-up girls carried on their backs little children

fastened to them by ropes of plaited bast. This enabled them to carry other loads on their heads.

These human beings were moving and running in all directions. We could not discover the nature of all this bustling which to us seemed quite confused. The city looked to us like a freshly dug-up ant hill. We all felt the same. Only on the following day did we realize in what way the city was different from all the others we had passed through so far. In this city there were no horses, or buffaloes. There were no carts or wheelbarrows. The only transportation was man: his back, arms, head and legs. The only invention that made the carrying of loads easier was the swinging bamboo pole.

Chungking left no room for aesthetic experience. But only after having seen cities like Chungking can one understand the irrevocability of the Chinese schism. Stalin had an inkling of it. But even he had never thought in terms of a hungry termite mound. To the Chinese leaders such a way of thinking must seem quite natural.

Perugia, end of July

I acquired a taste for Perugia only late at night when I found myself under the Etruscan Arch. High above it I saw the classical, walled-up arch of Augustus. Higher still, there was a beautiful and harmonious Renaissance arch and Arabic stone lacework. As in all Italian cities, I am struck by the piling up of all the styles. I like all impurities, even in architecture. I was most moved, however, by the romanesque cathedrals, which I usually encountered at night. Huge, unadorned stone walls, with empty circles above porticoes which the Gothic would later fill in with its rosettes. Churches here are closely surrounded by palaces and houses. On the hill on which Perugia is situated, there was a hard struggle, between the city and the Church, between the princes and the cardinals, for every foot of ground. Palaces and churches were erected almost opposite one another; their builders outdid one another in the sculpture of the tympanna. One could perform Shakespeare in every little square. I like the fierce hatred and rivalry of stones that one can see here with every step, that one can touch. I am also moved by the broken, humped noses I continually see in the streets. As if all the ice-cream sellers and vendors of ties have just descended from the canvasses of Perugino.

Assisi, 31 July

In Fellini's *Eight and a Half*, the most wonderful sequence, so far as I am concerned, is the overexposed—as if in blanc-majeur—scene with the cardinal who takes hot baths for his rheumatism in *thermae* near Rome. This sequence is intimate and hieratic in a way that is, I suppose, possible only here, in Italy. The cardinal with his legs in a basin of hot water, the steaming cardinal, the cardinal wrapped in towels, does not cease to be a cardinal.

There is another splendid sequence. The cardinal is old and tired. He is sitting on a garden bench; he falls asleep. The director is tormented by essential questions: what is art, what is life? He wants to ask the cardinal. He has to know what a Christian film is. But the cardinal does not listen to him. He has wakened from his nap. He is talking about birds singing: the male has lost his mate and there is despair in his singing. It is just like Fellini.

Catholicism in Italy is not only more familiar but also more cadaverous than elsewhere. In the vaults of every other church one can see skeletons or dried-up mummies of monks and nuns. Relics are sold in churches.

The windows of St. Clare's cell at San Damiano look out onto a green cloister garden fragrant with mint and almonds. In the window fresh red flowers are always placed. St. Clare has, of course, her own church in Assisi. In the vaults of the church is her tomb. She lies there embalmed, with a large crooked nose. At first glance I even took her for St. Francis, to the great indignation of a nun who stands there reciting her story. She stands there, all black, behind bars, and not even the outlines of her face are to be seen through her thick veil. She could be in a mask. The tomb of St. Clare impressed me as something halfway between a mausoleum and the Ku Klux Klan ceremonial.

Evening

In Assisi the pink hue of the soil and stone made the strongest impression on me. I had met a similar color only in Provence. There are places where the soil is almost red. There is a belt of red earth near Cabris. The road from Cannes to Aix-en-Provence, too, takes one through landscape of red stone and rusty soil. The pine trees, cypresses, and palms are soon left behind. The red landscapes of Provence are austere. The pink hue of Assisi is dipped in succulent green. The hills slope gently. There is sweetness on the ground and in the air. It was here that St. Francis talked to the birds.

Catholicism, like Marxism, has its two poles: the optimistic and the pessimistic; the confident and the bitter. Pessimistic Catholicism has inspired much better literature; it dramatized existence. Everything was doubtful: charity, even grace, above all, nature—nature in itself, and human nature, are flawed. That could be observed in all who passed through the dark corridors of Port-Royal. It is a most interesting fact that the Jansenist "heart of darkness" was always connected with stylistic clarity and precision. In this tradition, treatises on darkness were written with Cartesian logic. This also applies to Camus. The Jansenists waged a dispute with the Augustinians concerning the limits of grace. It was a theological and political dispute, but what theology and politics were really concerned about was nature. To what extent can nature be trusted? The essence of the dispute has not greatly altered since, except that history has been substituted for nature.

To what extent can nature be trusted; to what extent can
history be trusted? To what extent is nature deceitful? To
what extent is history deceitful? In Rousseau, the concept of
nature was substituted for the concept of history with complete naïveté; regarded almost literally. The emergence of
individual property was the original sin, and with it the flaw
in nature and the flaw in history began.

All this was, however, still the theological aspect of the
dispute; theological even in Marxism. Contrary to appearances, the real, political, dispute concerns the question of
whether paradise existed at the beginning, or will be accom-
plished at the very end, or has never been and will never be.
Four answers are possible: First, in the beginning and at the
end; this is the notion closest to the common Christian tradition. Second, only at the beginning; that on the whole was
the view of antiquity. The ancients regarded history attentively and had no illusions. After the golden age came
the silver age, which in its turn was followed by the bronze
age. Third, Utopian socialists and common Marxist tradition
predict paradise at the end of history; at least a dialectical
paradise which will be more and more paradisiacal. Fourth,
neither at the beginning, nor at the end—the view always
taken by libertines and pessimists, Christian and Marxist
alike.

Even before the war I was strongly attracted to Christian
pessimism; hence perhaps my later inclinations to practice
pessimistic Marxism. The Franciscan ideal had always been
for me, as for nearly everybody of my generation, very remote.
It seemed naïve, sentimental and modernistic. It seemed in
keeping with the fin-de-siècle, even in its visual aspect.

Just before the last war we all of us, believers and non-
believers, to a certain extent tasted Thomism. We dis-
liked St. Augustine intensely but treated him seriously.
Neither art nor ethics, it seemed to us, were there to serve
nature. They were to conquer, disintegrate, destroy nature,
or at least to disturb all that was natural.

These views were taught simultaneously by Breton and by

Maritain, though they were not aware of the fact that they propagated tastes that were to some extent identical. In 1938 I used to go and visit Breton; I also used to visit Jacques and Raissa Maritain. I was, perhaps, the only one, and certainly one of very few who were frequent guests of both of them; who attended at the very source, and almost at the same time, a surrealist course and a Thomist course. Only years later did I realize how similar the two milieus were, especially in their tastes. In 1938 both Breton and the Maritains invoked, as witnesses of poetry, Aloyzius Bertrand, the Romantische Schule, and Nerval at his darkest. In both houses, too, Max Jacob was admired and angry young Lautréamont was treated dead seriously. No matter what creed and ontology one subscribes to, one cannot escape from the prevailing tastes of one's time.

Between the "convulsive beauty" proclaimed by Breton and supernatural and (of course) transcendent beauty, which is the *form* of an object, there were more similarities than differences. Differences were in the tongue, but the saliva and the nourishment were the same. Neither the demonic Breton who cultivated the training of imagination, nor the mystic Raissa, nor Maritain, the last of the great scholastics, liked St. Francis.

The great and genuine philosophical disputes in the few years between the Spanish Civil War and World War II were held between followers of Augustine and Thomas, those of St. Kant and St. Hegel. Between the phenomenologists and the dialecticians of both denominations. Between the never-satiated devils of history and action, and the elusive angels of pure cognition. Husserl's angels were on the other side of the mirror and one could not even touch them; one merely banged one's nose against the glass.

In late spring, 1939, Stefan Żółkiewski wrote to me in Paris from Warsaw: "I am almost a Thomist now. I read the *Summa* avidly. I read and rage. It's very well written. My Persian cat gets fatter and fatter. You called him Emil Meyersohn, I remember. He gets all bristled and raises his splendid tail when I sit down to Thomas. If only one could chuck ontology out of it! If only one could be an intellectually honest Thomist and not believe in God. Maybe the old man with a beard is right, after all, when he says that the proof of the pudding is in the eating. O God of the conventionalists, how trivial this is! Emil Meyersohn bristles again and spits. He too wants his ontology to be accepted. To soothe my nerves I read *The Pickwick Papers* in bed."

Zołkiewski, of course, did not like St. Francis either. Not one of us did. That is why Cimabue so astonished me. On his great fresco in the lower basilica Francis has nothing about him of the gentle saint who talks to birds. He is demonic and tormented; thin, fanatical, with ruffled beard. This is all the more striking since on the same fresco the Madonna with Child is gentle, with slightly rounded cheeks, and even inclined to fatness, like Perugian women who quickly lose girlish slimness. Four angels standing nearby are also gentle, conventional, and still, somewhat elongated in the Byzantine manner. St. Francis is quite different, as if he had been painted from real life: dressed in a soiled habit, asthenic, tired, with flaming eyes, touched to the quick with God's hand.

Hagiographers maintain that Cimabue's St. Francis presents his true image. That was what he really looked like. After all, when his father made him angry, he undressed and threw his costly robes at his head. Perhaps the sweetness, gentleness and stillness of the gardens and cloisters of San Damiano is illusory?

AT NIGHT

For the last two days one could feel the approaching storm. Even at night the air was stuffy. I was invited to the theatre. The stage was situated high up, in a narrow passage between the house and a wall. The street came down steeply, paved with smooth stones. I was seated below. High up, on the stage, three women were trying to persuade a young boy to do something. One of the women was very beautiful. The performance was in a language I did not know. I could not even remotely guess what language they were speaking. Then only the women were left on the stage, among them the beautiful one. Later there was a crowd of men, shouting and throwing their arms about. Everything ended with a love scene, grotesque and obscene at first, then heartrendingly sad. From above, stones were thrown, slowly at first, then with violent speed, like an avalanche. The sidewalk on the right, along the wall, began to move. I could not understand how this was done. After all, the sidewalk and the house were real. The music was just percussion, very shrill, full of rising, broken syncopations.

Then the director appeared. He said that the first part of the performance was not important, but the second was an adaptation of *Doctor Faustus*; and this cannot be done in any other way, except by having the falling stones and the sidewalk moving alongside the wall, and the music of broken syncopations.

I was moved. It occurred to me that this was the true theatre I had always dreamed about; that once or twice before I had been to that theatre. But I could not remember what performance I had seen. Even when I woke up, I tried to recall for quite a while what the previous program of that theatre had been.

(1962)

A LITTLE TREATISE ON EROTICISM

Love looks not with the eyes, but with the mind.
                    A *Midsummer Night's Dream*, 1, 1, 234

During an evening with the Ionescos, Chiaromonte vented his dissatisfaction with the French nouvelle vague, particularly in its erotic aspect, as expressed by films and novels. He called it eroticism with the other person; there is no partner there, he said, it is really the eroticism of onanism.

To my mind it would, perhaps, be more apt to say that the partner does not exist as a person, as the subject. He or she has the existence and concreteness of an object. He is a thing, or rather is transformed into a thing.

It is possible, however, that Chiaromonte's arguments are more complex and more philosophical. The partner, indeed, does not exist. He or she is being *created*, is merely erotic imagination come to life. As in onanism, he or she is being created by one's own sexual ego. But erotic imagination never creates a fully developed situation, or a complete person. The erotic partner of imagination and desire is created or given only in fragments. Like a broken statue whose parts—torso, arms, legs, head or belly—we find or see in turn, as separate objects.

The same thing happens in the fulfilled eroticism of a sexual act. In darkness the body is split into fragments, which are separate objects. They exist *for themselves*. It is the touch that makes them exist *for me*.

Touch is limited. Unlike sight, it does not embrace the entire person. Touch is invariably fragmentary; it decomposes things. A body experienced through touch is never an entity; it is just a sum of fragments. They exist *apart*, as it were. They touch each other, but do not grow together. To put it more precisely, they continue to be contingent in relation to each other, but do not create a person. They are not a structure.

In darkness the body is given in fragments. I use the term darkness metaphorically. Eroticism always means being pushed into darkness, even if the act takes place in full daylight.

For that matter sight, like touch, gives a fragmentary vision during the act. It concentrates on a fragment of the body: on the eyes, the mouth, or the forehead, on the nape of the neck, or on the belly. The partner's body is given in a different perspective, from unusual angles, in magnifying close-ups. This is important, as in the case of details from well-known pictures, which strike us as new and different when photographed close-up. Fragments of the body embraced by sight during an act are, like touch, incoherent and disordered. The eyes open and close; a fragment of the body given in a big close-up has passed from sight.

I have seen a few abstract sculptures that managed to recall or transmit something of real eroticism. Though it may sound strange, this sort of thing happens less frequently in painting. The pictures of Max Ernst possess this kind of eroticism. I have lately seen a painting by Leonor Fini on which a real sexual act is so obscured and blurred that only its individual fragments pervade the phantasms of imagination. The act is implied, it exists literally and concretely, underneath it, under the texture, under the last of the painted surfaces. If film had more imagination, it could show perhaps the true eroticism of big close-ups of sight and touch.

In the close-up of sight, as if in a big film frame, one's own body and the body of one's partner change their proportions. (It is exactly this type of vision, made monstrous by close-up, that can be discerned in some scenes of Gulliver's voyage to Brobdingnag which have a clearly sexual implication. Swift expressed in them his anti-feminism, which was only part of his general hatred of the bodily aspect of man.) The body changes its proportion even more in literal close-ups, those big close-ups of touch.

The body is then being dissected, as it were, reduced to atoms, pervaded, touched from within. It has its stickiness and dryness, moisture, roughness, and temperature. Touch brings out the muscles and tissues, joints and gristles. It reaches the very skeleton, the bones, making them emerge from non-existence, as it were, and giving them up to senses and to consciousness; one's own consciousness and that of one's partner. The fingers get under the skin, as it were. Until now the body within was a stone; now it begins to exist. Touch becomes the vivifying section. But even in this instance touch retains its fragmentary structure and never creates a person, or, at any rate, creates one altogether different. The erotic "space" of touch is not a three-dimensional area of sight. Body becomes a glove turned inside out; it is experienced and perceived from within.

The function of language in eroticism undergoes a change too. Language goes back to its roots, to the moment of its birth. It is either non-articulated, a cry and onomatopoeic sound, as if it were only learning the names of things and actions. Or it is articulated and then its function is magic, or close to magic. The difference between a concept and an object, between a token and a thing, is blurred or disappears. Language becomes action, as in magic; i.e. it causes a thing or action to exist just by naming it, and gives them qualities that have been expressed in words. This erotic, or rather suberotic, language constantly breaks taboos. For taboos last longest in the sphere of language; it is almost invariably the relic of an era in which magic connections existed between a thing and its name.

Eroticism is always a cognitive act. In erotic cognition, the body is being dissected, and senses constantly verify one another. Sight becomes endowed, as it were, with some of the functions of touch, and vice versa. Eroticism is a constant appeal from sight to touch and from touch to sight; it is as if the real existence of one's erotic partner were being constantly questioned and required constant proof.

A partner created by erotic imagination consists entirely in the areas of sight and touch, intermingling with each other. He is the glove turned inside out. This applies in the same degree to the real partner as to the imagined one; to the partner of a fulfilled act as to the partner of an imaginary one. For this reason Chiaromonte is both right and wrong.

For in fact, it is four persons who go to bed together: the pair of real lovers and the pair of created partners; two bodies and two partners of imagination and desire, mutually created by each other.

Eroticism is the verification of the partner who has been created by oneself. In this verification, it is the body that will be the last instance and final resort. One's own body and one's partner's. Because one's own body, too, is on the outside, it is verified and experienced in the same way as the partner's. One's own body, too, is an object. One's body is a *medium* through which one takes and gives pleasure. Pleasure can be located, and so one can separate oneself from it.

But the paradox and sadness of eroticism consist in the fact that its absolute fulfillment is not possible. Verification is possible only during the act itself. To possess means just that. But the moment the act is over, the partner and his-her body are again apart. The body is a stranger again, it exists for itself, and not for me. The partner, real and created, the partner of the consummated act and partner of imagination, becomes ambiguous again. He-she has to be verified again. The verification is possible only through a new act, through another appeal to the body. Because body is the essence, and there is no other essence apart from the body. But the reduction to essence is possible only for a fleeting moment. The partner escapes again and cannot be permanently reduced to the body alone.

This probably is the reason for the failure of every passion, and possibly also for the defeat of the phenomenon we call love.

(1962)

MEDEA AT PESCARA

The Greek theatre from Piraeus had come with *Medea*. I
went to see it in Pescara by a roundabout way, through
Roccaraso and Palena, bypassing the Maiella ridge—the highest in the Abruzzi—from east and south.

Palena seemed to me the color of roasted coffee beans.
The place was empty, as if burned out. Little towns in the
Abruzzi look like swallows' nests, or rather wasps' nests.
Each of them is like a honeycomb plastered to a rock. In
Umbria and in Provence, too, little towns seem molded together, with their buttresses, steep walls, their churches and
castle which give one the impression of being stuck to one
another at the top. But in Umbria, villages and small towns
ascend the slopes of gentle hills, sink into the green; hills
become vineyards and olive groves. Here little towns are
washed by rains and swept by winds. They belong wholly to
this desert landscape, and at the same time bring some order
into it and provide food for imagination. Their beauty is
austere, they have the protective colors of soil and stone—
gray and yellow. Often they melt, almost imperceptibly, into
a large and empty rocky wall, or into heaps of yellow sand.
It is these stony walls, big heaps of stones and sand, misty
mountain tops and vast flat plains, shaped like huge plates,
that combine to give the intriguing effect of a waste, desert
landscape. Men and animals can hardly be seen in it. The
little towns seem deserted. Only occasionally can one see

little donkeys slowly mounting the steep tracks, with their excessive loads of brushwood. They are led by old women, dressed in black, with clothes arranged flatly on their heads.

The amphitheatre in Pescara is a new one, but it is situated out of town, and there is nothing in its immediate vicinity. Only the sea is near. The night I was there, a cold wind was blowing from the sea, while hot air still came from the mountains. The acting area consisted of large stone steps. On top of them stood the Doric portico of Medea's house, with a huge closed door. Above the portico the moon was shining, quite low, cut in half. It was covered by clouds in the second half of the performance, almost immediately after Medea said she would murder her children and her rival. Natural scenery gives unexpected effects occasionally, when all of a sudden the sky or birds start playing their part. In 1948 or 1949 I saw *Hamlet* performed in the courtyard of Elsinore castle. During the first great soliloquy some gulls flew just above Hamlet's head and a couple of them suddenly sat by his feet.

In the enclosed theatre there is no room for the chorus, even when the stage designer extends the forestage halfway through the orchestra. The entry of the chorus is artificial, but its continuous presence on the stage is even more so. One does not know whether to keep it there, or to let it come on and off the stage every time. In every performance of Greek tragedies that I had seen, the chorus had always been a disguised ballet. But the chorus in Sophocles and Euripides is not a ballet interlude, or an intellectual commentary. It is not external or added to the tragedy; it does not need any justification, does not have to jump or dance; if it does dance, then it is only for a short while. The chorus is not disguised.

Fourteen young women stopped on the stone steps. They had entered the way peasant women do, like the girls in Pescocostanzo when they assemble in the evening by the fountain in the town square. All day long they had poured over *tombolo*, heavy bags stuffed with hay and sawdust, onto which a newly begun lace is pinned. Lace is made by the arduous and patient manipulation of small wooden bobbins with threads. These bobbins are called *fazzoletti* here. The same kind of lace has been made in a like fashion in our country, from Zywiec to Zawoja, in all the hungry mountain villages under Babia and Barania Góra.

I do not know what impression *Medea* makes in the marble amphitheatres of Greece. Perhaps it seems monumental and remote. Here in Pescara, from the very first scene Medea and the chorus of young women seemed to belong to this soil, this landscape. Medea was in buskins, I suppose because the part was played by a tiny actress. She was an ordinary Medea, humanly unhappy, and humanly vindictive; she was like those peasant women. There was something about her that reminded me of those women, stiff and erect under the fifty-pound loads on their heads, I saw returning to their villages at noon, fatigued but still full of dignity. There was something about her, too, of that night when the cold wind from the sea blew—making everybody crouch in their stone seats —alternating with the stifling hot wind from the Maiella ridge.

The action of Euripides' *Medea* lasts a night and a day. But here the real time and the time of performance were the same. A few hours of such a night were enough in which to accomplish mad deeds that would seem impossible in the daytime. Daylight would disperse madness like the mists that drowned Pescocostanzo in the mornings.

Not only time was condensed. Just as essential was the unity of place; ordinary and natural, there was nothing of contrived poetics about it. I remember how amazed I was to see on my first visit to Rome that the Forum Romanum was so small. Just a few hundred steps from the Capitol and the Tarpeian Rock to the Arch of Titus. I went around that arch some distance away from it and spat, like an orthodox Jew. Kings, patricians and plebeians, republicans; all the tribunes and all the consuls, the Ides of March, Nero and Caligula—that square between two hills was enough to pro-

vide the setting for almost the entire history of Rome. Just
one setting. The Acropolis is even smaller than the Roman
Forum. Corinth was certainly no bigger than Pescocostanzo.

On the little square in front of Medea's house one could
hear the groans of Glauca being burned alive. In the last
scene, Jason ran in, out of breath; he had run the hundred
steps from the royal palace. Earlier still Aegeus had appeared;
he had come directly from a small harbor where he had left
his boat. That fishing harbor could almost be seen from
Medea's house. Something similar happens also in Racine,
as Roland Barthes pointed out in his last book. In nearly
every tragedy, a ship is waiting in the harbor with sails set.
One need only lean out the window to see it. The ship
means an escape. But the true heroes are shut in the palace.
The palace is both prison and asylum. They cannot go away.
If they could go away, there would be no tragedy. Only their
confidants are free to go. Of the true tragic heroines Berenice
is the only one to depart. But her departure is equivalent
to death. We may call it a white death, in a tragedy that—
according to Norwood's classification—is a white tragedy.
Berenice's departure means a delayed death, like a time bomb,
or a delayed action mine.

The unity of place in an enclosed theatre always seemed
to me artificial. Here, however, everything is close at hand.
In the *Medea* at Pescara night was really night, stone steps
were stone steps, the nearby sea was a nearby sea. It was the
same with *Hamlet* at Elsinore, which suddenly revealed its
realist character. *Hamlet* revealed itself through architecture;
at least one possible *Hamlet* did: the Renaissance *Hamlet*.
It is the *Hamlet* that the theatre attempts to demonstrate
most frequently with the least success. *Hamlet* proved itself
in Elsinore not only because Shakespeare placed the action
there, but also perhaps because the performance began at
dusk; in its second half, the beam from a lighthouse placed
in a tower of Elsinore castle swept the scaffolding erected in
the courtyard with its light, yellow and red in turn. Hamlet's

father's ghost appeared on real battlements and his voice reached the audience from there. Wyspiański, with his unerring theatrical imagination, knew that *Hamlet*—a play written for the Elizabethan stage with its upper galley—can be performed to advantage in the courtyard and galleries of a Renaissance castle.

Medea does not address the gods. They do not exist for her, just as the world does not exist, or even the children. For her they are Jason's children. More than that, they are Jason himself. She kills them not only to revenge herself on him, but because she cannot kill Jason; she kills Jason in them. But actually even Jason does not exist for Medea. Only she exists; she and her defeat. She cannot even for a moment talk or think about anything else. She is locked within herself with her misfortune, as if inside an egg. Medea's mad monomania is undoubtedly a Euripidean discovery. It makes the tragedy psychologically complete; it makes the tragedy possible. Monomania singles Medea out, separates and cuts her off from the real world. Through her monomania Medea is alone. Heroes of tragedy have to be alone.

But the women's chorus is of this world. They have come from the village, from the small harbor which is also a village. They have come to commiserate with Medea. She has been deserted by her husband; now they want to take her sons away. In its first odes the chorus complains of the injustice of the human lot and says that bitter is the life of a girl who remains unmarried, and bitter the life of a woman who marries. The women are on Medea's side and will remain so to the end. But gradually they become more and more terrified. Terrified not only by Medea's designs but by the ordeal sent her by the gods. The women's gestures become more and more ritual, liturgical. They fall on their knees, begin to beg for mercy and pity, but not for themselves. They beg for mercy from the god who takes revenge on Medea, Jason, Creon; who takes vengeance on children for parents' misdeeds, and on grandchildren for those of their grandparents.

Perhaps because I did not know the language, it seemed to me that the women, who went to the top of the stairs, to the shut door of Medea's house, began to recite the litany to the Virgin, or to the Heart of Jesus. They were praying and their prayer was one long moan.

A few days earlier, on the way back from my evening stroll, on the stone steps in front of the collegiate church of Santa Maria del Colle I had noticed a group of women, dressed in black, reciting a litany. It had been the same kind of moaning as I heard now. The words "have mercy on us" had been shouted almost like a cry of despair. The door of Santa Maria del Colle remained closed. God had literally locked himself in.

The day after the performance of *Medea* I went to the old fishing harbor in Pescara. In the square, by the entrance to a small house, stood a tall column with the statue of the Virgin. The column and the statue were ugly. They had been erected between the two world wars. On the column was the inscription: "Mary, Queen of Heaven, Mary who rules the thunder, do not kill the sons of Pescara." For the last two weeks it had been raining heavily in Pescocostanzo. The harvest had been soaked; the hay could not be brought in. Yesterday, and the day before, bells rang in all the churches of Pescocostanzo. They rang for two hours, from seven to eight in the morning and from three to four in the afternoon: seven bells of the splendidly gilded fourteenth-century Santa Maria del Colle; two shrill little bells of the new church on the rock—San Antonio Abate, and—loudest of all—four bells of the dei Fratri convent, with their monotonous and ominous sound. They had rung so that God would take pity and avert the calamity of rain from Pescocostanzo. Today they rang again; they will ring tomorrow and the day after tomorrow.

The persistent, mournful and fierce ringing of bells might end the Greek tragedy with which the Greek theatre from Piraeus came to Pescara. The bells of Pescocostanzo have been ringing to appease the same god who punished Medea and the family of Jason. For it is men who are always guilty; never God. God has not changed here for three thousand years.

(1962)

ENCOUNTERS, 1965

I first went to see *The Lesson* and *The Bald Soprano* some eight years ago. During my subsequent visits to Paris I went three or four more times to the little theatre in the rue de la Huchette in the evenings, to find out if everything was still as it had been. *The Lesson* and *The Bald Soprano* were still being performed. Last autumn I decided to see the performance once again. There was no change, except perhaps that the little theatre was more untidy than before. Even the audience was the same, as if the same spectators had been coming here for seven years with the same regularity as Mr. and Mrs. Martin had been coming to see Mr. and Mrs. Smith. Again I saw a couple of puzzled tourists and a gentleman from the provinces who did not laugh at all. Only the students' beards were longer than before, and the girls' hair shorter.

I had seen *The Bald Soprano* twice before: at the same theatre eight years ago, and then in Warsaw. But it seemed to me as if I knew it by heart, as if it had always existed, instead of having been written only recently. It didn't occur to me until later that for many months I had been talking at home in the "bald-soprano" manner, for hours at a time. "It's amazing, it's extraordinary, what a coincidence, you have a daughter called Teresa, and I have a daughter called Teresa." After eight years *The Lesson* seemed to me more violent, more cruel, more masochistic than before. I was not sure whether the Pupil was still being played by the same actress. When I had first seen her, she seemed so childish.

After the performance I went to see the Ionescos. "Of course, it's the same actress," said Eugène. "*The Lesson* will go on being performed for another fifty or seventy years. One day the Pupil will die. I mean really die, not just on the stage. She will go to heaven, and St. Peter will sternly ask her: 'What did you do in life, my child?' And she will reply, 'What did I do? I was eighteen when I began to act the Pupil in M. Ionesco's play at the theatre in the rue de la Huchette. Then I got engaged, to be married, and I went on acting the Pupil. Then I got married. I went on acting the Pupil. Then I got pregnant and for three months I stopped acting the Pupil. Then my daughter was born. I went on acting the Pupil. Then I got a divorce. I went on acting the Pupil. Then I got married again. I went on acting the Pupil. Then my son was born. I went on acting the Pupil. Then I got divorced again. I went on acting the Pupil. Then my daughter had twins. I had to leave Paris for two weeks. Then I went on acting the Pupil.' And St. Peter will say, 'M. Ionesco can hardly wait for you; he is attending a rehearsal of *The Lesson*.'"

Ionesco looked at me, became very sad all of a sudden and said in a choked whisper, "It's not true; I shall not die."

*

There has to be the Ghost in *Hamlet*, said Peter Brook. I had just come back from Stratford where I had seen the latest *Hamlet* produced by Peter Hall. I did not like the Ghost. At first he seemed awesome, swept through a door half his own size; he did not walk but glided, huge and shapeless. He was uncanny, but only for a little while. Soon his stature was reduced to a theatrical trick. Before long I guessed that the Ghost was played by two actors: one was riding a specially constructed bicycle, hence the gliding rhythm; the other was standing on his shoulders. The Ghost on a bicycle became ridiculous. I have never *seen* a really good Ghost in *Hamlet*. Only once, in the courtyard of Elsinore castle on an occasion I have described previously, did I like the way the Ghost was presented. The reflector from a light-house, situated in a castle tower overlooking the sea, swept the wooden scaffolding with its light; sea gulls flew just over the actors' heads. The effect was that of a market fair, and yet real. The Ghost spoke in a hoarse voice from distant galleries; but although the spotlights followed him, there was nothing to be seen. I also liked the way the Ghost was treated in an Italian *Hamlet* produced by Zeffirelli. He had designed the sets himself: a black background and an empty stage, with a round hole near the proscenium arch. Through that hole, as if through a trap on top of a winding staircase in the castle tower, halberdiers entered, and so did Laertes. The empty stage was immediately changed into the upper battlements. The Ghost was Hamlet's shadow when he stood with outstretched arms; the shadow, thrown against the backdrop, grew larger and smaller, running across the black horizon, flashing against the dark.

I told Peter Brook about this, but I failed to convince him. He wanted a genuine Ghost who would awe the audience, for a little while at least, the way Elizabethan audiences must have been awed by a real Ghost. He wanted a Ghost derived from the liturgy and from Artaud. At about that time Artaud became the ghost who haunted Brook and other men of the theatre in a most violent manner. Brook sometimes looks like a big cat; suddenly there is fire in his eyes and he tautens as if preparing for a jump.

"The Ghost *must* cause a shock. He does not have to be big. Have you seen a scorpion? Everybody starts back at once on seeing one. You are afraid of cockroaches; they are revolt-ing. So is a bat when it suddenly flies into a room and bangs itself about, blindly. Look at these statuettes." In a glass case in the corner of the room stood two little demons, probably made of jasper. "They are demons from Sumatra. Aren't you afraid of them?"

I was not afraid of them. The gods or demons had round protruding little bellies and excessively pointed heads. There was nothing fearsome about them. Brook switched the main light off, took the smaller demon away and placed the other one near the glass so that it cast a shadow. Then he placed the lamp on the floor, adjusted its position. The demon grew larger, had a round head and a beast's muzzle. It was revolting and fearful. I shuddered and began to be afraid.

*

I met Helen when she came out of the water. We bathed every night in the moonlight. The sea at Aghios Nikolaos was even saltier than elsewhere in Crete. It was so buoyant one cold swim for hours. Even at night the sky was light, only the mountains seemed to be nearer. Helen was Richard's wife. They taught me to drink retsina, the rough wine that tastes of resin. We did not know anything about each other, but from the first day we addressed one another by our Christian names. Everything began with the gold mask of Agamemnon. His wry mouth was set in a grimace. Of gold, and possibly a death mask, it was yet a human face with its taunting smile. The face of someone who was alive when the Greeks were setting out for Troy. We discussed that mask for hours. We could see Mount Ida; we went to the palace of Minos; we went by car to see the wall built by the Cyclops. Everything became close and real. Agamemnon had a human face with a taunting smile. Richard had brought with him an aqualung, fins and a harpoon. In the evening he hunted fish on the bottom of the sea. Later he took them to a little restaurant, called Rififi because some film people had once stayed there, to be fried. We ate fried fish, drank the golden retsina, and talked about the wry mouth of Agamemnon.

Richard took me to Delphi. On the way we passed through Thebes. A few miles from the town is the crossroad where Oedipus met the cart in which an old man was driving with his servants. Oedipus did not want to give way; a scuffle began, and he killed his father Laius, not knowing the old man's identity. It is an asphalt road, with warning signs at the crossroads. The sky is white, as always in Greece; the mountains—rocky and deserted—are near; they seem yellow, as if burned out by the sun.

"I was first told about Greece," Richard said, "by a friend in New Orleans. Her parents were Greek, but she was born in the States. She visited Greece for the first time a few years ago. She spent a couple of months here but did not seem to like it. The ruins are nice, she said, the sea warm, but it is a poor country and there is nothing much to see. She went to the town where her parents had been born. There were a couple of new houses, she said, and while she was there they were installing electricity. I wanted her to tell me what the town was called. Somehow she could not remember. It was a strange name, she said, Thebes or something." We went through Thebes. The town was indeed dilapidated and ugly.

It was only when we were taking leave of each other in Athens that we exchanged surnames and addresses. My companion was Richard Schechner, editor of the *Tulane Drama Review*. We wanted to have a chat about the theatre, but there was no time for that.

HAPPENINGS IN EDINBURGH, 1963

I first visited Edinburgh three or four years after the war. I remember almost nothing of that visit except that Edinburgh was nice. Just nice, nothing more. And, like Kraków, it had style. In 1963 I spent a week in Edinburgh. It was cold and rained all the time, day and night. I stayed in the district of Newington, almost out of town. From my window I could see a big, flat, green hill. Most of the time the hill looked gray, however.

I went into town every evening. The rain was annoying; the drizzle seemed wetter than ordinary rain and penetrated to the bone. The city was strange, somber, tightly closed. The streets were dark in spite of gaudy shopwindows filled with masses of tartan blankets and Scotch wool pullovers. No one stopped at the windows. No one even turned his head to look. It struck me at once that people were taller here. I often went by fair-haired giants with blue eyes and soft wavy beards. They were leading giantesses, fair and blue-eyed like themselves, by the hand, in the country manner. Sometimes they stopped to pat them on the back or buttocks. They did all this slowly, silently, solemnly. In nearly every doorway stood a motionless couple who seemed to be glued together. They did not even kiss. In their immobility they reminded me of copulating insects. One spring in Obory I saw the gold-and-green larvae of beetles joined by their abdomens. Every now and then they moved very slowly along the trunk of a tree or the twig of a bush, made little movements with their jaws, and sank again into immobility for long periods of time, joined together like some odd Janus with two heads and one trunk. There was something frightening and ecstatic about that insect love-making. The human larvae stood thus joined together till late at night, in spite of the non-stop rain and the sharp gusts of east wind. The insect-like impression was magnified by their dress. Men and women were dressed alike in tight-fitting jeans and thick rough pullovers. Their heards were bare and their eyes closed.

The hill I could see from my window was not the only one. Edinburgh is situated on hills; they are in the city itself and all around it. On the hills stand huge Gothic structures. At night and in the rain they seem even larger, suspended in the sky halfway between the dark city, sullen and tightly shut below, and the low-hanging ceiling of clouds. They are all equally gray, built of the same kind of stone: the cathedral, a dozen churches, and the castle where every evening at six a piercing wail of bagpipes and shriek of fifes accompany the changing of the guard.

These big Gothic buildings seem to belong to another city. Strange, desolate, and huge, they exist in a different dimension. For a while I had the impression I was wandering on a large stage where they had forgotten to remove the backdrop after the last show. Down here sets were already standing for a new and quite different play. A railway line runs across the center of the city. From the viaduct one can look down to the tracks and a big, usually quite empty station. Between the two thoroughfares is a flat stretch of railway buildings. In this setting one can perform *A View from the Bridge*.

The extras were there already: the motionless couples stuck together in every dark doorway, between shopwindows full of blankets and mohair pullovers. Over these blankets and pullovers, over heaps of shawls and gloves, socks, checked stockings and ginger-and-green handwoven jackets one could see—in every part of the town—the huge superfluous Gothic backdrop, left here by mistake.

The backdrop also belonged to a play, only for a long time I could not recall its title. But I knew it; I knew these sets. It occurred to me only on the evening before I left, when suddenly, in the rain and fog, stone steps emerged in front of me, barred halfway up with a massive iron grid. High above, two spires seemed to be rising from the top of the steps. Higher still, a hill shaped like a flattened cone was visible, white in the moonlight, as if covered with snow.

Five or six months earlier, when I was in Venice, Gordon Craig had shown me reproductions of his theatre designs and drawings. He moved his finger, stained yellow, twisted with arthritis, across a drawing representing stone steps leading up to a flat semicircular courtyard from which towered two half-derelict spires, spiny like hedgehogs. Craig stopped his finger at the very top of the drawing and suddenly began to laugh. His chuckle turned into a senile cough. "Here"—he pointed to a broken arch and black bars thickly drawn by charcoal crayon—"here was Duncan's chamber." Again he moved his bent finger around the drawing and pointed to other stone steps—the whole design was composed of stairs, bars, and broken Gothic spires—down which Lady Macbeth was to run.

We were standing in front of a stone gate barred with a massive iron grid; beyond it we could see a red light. "It must be here," said Candida. For a moment I thought it was the very gate the drunken porter opened at dawn to Macduff on the night of Duncan's murder. But it was only the light of a pub.

It was in Edinburgh that I started going to pubs regularly. For a long time I could not understand the pleasure derived from drinking while standing almost in silence and during strictly limited hours. Only on my second or third stay in Britain did I slowly begin to relish the strange liturgy and ceremonial of pubs, and even the black and very bitter Guinness stout. The pub limits social relations to the minimum while drinking, but it invests that activity with a certain social sanction. One drinks in privacy but never in isolation.

The strictly defined and rigorously observed licensing hours turn a simple "dropping in" for a beer, whisky, or gin and tonic into an almost sacral or at least—as sociologists say—institutionalized activity.

We met in the pub shortly after the end of each day's proceedings, precisely at a quarter past five; the three of us, that is: Candida, Jovan, and myself. Jovan was a playwright from Belgrade; Candida had come to Edinburgh with a television team; she was a kind of script girl. She was tiny, had a very delicate complexion and laughing eyes with golden dots in them. One of her grandmothers was Scottish, the other Irish. From the very first day there was a common bond between us: an ironic attitude to the conference at which almost a hundred of us were gathered from all parts of the world, from Canada to Equatorial Africa, from India to Spain, and seated under spotlights at McEwan Hall. Tickets for the conference were being sold for one pound ten shillings each. For an additional two shillings and sixpence one could hire headphones and a little receiver if one wanted to hear simultaneous translations of the proceedings into German or French. We were made into an intellectual circus for four thousand spectators. For almost a week, from two to five, we discussed set topics according to a set schedule; the parts were more or less distributed, we were being filmed and recorded non-stop. Like expensive trained animals we argued, ten or fifteen minutes to a subject, about Brecht and the theatre of the absurd, freedom and duty in art, censorship and commercialization, the national and the universal theatre.

We were not the only ones to get bored. The Americans were even more bored. They had moreover been obsessed for some time now by the *happening*—improvised and spontaneous theatre which was to liberate pure theatrical phenomena. In a happening there is no stage or auditorium, author or actors; there is only the crowd and theatrical provocation.

On the penultimate day of the conference some trucks drove up in a small square by a side entrance to McEwan Hall and began to unload car tires in large quantities. Soon they formed quite big and picturesque heaps. At the same time the roadway was quickly dug up by pneumatic drills; temporary wooden bridges, miniviaducts and small tunnels leading in all directions were put up. The little square turned into a strange labyrinth. During the first intermission we were let loose into the labyrinth. The youngest of the American theatre directors madly banged an empty gas can with a hammer. Mobile television cameras drove up nearer. The participants of the conference—their air fares paid from the four corners of the world—were jumping like rabbits from tire to tire. I did not understand a thing. I asked everyone in turn what it all meant. They replied that theatre was being made, that this was a happening, that according to Zen philosophy . . . And after all, television cameras were upon us . . . Everybody was in a state of happy excitement. Only Jovan stood apart. "In Belgrade," he said, "the roadway is also continually dug up. Maybe that is a happening too."

That was not the end of surprises. Two hours later, when a young Hindu dramatist, a great admirer of Stanislavsky, began to talk about acting, almost directly over his head, on the balcony where the spotlights were situated, a girl appeared in the nude. She was accompanied by a couple of ten-year-old boys with close-fitting hats on their heads who blew flutes for all they were worth. Two American directors had persuaded an eighteen-year-old Edinburgh model, a lovely big blonde, to walk in the nude along the huge gallery of the hall. The Hindu, who did not see the girl promenading above his head, attributed the commotion in the auditorium to the effect of his speech. At this very moment he said: "The paramount task of art is to represent the naked truth."

The girl was soon conducted out, and after a short interval the proceedings were resumed. That afternoon I was to speak about Joyce and the origins of the theatre of the absurd. But I gave it up. I had a date with the Irish.

"It's here," Candida said. This pub was different from all the others I had seen. Almost empty and very dirty, as if it had not been tidied up for a week. The walls were adorned with brightly colored prints of oil paintings. A splendid officer in a huge black sheepskin-lined coat, setting spurs to a horse on the bank of a flooded river, for a short while seemed to me to be Prince Józef Poniatowski jumping into the Elster. Even his whiskers were identical, but—as was clear from the inscription —this was an Irish general whose name meant nothing to me. Another picture represented an old, gray-haired officer dressed in tight white trousers and a coat with huge epaulets, who was detonating a fuse in order to blow up his redoubt. But that colonel, or general, was not a Pole either. Behind the counter three men were engaged in so fierce a discussion that they did not even notice when we entered. Candida talked to them in whispers. We were conducted first up, then down very narrow stairs to a very long, narrow room full of people. Candida said something again. They all got up; we were passed around. Unknown men kissed us on the mouth, women took our hands and shook them firmly. The place was so dark with smoke that for a long while I could not see a thing. The thick pullovers, soaked with rain, were steaming; the steam clouded the mirrors. It all looked like an amateur performance given in a fire hall. Men were sitting cramped on simple benches. They were, most of them, small, plain, red-haired and freckled. Women were mostly sitting on the men's knees or even on the floor. We were given a large mug of beer and a glass of gin each. Room was made for us beside a tiny platform, or rather a step made of boards nailed to- gether. We were guests of Dominic Behan, the younger brother of Brendan, who had almost drunk himself to death and was spending his last days in an institution.

Dominic was singing. He had a clear, romantic voice, rather high-pitched for a man. I did not understand the words, but it must have been a ballad for at the end of every stanza all those present took up the refrain, melodious, strange, like children's counting chants, and always the same. After Behan, a young girl with hair as red as a carrot mounted the tiny platform and recited an extremely long poem in a very affected manner. It must have been a patriotic poem for she was very much impressed by it, and so were all those around her. Then a boy got up and began to sing in English. He had a pleasant, somewhat childlike voice, but they all sprang to their feet and began to protest. Dominic got up, waved his arm to silence the assembly and said: "In the house of captivity we shall not sing in the language of the enemies of our fathers."

For a long time I could not grasp the principles by which this community was ruled. After all, they talked English all the time. Only in the morning, when the Edinburgh night was drawing to a close, did I realize that Irish was not just a language for the people here; it was something less and something more: poetry, theatre, liturgy. For a long time, too, I could not get an idea of the social class these people belonged to. Men and women alike were dressed very simply, some even with striking carelessness. They looked like workers. But appearances proved deceptive again. The man with a massive neck and a broken nose who seemed to me a porter gave me in the small hours an extensive lecture on Celtic cemeteries and on the aorist tense in Welsh and in Sanskrit. He was an archaeologist.

On the floor next to me two girls were sitting in an affectionate embrace. The older of them, big and dark, was dressed in drill trousers, torn through at the knees, and had straw in her hair. The younger, very pale, who kept looking at her companion all the time, held a large violin case which she did not let go for an instant. Her eyes were half-closed. Candida knew these girls. They were sisters; daughters of a bank manager from Dublin; the younger had just graduated from a music school, with honors. They had come to Edinburgh for the festival and for the last week had been following Dominic from pub to pub, through the apartments of all his friends, fascinated and spellbound. There were more people like them in that Irish group.

On my other side a woman with charcoal black hair was sitting on a small stool. She was dressed with a gaudy cheap elegance. Suddenly she started to talk to me, in French. "I came here from Amalfi fifteen years ago. What an awful country. My husband is a Scot. He works in the biggest hotel in Glasgow and makes good money there. He is a cook."

On the tiny platform Dominic was singing a lively folksong. It must have been bawdy because the girls were giggling and covering their eyes with their hands. The Italian woman was beating the lively rhythm with her small bony fists on the back of a red-haired Irishman. Then she glued her face to his unshaven cheek. "What an awful country," she said. "But the people are charming."

Dominic had his theatre in Edinburgh, or rather, during the festival, he opened his own little cabaret show under the title *Behan being Behan*. The show opened at one in the morning and lasted till three. He performed in a dilapidated dance hall with an improvised stage and a couple of spotlights. The fairly big hall was only half filled, and very few spectators paid for their tickets. I knew almost everybody in the audience. They were the people I had met in the pub. Gradually I began to decipher the guiding principle of the group. I had been with them since five in the afternoon. Most of them had been together for a week. They camped in the houses of their friends, met for rehearsals in the mornings, spent their afternoons in the pub, at night got together again at Behan's.

He was truly indefatigable. In the pub he had seemed younger; now I realized that he must be over forty. He sang, danced, told Irish anecdotes and some biblical stories maybe; on several occasions during the show he came down from the platform to kiss Jovan and myself on the mouth. We were his guests. Apart from Dominic two young Jews from New York took part in the show; they told jokes in Yiddish. A young Greek girl was also part of the company. She danced gracefully. I met her a few weeks later at the London airport. She had come for a summer course in English, met Dominic, and joined his troupe.

In the intermission we were given beer and gin again, and they would not let us pay. For that matter, no one paid for

himself; everyone treated others or was treated himself; everyone threw what money he had on the table—shilling pieces,
half crowns. Women drank from the same mugs as men. I was
dead tired. But Candida, usually somnolent and lethargic,
suddenly came to life. Jovan, too, would not let me go
home. There were still a couple of hours left till morning.
The Irish night was still young. When the show was over
we went first to a picture exhibition. Before Dominic all doors
opened, and all glasses were filled. The exhibition consisted
of landscapes, painted with moving simplicity; it was an exhibition of Irish Sunday painters.

In the morning, when we were in a third or fourth place,
I lectured on Mickiewicz to the two sisters; the dark one who
had her trousers torn, and the fair one who still would not let
go her violin case. They listened very attentively and seemed
to understand everything, undeterred by the fact that I was
reciting Mickiewicz in Polish.

There is a narrow street in Paris, not far from Saint-Germain, between the rue des Beaux Arts and rue de la Seine. Its
name escapes me. In it there is a small house in which
Racine died and a three-story house in which there was once
a printing press owned by Balzac. There are plaques on both
houses. Over ten years ago I visited some friends in Leningrad,
in an alley situated in the old quarter of the city, not far from
the Neva. I recall a wide rotting staircase smelling of laundry
and a labyrinth of dark corridors through which one crossed
to an open porch. That was not the end of the way. One had
to pass through two crowded rooms in an alcove, half of
which was occupied by a heated stove. I do not quite know
why, but it is in this house that I could best visualize Sonia
and Raskolnikov.

Before the war my wife used to take me to the Parc
Monceau, where young Marcel had played with Gilberte.
Three years ago friends took me on a Sunday for a walk to the
docks along the Thames. We did not meet a soul for hours.
On either side of narrow streets storehouses, which must have

been built in the early nineteenth century, stretched for miles. On the Thames side, there were shoots on the second floor so that sacks could be thrown directly into vessels. In those empty streets, those yards overgrown with grass, Oliver Twist could have walked. And so it happened on a few occasions in my life that I was able to touch that raw material from which the world of a writer originated. Sometimes it was a room, sometimes a street, once even a barbershop window on the outskirts of Paris that suddenly revealed Apollinaire to me. I read *Ulysses* for the first time before the war, and then twice again. But the work was alien to me. I could not visualize it anywhere. Not in any town; not in any landscape. I did not know that one could discover Walpurgis Night in an Irish pub. Even in Edinburgh.

The next day was Sunday. Dominic woke everybody up; we went to Mass: the two sisters, the lecturer in archaeology I had taken for a porter, the two street vendors of ties, with whom I had a great discussion at dawn concerning Goya's "Naked Maya" and Cranach's "Venus in a Cardinal's Hat." Dominic took Jovan, Candida, and myself up to the loft where he played the organ; Candida blew the organ as best she could.

That afternoon, evening, night and morning had nothing in common with a London party, or a Parisian partouse, or a Polish drinking bout. Perhaps there was a Polish flavor about it; but it was a romantic Poland of over a century ago that one was reminded of. All these men and women had their homes, occupations, professions, positions in life. They were joined together only by that unreal, mad, utopian Irishness, which in reality did not mean anything at all, which was pure make-believe, yet on that morning, when we walked embracing one another with Dominic, it seemed to me the very essence of life.

MARCEAU, OR THE CREATION OF THE WORLD

Marceau imbues the air with gravity. The world has to be created on an empty stage. At the beginning there is the physics of mime. From the very first gesture the world is matter. At the beginning there is only the pull of gravity. The most literal mime of a man climbing the stairs would be a man climbing the stairs. Marceau creates the stairs, leans against invisible banisters, climbs. This simplest of mimes has from the outset the characteristic style of the genre. A gesture must not be literal because the stairs are not real. A gesture must be condensed and generalized, metaphoric and elliptical. Mime does not mean imitating a man climbing the stairs, because it contains all the stairs in the world. Mime expresses the physical world and the concreteness of movement. The man walks against the wind; the wind pushes him, blows him over. Marceau makes air and wind materialize, gives them consistency and force.

The art of the equilibrist, juggler, or acrobat consists in abolishing the physical concreteness of the world; it defeats the force of gravity. Marceau lifts invisible weights, juggles with non-existent plates. He has to begin by giving them material concreteness; he has to create the force of gravity anew. Miming physical actions is possible only in air that has a definite consistency. An invisible rope has been stretched across below the circus top. Marceau slowly raises his foot; his leg is trembling under the weight of his body. He is standing on the floor all the time. It is the air that sinks and becomes an abyss under him. The physics of mime is followed by the poetry of mime. A clown with a tormented expression on his face is standing on a rope under the circus top. He is afraid, but he has to smile. He smiles. The expression on his face, fixed till now, begins to change. His ridiculous beetle-brows begin to rise, his mouth sets in a grimace. The drama begins—comedy and tragedy, sublime and clownish.

First the force of gravity was created, then physical objects. Now the empty stage is full of people. It is a fairground, a square, a park. A few gestures of the hand and two women are sitting on the bench, knitting; the arms are crooked and a nanny is pushing a baby in a pram; a boy waits for a girl, meets and embraces her. Mime creates the atmosphere, the location, the situation. What joy to guess the meaning of a gesture, what a leap of the imagination. The silent language of mime has the precision of a drawing and the ambiguity of poetry. The sign and the concept are never exactly equivalent. That is why it is so difficult to describe a mime. It is like trying to make something unambiguous out of something ambiguous. It is like summarizing a poem. The language of mime consists only of metaphor. The fluttering hand is a butterfly. But there is also Marceau's real hand, and the hand of the butterfly catcher represented by the clown represented by Marceau. The butterfly dies and the hand goes dead. But the butterfly was Marceau's hand. The death of the butterfly is his own death.

The white mime is Watteau's Pierrot and the sad Chaplin; he is the jester, the clown and the harlequin, the bitter philosopher, and the little man exposed to the cruelty of men and inanimate objects. At the beginning there was the empty stage and the man in the white suit. The world was created, starting with the purely physical and material, to include all human situations. Within two hours every tragedy and every comedy have been performed. We have seen both the physics and the poetics of mime; all that can be said by mime and through mime. It seemed that the limits of art, and of this genre, had been reached. But no. Not yet.

The maker of masks tries them on. There are happy and sad masks, grotesque, distorted, terrifying masks. The maker enjoys them all. He has plenty of them. He puts the last one on. The mask gets stuck to his face. He tries to take it off but cannot. He runs up to the mirror; he sees the clown. The most horrible of all masks has now become his face. The fool's mask, stuck on his face, is set in an idiotic laugh. At last he manages to tear the mask off. He has his own face back. But he has already crossed the frontier. Now he knows all: he has come to know the tragicomedy of life.

Let us imagine this scene played by an actor, with real masks. It would be deeply moving. It would be as I have described it. But Marcel Marceau plays it without masks. All the masks are facial grimaces—grimaces of his own face. The horrible, grotesque mask is also just his own face. And his own face, the first face, the face of the maker of masks, is only the tormented face of a clown. His own face is a mask. So there is no face and there is no mask. Mask is face, face is mask. All faces and all masks.

Marcel Marceau has reached the point at which modern art achieves greatness at the price of renouncing falsehood. To do this art must be completely laid bare. Mime is make-believe, putting on masks. Marcel Marceau, at the furthest point of his art, creates the absolute mime in which the frontiers between mask and face, make-believe and truth, have been obliterated. Marcel Marceau creates the world and shows that the world is a mime. I do not think one can go further than that.

(1963)

STRANGE THOUGHTS ABOUT KAFKA

To the right of the road leading from Kraków to Nowa Huta, about half a kilometer from the first blocks of the new town, there is a park. I was there in December; the day was foggy, the first snow had just fallen. The park was empty, if one can call a large, flat field with some benches but without an enclosure a park. There is not one tree, not even a bush. There may be lawns, but I could not see them for the snow. Just a white empty field with black benches, placed quite chaotically, as if someone had thrown them around haphazardly. A few of them were arranged in an unshapely polygon, as if they had approached one another for a chat. In the fog they had a ghostly appearance. I had the feeling a drama had been performed here, but I could not guess its meaning or plot. There was something Kafkaesque about the landscape.

During the same visit to Kraków, I went to Noworolski's café in the Cloth Hall earlier than I usually do. It was not yet eleven. Later the place is always full, but at that early hour, only the tables by the walls were occupied; those in the center were empty. I rushed to the only free table by the wall. Newcomers were arriving all the time. I could see their anxious looks: they were looking for tables by the wall, or by the window. Then, reluctantly, anxiously, they took their seats at the center tables. Never before had I paid any attention to this phenomenon. Suddenly I had the impression that we were all insects, ruled ruthlessly and des-

potically by "walltropy." I had a good corner seat, I was safe
on three sides. I felt like a huge insect hidden in a hole. I was
again reminded—I did not know why—of Kafka. Perhaps the
reason was a sudden awareness of fear.

I saw *The Trial* on the stage a few weeks later. I was
immediately struck by its "theatricality." I do not mean the
theatrical qualities of the stage adaptation, but the intrinsic,
natural theatricality of the story's substance. An ordinary
novel takes place in a room, on a train, during a walk, or
nowhere. Kafka's stories take place in a setting. The setting
is not a chance one, external to the action. On the contrary,
one cannot imagine Kafka without his particular settings.
It is never a natural one—there is no nature in Kafka—but it
is never a neutral, indifferent room either. Objects are often
meticulously drawn: a bed, a wardrobe, a door, photographs
above the bed, a blouse on a hanger in Miss Bürstner's
room, or the bar counter at the inn in *The Castle*. All these
objects not only exist, they mean something as well. But
besides them there is nothing.

The precise and meticulous scenery ends abruptly; there
are holes in it. It opens onto the town, the field, the castle,
the staircase, the corridors, the attic. It is like a stage set and
is constructed on the same principle. It includes real objects
and dummies, is realistic and make-believe; it has its stage
and wings; it exists and is leading somewhere. It is—and it
represents something. Like the benches in that strange park
near Nowa Huta. It is a lyrical and dramatic set.

At the same time it is the stage set of a nightmare. We say
sometimes that a person or event or image is nightmarish.
The first meaning of the word "nightmare" is a bad dream.
Dream scenery is rather like stage scenery: objects in the
main stage area are very clearly marked in both, they exist
and they take part in dramatic action. Often there are also
doors, stairs, corridors; but behind them there is nothing,
just as in the theatre, or in Kafka. Objects are themselves
and at the same time represent something else; they are
more than themselves. When we talk about dreams we ask

what they mean. There is no dream without its scenery; just as there is no theatre without a set. In a nighmare the scenery is particularly vivid. We are short of air, we are stifling; suddenly we find a door with the notice: "Entrance to the Clerk of the Court." We walk up the stairs, we grope around some attics. One of the most striking features that distinguishes a dream—particularly a bad dream—from waking experience is that in a dream we cannot leave the place in which we are. In real life we can leave the room, unless we are locked in. But in a dream our movements are limited. This may be the reason why we so often use the word "nightmarish" in regard to situations that we cannot extricate ourselves from. We talk, for instance, about nightmarish conferences when we cannot leave the conference room. From the days of the German occupation we remember what a nightmare the curfew was. Being locked up is always a nightmare. Kafka's world is a locked-up world.

In waking experience we can escape with our thoughts, even from pain, even from fear. There is no escape from a nightmare. In a dream there is no future or past. We can dream that we are dreaming, but there are hardly any dreams in which one dreams about what was or what will be. A dream, still more a nighmare, has only one tense: the present. In Kafka's world there is also only the present tense. Joseph K. in *The Trial* or the surveyor K. in *The Castle* do not recall the past, do not think about the future; they are in their cruel present all the time.

Kafka's prose hardly ever relates thoughts. The characters are there, they talk, experience things, but they do not think. Or at any rate, we do not know what they think. Just as in a nightmare or in the theatre. It is a kind of prose that operates solely through scenery and dialogue. Hence the infernal intensity of Kafka. After all, the present is the most intense of tenses; and only the present is really dramatic.

Apart from the main protagonist, Kafka's characters are guided by the laws governing dream characters. In a dream, all the people we meet perform a part in relation to us; we can talk to them, but we do not know who they really are. In a nightmare they are always stronger than we. It is they who develop the action, tell us to do things, take us somewhere. We protest, but we are powerless. Or we struggle, but they win. It is as if we were in a theatre: the action does not depend on us. We have been put on trial, but we do not know for what, by whom and where. We resist, we shout our protests, but we have to submit.

There are nightmares in which we are aware of the absurdity of the action in which we have been entangled. These are the worst nightmares. We have a tiny hope, we grasp someone's hand, we see a light appearing at the moment when a knife is to pierce our heart. But the scenario of the nightmare has not been written by us.

Dreams are a distorted reflection of reality. And not only distorted, but also condensed. Dreams are not irrational. In our dreams we are frightened by things that really are frightening. Kafka's somber greatness lies in the fact that he demonstrated the substance of our modern terrors through nightmares. But there are dreams dreamed before their time —precursor dreams. Kafka began to write *The Castle* and *The Trial* in 1914. The era of concentration camps with their crematoria had not yet begun. To be locked up. Not to be able to escape into either the past or the future. To be just a number. To come to believe in one's guilt, in one's trial. That is the worst nightmare, indeed.

(1958)

A NOTE ON BECKETT'S REALISM

Winnie is buried to her waist. *Happy Days* opens with the terrifying sound of a bell. A moment later the bell rings once again. Winnie wakes up, raises her head, opens her eyes. What does the bell signify? Winnie talks about the bell often and waits for it to ring throughout the entire first act. The bell rings when it is time to get up and when it is time to go to sleep. When I was in the hospital, there was no bell; the nurses woke us up and also turned out the lights at night. But there was a bell when I stayed in a nursing home. The bell had a horrifying sound and woke us up every morning. The bell also rang at night, and when it had rung, we were not allowed to have the light on.

In the first act of *Happy Days* the bell rings twice, at the very beginning. In the second act it rings several times and breaks Winnie's monologues. The reason for it is simply that in the second act time passes more quickly. The longer one has been ill, the more quickly the time passes. The first act is long and lasts one day. The second act is shorter nearly by half, but it covers several days. The longer one has been in the hospital, the more time becomes divided into the short stretches between waking and falling asleep. Winnie says:

> I used to think . . . (*pause*) . . . I say I used to think there was no difference between one fraction of a second and the

next. (*pause*) I used to say . . . (*pause*) . . . I say I used to
say, Winnie, you are changeless, there is never any difference
between one fraction of a second and the next.

The world in which Winnie and Willie are dying is a
closed one; on only one occasion do two visitors stray into
it. But it is not an imminent world; it is regulated from
outside. Outside the world of Willie and Winnie there is the
bell. The bell is transcendental. The agony of Winnie and
Willie is happening within time.

On her left side Winnie has a big black handbag, on her
right a collapsible parasol. The parasol has a very long
handle which can be pulled out. I have seen parasols with
such handles used by paralytics. I have also seen such handbags by the sides of women who had not left their beds for
months. In the bags they had mirrors, combs, toothbrushes,
and many other strange objects. In the morning they too,
like Winnie, opened their bags, took out the mirrors and
looked at themselves in them:

—good Lord!—(*pulling back upper lip to inspect gums*)—
good God!—(*pulling back corner of mouth, mouth open*) ah
well—(*other corner*)—no worse—(*abandons inspection, normal speech*)—no better, no worse—(*lays down mirror*)—no
change—

The paralyzed women used to take out their mirrors, observe their gums, do their make-up, take out their combs,
lose their combs or mirrors, open their bags and look for
something in them. They all had big bags. Beckett is more
than economical in his choice of objects—the world consists of people and of objects, the world, outside of which
there is only the bell. Beckett is precise and exact in his
choice of objects when he uses a comb, a mirror, toothpaste, a medicine bottle. Winnie throws the empty bottle
away, breaks the mirror. The world of Winnie and Willie is
not a closed one, however, because the objects reappear.

(*Pause. She takes up the mirror.*) I take up this little glass,
I shiver it on a stone—(*does so*)—I throw it away—(*does so*

far behind her)—it will be in the bag again tomorrow, without a scratch, to help me through the day.

Why do objects in this particular world reappear? Because the nurses put medicines in in the morning and at night on their paralytic patient's bedside tables and buy them combs or mirrors. The patients put them in their handbags, lose them, search for and break them. The world is easily reduced, not to a man's own self, but to what surrounds it. Everyone who has spent a longish spell in a hospital, nursing home, or prison knows this by heart. The world is very easily reduced to a big plastic bag filled with such things as toothpaste, a comb, a mirror. In the reduced world of Beckett even a fly lighting nearby for a while is carefully watched: it is important, like the flea in *Endgame*; it is watched in close-up; it is holding a small white ball in its little legs. This too is important.

To be together in the world of Winnie and Willie does not mean to see one another, or to be able to see each other. I have watched paralyzed patients in a hospital room who for months could hear one another, could even talk, but never saw one another, or could see one another only occasionally, when the pillows were arranged in a special way. Often, one patient could see another but was never seen by him.

Can you see me from there I wonder, I still wonder. (*pause*) No? (*back front*) Oh I know it does not follow when two are gathered together—(*faltering*) in this way—(*normal*)— that because one sees the other the other sees the one, life has taught me that . . . too. (*pause*) Yes, life; I suppose, there is no other word.

This reduced world in which certain objects keep reappearing and the bell is the only sound coming from outside is filled with voices. The patients speak their monologues and read newspapers. Monologues of others are to them only a buzz. Newspapers, read aloud, are also a buzz, which still comes from the world but does not really mean anything any more. Newspapers are of another time, and that is why in hospitals one can read tomorrow's newspapers just as well as yesterday's, and those of a week, or a year, ago. Newspapers have no dates in a hospital. In a hospital one reads classified advertisements just as avidly as dispatches and headlines on the front page. They are just a buzz and do not mean anything. Willie reads aloud: "His Grace and Most Reverend Father in God Dr. Carolus Hunter dead in tub." Willie reads aloud: "Wanted bright boy." Willie reads aloud: "Opening for smart youth."

In the second act Winnie is completely paralyzed. She can move only her eyes. Now time begins to move faster and faster. What is time for Beckett? The simplest pre-Einstein definition compares time to points on a straight line. Time is continuous. Given two moments of time we can say that one of them must be earlier, the other later. Time runs one way, is unidirectional. This "unidirectional time" occurs in *Endgame*, *Krapp's Last Tape*, and *Happy Days*. It means aging, decay, dying. It contains both the "earlier" and the "later." But Beckett uses also another kind of time. Beckettian characters know a *present* and a *past*; but all that happened in the past did not happen "earlier" or "later." Everything that *was*, is two-dimensional, simultaneous as it were; sometimes part of what *has* happened earlier, at other times, later. There was a shed; Winnie kissed somebody; someone kissed her; a gentleman came, he was called Shower, or perhaps Cooker; Willie proposed to her; someone had a doll; the daughter had a doll; a mouse jumped on the daughter's leg; someone wrote a poem; Winnie kissed someone; nothing was earlier, nothing was later. The world in which Winnie and Willie live seems, sometimes, to have no gaps, no empty places; it is tightly filled with voices, objects, memories. But all these voices, memories, objects are loose; they intermingle haphazardly, to no purpose, like necessary and unnecessary trifles crammed together in a big plastic bag. In this tight Beckettian world the existentialist metaphor seems crystal clear for the first time: consciousness is a gap in existence, a bottomless pit.

Beckett is very consistent in his choice of objects. Winnie takes a revolver out of her bag. In the second act the revolver lies on the mound close by her. Why the revolver? The world of Winnie and Willie is a closed one, yet one can escape from it. One can leave it. But what for? In any case, the bell will ring. But before it rings, there is still so much happiness to be had. Our misery is always matched by our happiness. Winnie has been paralyzed up to her neck. Willie can still crawl. But Willie will not be able to crawl up to Winnie. He will, however, be able to look at her. A gap in existence will then be able to say to another gap in existence, "My Winnie."

The world of Beckett is precise and verifiable, subject to every rigor; even to realism. This kind of realism can be called infrarealism, or subrealism. In a Beckett play, a wide generalization, the total and absolute human situation always corresponds to a real, concrete, individual situation. That situation can always be shown. It can be performed. In a production of *Waiting for Godot* given at Tunis, the tree that bloomed was a fig tree. Under the fig tree two fellahs wrapped in burnooses were waiting for Godot. But the action of *Waiting for Godot* does not take place in Tunis; and that of *Happy Days* does not take place in a hospital for paralytics. Or rather, it takes place not only there.

(1965)

ON THE RELEVANCE OF MOLIÈRE

1

In an Arabic production of *L'École des femmes* I saw in Tunis, Arnolphe wore a red tarboosh with a green band around it. The green band meant he had made a pilgrimage to Mecca. Arnolphe was full of dignity and refinement, rarely flew into a rage; and only on one or two occasions did he level a long black stick with a bent silver handle at his servants. For the most part he was smiling, ironical, had an air of superiority, was certain of his absolute rights. He was a merchant, an honest and experienced merchant. Agnès was his property; he had bought her as a child, was supporting her and bringing her up to be his wife. She should be obedient. She could be stupid. She must not know too much.

Arnolphe had white stockings and walked about, like all merchants, in a white, uncut, very wide tunic reaching below the knees and worn over the shirt. He was less ridiculous and far more dignified than French Arnolphes. At one point he reminded me of a most remarkable perfume seller in Tunis who had entertained me with a philosophical discourse for an hour and treated me to peppermint tea for a long time before, without any hurry, he began to produce little bottles of oriental scents. The custom had to be conformed to, though he knew full well that I would buy no more than one little bottle of ambergris for a couple of denarii. Here, in the theatre, the sickly smell of perfume and sweets emanated from the stage, from the auditorium, from the town. The Arab girls sitting next to me were dressed the same way as Agnès, and their black eyes glistened just like hers. They wore ornamented, richly embroidered dresses, over which they threw white shawls. Only a few were dressed in the European fashion, but even those who were traditionally dressed did not veil their faces, at least not while the performance was on. The wooer of Agnès was also dressed in the European, or rather Italian, fashion. He too did not differ at all from the group of young, suntanned, swarthy Arab boys sitting next to me. In that Arab *L'École des Femmes* the stage and the auditorium looked alike. Aly Ben Ayed transferred the place of action to Sidi Bou Said, a little town a dozen miles from Tunis, a town where everything was white and blue. There, on a little square, between two small houses whose barred windows were like fine cages, a modern Arab wooer in European clothes led a worthy Arab merchant up the garden path. Behind the cage windows stood the Arab Agnès. As in Molière, the windows opened and the letter reached the boy: not only did the actors and the spectators wear the same clothes, the same comedy was being performed on the stage and in the auditorium. A modern comedy about a girl's erotic—and not only erotic—emancipation. After the performance, women and girls ran up to the stage, shouted and clapped their hands: Molière's Agnès in Arab dress was their own modern heroine.

In Tunis I witnessed for the first time how Molière became, in eighteenth-century Poland and in many other countries, a contemporary native playwright. Bohomolec was the first to discover that Polish Parisians could stand for *Les Précieuses ridicules*, Warsaw for Paris, the middle rank of the Polish gentry for the French bourgeois. That discovery was crucial for the development of Polish comedy in the Age of Enlightenment. The method was applied to other plays of Molière. As for *L'École des femmes*, Boguslawsky—like Aly Ben Ayed nearly two hundred years later—transformed Arnolphe into a

Warsaw nobleman, Mr. Rich, who leased for Agnès a
secluded little mansion in a Warsaw suburb. The wooer, too,
was a contemporary; he was serving in the army, and in a
Warsaw regiment to boot.

The Polish Molière was performed in native national
costume, just as the Arab Molière is performed today in the
dress worn in the streets of Tunis. In both these national
guises, Molière was not and is not made topical in any
artificial way. He is simply present in current conflicts, in
similarly prevailing customs, in the very substance of life.
But Molière, who can so easily, almost effortlessly, be shown
in the guise of different contemporary costume, certainly is
not a Molière for all time. It is a Molière once topical in
Poland, still topical in the Arab countries. It is a kind of con-
temporaneity not to be found any more today; or at any rate,
not to be easily found. One can perform Molière in modern
dress, and he was so performed in Paris recently. But to
perform Molière in modern dress today is quite different
from the eighteenth-century adaptations; it means a search
for the everlasting Molière, not a Molière in costume, but a
Molière rid of costume, or at any rate of costume implying
a particular era. This kind of Molière can be topical too, but in
a different way.

2

In his excellent studies published under the title *Mimesis*,
Erich Auerbach begins his analysis of Molière's Tartuffe by
recalling the portrait of a religious hypocrite drawn by La
Bruyère in his *Caractèrs*:

> The *faux dévot*, La Bruyère says at once, does not speak of
> "*my hair shirt and my scourge*; on the contrary; he would pass
> for what he is, for a hypocrite, and he wants to pass for what
> he is not, for a devout man; it is true that he behaves in a
> way which makes people believe, without his saying so, that
> he wears a hair shirt and scourges himself."

Onuphre in the *Caractèrs* is a perfect and impeccable hypocrite. La Bruyère's polemical intention is beyond doubt. He was clearly alluding in a critical way to Molière's Tartuffe:

If he finds himself on a good footing with a wealthy man, whom he has been able to take in, whose parasite he is, and from whom he can draw great assistance, he does not cajole his wife, at least he does not make advances nor a declaration to her; he will run away, he will leave his cloak in her hands, if he is not as sure of her as of himself. Still less will he employ the jargon of devotion to flatter her and seduce her; he does not speak it from habit, but from design and according as it is useful to him, and never when it would serve only to make him extremely ridiculous. . . . He has no idea of becoming his sole heir, nor of getting him to give him his entire estate, especially if it is a case of taking it away from a son, the legitimate heir: a devout man is neither avaricious nor violent nor unjust nor even interested: Onuphre is not devout, but he wants to be thought so and, by a perfect, though false, imitation of piety, to take care of his interests secretly: hence he never ventures to confront the direct line and he never insinuates himself into a family where there are both a daughter to be provided for and a son to be set up in the world; such rights are too strong and too inviolable: they cannot be infringed without scandal (and he dreads scandal), without such an attempt coming to the ears of the Prince, from whom he hides his course because he fears to be exposed and to appear as what he is.

The portrait of Onuphre has the cold perfection of the abstract. La Bruyère systematized human beings in the manner of a naturalist. Molière's characters are sometimes theatrically clear, particularly those taken over from old French farce or from the Italian commedia dell'arte. One can find in Molière almost all the Italian *lazzi*, even in his great comedies, which are really dramas. Alceste almost beats his servant with his fists; Orgon crawls under the table. But none of the great characters in Molière is psychologically clear; every one of them is flawed, has his own secret, his own shadow line.

Baudouin gave his Polish adaptation of *Tartuffe* the title

Swietoszek Zmyślony. "Zmyślony" in eighteenth-century Polish meant "false." But what does it mean: a false hypocrite? A hypocrite pretends to be a pious man, so he is not pious. The French language is more precise: "faux dévot" means a hypocrite. A false hypocrite would be "un faux faux dévot." A false hypocrite means someone who pretends to be a hypocrite, so he is not really a hypocrite. It seems that Baudouin may have unconsciously expressed the basic ambiguity of Molière's Tartuffe.

If La Bruyère's Onuphre is a perfect hypocrite, Molière's Tartuffe is an apparent hypocrite. His passions are stronger than the mask he has assumed. All passions: power, money, and women. All passions, and that is why he must lose. But perhaps for this reason it is Tartuffe, and not Onuphre, who is a more genuine hypocrite than the real hypocrites. *Onuphre* could be a comedy of character; Tartuffe belongs simultaneously to drama and to farce. Tartuffe is fascinating because his face is truer than his mask. This is a measure of Molière's greatness.

Molière's Tartuffe has shining red cheeks. But there is an ambiguity even in his physical appearance. Theatre tradition has left us some very different Tartuffes. I have seen big fat Tartuffes as well as thin stooping ones with pale faces. But Tartuffe in the theatre was always older than the young Madame Orgon; he was always slimy, sticky as it were. Then, seven years ago I saw a performance of *Tartuffe* in the Warsaw Drama School that was a revelation. School performances very seldom bring surprises, hardly ever revelations. But that particular performance revealed a new *Tartuffe* to me.

Tartuffe was played by a slim young boy with an oval face. He was dressed in a kind of short violet surplice and looked like an altar boy or a young sacristan. He was tender and full of charm. He reminded me a little of Gérard Philipe. But who would cast Gérard Philipe in the part of Tartuffe? That evening I saw in the young hypocrite Stendhal's Julien Sorel practicing the art of hypocrisy in a seminary. Tartuffe was a young boy, full of disturbing and dangerous charm, making advances to a mature woman, just as Julien Sorel made advances to Madame de Rênal. He was not a hypocrite, but forced on himself the discipline of hypocrisy as an exercise in will power. He was precisely the false hypocrite. He wanted to gain the world, money, and women. There was in him something of Don Juan, who also assumed the mask of hypocrisy. After all, Molière wrote *Don Juan* soon after *Tartuffe*. This Tartuffe I saw now was already a little demon in the mask of a conformist.

Perhaps one should not entirely disregard the judgments of theatre and literary critics. After all, Thibaudet showed long ago the affinities between Julien Sorel and Molière's Tartuffe. In the essay I have quoted Auerbach writes about the cruelty of Orgon. Religious belief only helps him to justify the family tyranny he practices. Orgon seems more of a menace than Tartuffe. He is only seemingly deceived and can only pretend to find a justification for his behavior in his naïveté or even his good faith. I think Molière hated Orgon more than he hated Tartuffe. Orgon's stupidity is as gigantic as Père Ubu's. They are both exemplary bourgeois, except that Père Ubu became a king. Let us now imagine Orgon as an absolute ruler. I should like one day to see on the stage Molière's *Tartuffe* with Julien Sorel and Père Ubu in the leading parts. This is another aspect of Molière's relevance for our time, a relevance that means more than just dressing the actors in modern clothes. With *Tartuffe* begins a Molière who fascinates and disturbs us still.

3

Don Juan was censored immediately after its first night in 1665 and had only fourteen more performances. It was not until the middle of the nineteenth century that the play returned to the French stage, and even then it was seldom performed, as if theatres were ashamed of it. At that time

Don Juan did not rouse any interest among audiences or critics. The real discovery of *Don Juan* came a hundred years later, when Jouvet produced it in 1947. Almost three hundred years had passed since the original production.

One can easily imagine a Molière who did not write *Don Juan*. It would be an easier Molière but a poorer one by far. *Don Juan* is not a work that could be attributed to Molière the moralist or Molière the classicist. Even the Romantics failed to appreciate its quality. *Don Juan* is a play that obviously did not fit either the eighteenth-century or the nineteenth-century theatre. Only Mozart admired it. In the nineteenth-century theatre *Don Juan* really existed only as an opera.

Don Juan is, indeed, unlike any other play by Molière. Only in the very greatest writers can one find one or two works, sometimes just a chapter or a few lines, unlike anything else they have written. For Shakespeare, *Troilus and Cressida*, and perhaps *Cymbeline*, were such plays. *Don Juan* is Molière's most disturbing play, although *Le Misanthrope*, probably begun earlier and finished a year later, is full of puzzles. Molière is a clear writer, on the surface at any rate. Every play of his has a moral that does not seem to give rise to doubt. Misers are mocked; so are fools and ignoramuses, prigs, pedants and dogmatists, hypocrites and prudes, jealous old men and inhuman fathers, courtiers, snobs and flatterers. All Molière's plays, except *Don Juan* and *Le Misanthrope*, have happy endings. Tartuffe is punished; we may not believe in that punishment, but it does not raise any moral doubts in us. Don Juan is punished, too: the earth opens under him and the fires of hell envelop him. Tartuffe is punished by the sovereign and taken away to prison. Don Juan is punished directly by God. It is easier to believe in temporal than divine justice. *Don Juan* is from the first to the last scene an ambiguous play. So is *Le Misanthrope* for that matter. In *Don Juan* spirits appear and statues talk. But it is a rationalist and a liberal who sits down at table to a meal with a talking statue. The rationalist loses the duel with ghosts. Scarcely has he disappeared below ground, however, than the pious Sganarelle in the very same spot is bemoaning his fate. It was a stroke of genius on the part of Molière to change the clown accompanying Don Juan into the defender of social order, religion, and piety. Molière's Don Juan rejects all the principles of the social order: family, woman's honor, the moral order, heaven, hell, and supernatural forces. He does not even want to pay his debts. Don Juan does not recognize any authority and does not believe in anything. Sganarelle recognizes all authority and believes in everything: in God as well as in the devil and in werewolves, in money and in force, in Providence and in the whip. He is an absolute conformist. Sganarelle abases himself before society, is a fool and a coward, but he never ceases to be human. Don Juan is independent and a rebel and for this reason seems inhuman. There is no room for him in the world. Just as there was no room for Alceste, although for different reasons. It is Molière's Sancho Panza who remains, and the play ends with his pitiful lament. He too has been deceived. Molière's Don Juan scoffs at even common sense. In Molière's dialogue with the world, Don Juan's with his servant, Sganarelle, as Eric Bentley has rightly observed, represents the audience.

If Don Juan is really punished, then God exists. But in the theatre there is only a theatrical God, and Don Juan disappears down a trap door. Of all Molière's plays this is the one most remote from all the rules, the only one in which machines intervene, the only one that ends with fireworks. Molière took the plot from the Spaniards and the Italians; the machines from the theatre of the baroque. Like the mystery and miracle plays, this mocking comedy takes place between heaven and hell. Something of a mystery play remains in it, though it is a blasphemous mystery. Don Juan challenges not only men but also God. He is not a mere seducer. For him love has to be a sacrilege. He wants to have God for a rival; otherwise, pleasure for him, as for the Marquis de Sade, would be insipid and cruelly boring. Don Juan's

greatness lies in the fact that he does not surrender until the
end. For me the ambiguity of the ending is one of Molière's
most astonishing discoveries. Don Juan is punished not by
God in whom he does not believe; he is punished by a
machine. As Camus wrote:

> What else does that stone Commander signify, that cold
> statue set in motion to punish the blood and courage that
> dared to think? All the powers of eternal Reason, of order, of
> universal morality, all the foreign grandeur of a God open to
> wrath are summed up in him. That gigantic and soulless
> stone merely symbolizes the forces that Don Juan negated
> for ever. But the Commander's mission stops there. The
> thunder and lightning can return to the imitation heaven
> whence they were called forth. The real tragedy takes place
> quite apart from them.

4

In Alceste's third reply, Barrault turns his back on Philinte,
violently stamps his feet, raises both his hands, rolls his eyes.
He is a comic figure. At the same point in the first scene of
Le Misanthrope, the great actor Molé, who acted Alceste
toward the end of the seventeenth century, broke the chair
on which he had thrown himself on his agitated entry. With
that third speech the part of Alceste really begins for an actor,
and the type of acting adopted is at the same time an interpretation.

There are two basic interpretations of the part of Alceste.
He can be choleric or melancholic. Molé was ill-tempered
and choleric. He broke chairs. He was comic more than anything. He was a "splenetic lover." Baron, who took over the
part of Alceste from Molière, was a melancholiac. He was
noble, generous, and ironical. He was dressed in a costume
with green ribbons. Baron originated the tradition of an intellectual, tragic Alceste, an Alceste full of contempt and grief
Such an Alceste could have been close to the Jansenists'
hearts. He was sermonizing and intransigent.

The Baron tradition is the older of the two, but Molé—according to theatre historians—was nearer to Molière's own interpretation of the part. Molière delighted in playing the parts of clowns. His Alceste was certainly a comic figure, at least as far as acting technique was concerned. This was the tradition Barrault went back to in his performance of 1954. He was even made up to look like Molière in the engraving by Mignard. He adopted the characteristic mannerism of carrying his head low as if he wanted to hide it between his shoulders, a mannerism observed in the acting of Molière. Barrault was first comic, only later tragic. But he was comic for a long time, even as late as the fourth act when he ran across the stage on his knees proposing to Éliante.

Alceste's comicality offended Rousseau. Alceste is funny, so Alceste is made ridiculous. A noble man is made ridiculous, so the play is immoral. He is made ridiculous to amuse the audience, so theatre is immoral. Rousseau interpreted *Le Misanthrope* as a contemporary play. Perhaps even more, as a play about himself. He was the first writer to identify himself with Alceste. Hence there is a very personal tone in the analysis of *Le Misanthrope* in his famous *Lettre sur les spectacles*. He wrote:

> A noble man is he who delights not in the manners of his age and the malevolence of his contemporaries. Just because he loves his neighbors, he hates the evil in them which they do unto one another, and the vices from which that evil stems. Would he be more human had he been less concerned with errors men commit, less indignant at iniquities he witnessed? With equal truth could one assert that a good father loves other men's children more than his own because to his own he does not spare reproaches, while to the others he does not say a word.

And a few lines farther on he said:

> He is not then a hater of men but of the malice of some and of the approval that malice finds with others. Were there no scoundrels or flatterers, he would love all mankind. Every de-

cent man is a misanthrope in this respect. Or rather, those
are misanthropes who think otherwise. I do not really know a
greater enemy of mankind than everybody's friend who, ever
delighted at anything, encourages the evildoers and, through
his evil courtesy, flatters the vices that are the source of all
confusion in society.

Rousseau identified himself with Alceste to such an extent
that he used almost his very words. He went on conducting a
discourse with Philinte, whom, perhaps, he also saw at that
time in Diderot. He wrote his *Letter* after he had definitely
broken his friendship with him. He fell in the same traps that
Molière had set for Alceste. He was indignant at the fact that
Alceste was funny, and in his indignation became ridiculous
himself. Just as Alceste had. After all, he was Alceste too.
He wanted to be "himself" and live in the world. He
wanted to be "himself" and frequent the salons. One can
change the world, but one cannot change a court or a salon.
When one is "oneself" at a court or a salon, one is ridiculous.
Alceste personified for Rousseau his own antinomies; he rejected the society in which he could not live, and without
which he could not live either. Alceste's wilderness is Rousseau's state of nature. Rousseau's biography, as Bronisław
Baczko put it, was a paradox experienced by himself. For
him Alceste was his own paradox walking on the stage.

In 1758, the same year that Rousseau published his *Lettre
sur les spectacles*, Diderot wrote his discourse *De la poésie
dramatique*. Rousseau identified himself with Alceste; Diderot
almost identified himself with Philinte. At any rate, Philinte
was much closer to him. He was impetuous and an ideologist,
but he valued the charms of the salon. And he remembered
the long hours he had spent tête-à-tête with Catherine in a
locked room. Philinte, who understood everything, was for
Diderot a philanthropist, that is, a true friend of mankind:

> Let us suppose that posters announcing *Le Misanthrope*
> had not been stuck up and that the play was performed with-
> out publicity. What would happen if Philinte had as decisive

a character as Alceste. Could not the spectator rightly ask, after the first scene at least, where as yet nothing shows who the principal character is, what is being performed: *Le Misanthrope*, or *Le Philanthrope*? How does one avoid that difficulty? One sacrifices one of the two characters. In the mouth of one is put everything that enhances him; while the other is made to appear clumsy and a fool. Would not the spectator feel the defect, however, particularly when the principal character is at a disadvantage, as happens in the example quoted above?

He goes on:

In spite of that the first scene of *Le Misanthrope* is a masterpiece. Yes. But let it be done by a man of genius who would give Philinte so much presence of mind, determination, eloquence, integrity, love of mankind, indulgence for human vices, compassion for human weaknesses, as a true friend of mankind should have. And then you will observe that, without altering anything in the part of Alceste, the theme of the play becomes blurred. But why does this not happen in reality? Is Alceste right? Is Philinte wrong?

Molière was wiser than both Alceste and Philinte. But it was a most bitter wisdom. The conflict is unresolved and cannot be resolved. In the end it boils down not to the superiority of intellectual arguments but to a choice. Alceste chooses. Just like Racine's heroes he refuses to accept the world. A comic figure becomes a tragic hero. This seemingly objective play is at the same time highly personal. Alceste chooses for Molière. Molière knew that a theatre manager could not go away into a wilderness; that he could not go away or escape. He knew all Philinte's arguments, but he certainly wrote the part of Alceste in the first person. He gave him the awareness of his own defeat. With the difference that he was not only Alceste.

Don Juan experiments with evil, provokes men and God in whom he does not believe, rejects all conventions and breaks all rules. Alceste wants to speak only the truth and to change Célimène. The action of *Don Juan* takes place between heaven and hell. The entire action of Le Misanthrope takes place in a drawing room in the course of one day, from morning to evening. The defeat of Don Juan is pathetic and theatrical; Alceste is defeated only inwardly, but because of that, perhaps his defeat is real. There is an astonishing incompatibility between his defeat and what has really happened. He lost the suit but he can still win it. Célimène does not want to go away with him, but she is still willing to marry him. It is not even certain that she has been unfaithful to him. There is gossip in the salons, but why should it be otherwise? The court consists of opportunists, sycophants, informers, envious men, for such is the nature of courts. Nothing has really happened though everything has been played out. It is just that one cannot go on living in that country. Everything in the play is transparent, but it is the transparency of water. Nothing can be got hold of, everything slips through the fingers, only the bottom can be seen with a terrifying clarity. Perhaps the only sound comments on Le Misanthrope can be found in La Bruyère. As when he writes about women in a way that brings to mind Célimène:

> Women's whims are the antidote to their beauty, so that it may do less harm to men, who, without such a remedy, would never be cured of their love.

And yet another quotation directly relevant to the real content of Le Misanthrope:

> There is a country where all joy is conspicuous but false, and all grief hidden but real. Who would imagine that the anxiety to be present at entertainments, the raptures and applause at Molière's or Harlequin's comedies, the banquets, the chase, the ballets, and carrousels, conceal so much uneasiness, so many cares and such various interests, so many fears and expectations, so many ardent passions, and such serious matters of business.

(1966)

THEATRE AND LITERATURE

The first French collection of Meyerhold's essays was titled *Le Théâtre théatral*. These words "theatrical theatre" can have many meanings, but two at least are highly significant: theatre that is to be staged rather than read, or theatre that is first of all "spectacle." It was E. Gordon Craig, so far as I know, who introduced the notion of "the art of the theatre"—the great realm of light, setting, music, movement, and, last, text, in which the director, like God, is the great and almighty Creator. Meyerhold not only revised the order of the scenes in the plays he directed, but sometimes, as in his production of Gogol's *Inspector General*, added to the original text fragments from the author's other works. Leon Schiller, the greatest personality in the Polish theatre during the two wars is said to have declared once that his greatest dream was to produce four pages of classified advertisements from the *Warsaw Courier*. (And the *Warsaw Courier* is about one quarter the volume of the Sunday *New York Times*.)

It was very characteristic of the theatre in the interwar period for directors to use the text of even the great classics merely as raw material. They felt that theatre could be created out of half-finished literary products, or out of "super-literature." In either case the director shaped the dialogue to suit his theatrical vision. During this period the great theatres were rarely closely connected with contemporary dramatists, as the Artistic Theatre (MCHAT) in Russia had

been connected with Chekhov and Gorky, or the Jouvet Theatre in France with Giraudoux. The leading theatres then were
known for their directors: there are a Théatre Copeau and a
Théatre Baty in France, a Piscator Theatre in Germany, a
Meyerhold Theatre in Russia, a Schiller Theatre in Poland,
a Burian Theatre in Czechoslovakia.

In this period, often called the time of the great reform,
many directors seemed to feel that for theatre to develop, old
theatre buildings, and particularly the stage "à l'italienne"
had to be demolished. New theatre architecture is certainly
always necessary, but, as it turned out, the entire avant-garde
drama could be staged in a conventional theatre with only
minor changes of the stage. Beckett and Ionesco, Dürrenmatt
and Genet can be performed everywhere, even on a simple
wooden rostrum. Even Brecht's plays can be produced according to the strict rules of his Berliner Ensemble without a large
theatrical machine.

Contemporary directors, especially the leading ones, are
once again seeking to "theatricalize" the theatre. But in our
day theatrical as well as dramatic styles are named after playwrights. We have a Beckett theatre, a Ionesco theatre, a
Genet theatre, even a Marat/Sade theatre. These terms mean
something more than plays by Brecht, Beckett, Ionesco,
Genet, or Weiss. They impose their own types of production,
style, and acting, and the common term, the "theatre of the
absurd," actually means the dramaturgy of the French avant-
garde of the thirties and its followers. The theatrical inspiration for the greatest directors today comes from modern
dramaturgy or from modern literature.

This close connection between theatre and literature has
developed since World War II. I have often wondered which
writers have most influenced the contemporary theatre in its
three main directions: the theatre of the absurd, the theatre
of cruelty, and the happening. To my mind it has only very
recently been possible to attempt a reply to this question. One
could not imagine this revolution in drama occurring without
Kafka and Joyce.

Compared to poetry and the novel, drama seemed for a long time to lag behind, as if it could not divorce itself from the nineteenth century. The theatre still operated in another sphere: it still described and represented, while the leading poetry explored and experimented with the possibilities inherent in language. To experience the possibilities of language, to destroy its given structures, to reach new structures—all this really meant analyzing consciousness and subconsciousness. In novels, too, plot and character were beginning to be discarded; at any rate, unambiguous plots and characters were. Novelists strove to find extreme or eschatological situations. *Ulysses* and *The Trial* are in a sense books dealing with the whole of existence. The "Night of the Walpurgis" from *Ulysses* is written not by accident in dialogue, and it is in reality the greatest drama of the theatre of cruelty and of the absurd.

The material of the new drama, on all levels from language to plot and situation, is in fact the same as that of post-Joyce, post-Kafka literature. Even the elements of the circus—clown play, surprise and shock—that we find in happenings are of a literary kind, and there can be no doubt of their surrealist or expressionist parentage. The first happening was in poetry, when, in the Dadaist period, Tristan Tzara pulled scraps of newspaper out of a top hat and from them created a poem.

It was a time when all the arts strove for purity; poetry to be pure poetry, literature to be pure literature, and theatre to be pure theatre; even the film dreamed of being a pure picture. This dream was both classical and aesthetical, it was the last expression of the old faith that the artistic genres were all created separately out of nothingness, just as God created the species of animals in Genesis. But our lives, our world, and our consciousness are not pure; so why should art be pure?

The novel, like poetry, has become more and more an experiment in language. It now plays all the registers, from breaking up the sentence to breaking up language taboos. But at the same time the novel has intermingled more and more with the essay, philosophy, and sociology in its themes, means of narration, and in language. Even some scientists have begun to see their disciplines as similar to art or literature; mathematicians, physicists, and finally, Lévi-Strauss, who claims that scientific anthropology is a new realization of the old myths.

The same processes of integration and disintegration have affected the new drama and the new theatre. They are depoeticized poetry, philosophical grotesque, or—to risk another term—a tragifarce of archetypes, a mixture of poetry and vulgarity, a metaphysical mime, or a philosophy of existence expounded in images and examples. After Beckett's *Endgame* it seemed that one could go no further. But in fact one could. It is enough to show just one woman being buried deeper and deeper in the sand.

If we look at Beckett's *Happy Days* as a literary text, we find it consists in equal parts of dialogue and stage directions. As literature it is very theatrical; as theatre, very literary. The central situation is a metaphor or a parable that is both theatrical and literary, unrealistic and concrete; but it can and should be staged, for it realizes its full expression only on the stage. In *Happy Days* we have "theatrical" theatre stripped of all the old tools. The one-time opposition between theatre and literature takes on new significance; the two words "theatrical" and "literary" come to have different meanings. Theatre begins to be literary to a high degree, but literature—the best and truest literature—begins to be less and less "literary."

In a very general sense one could say that literature performs two functions: it creates myths and it demystifies. There were periods in which the myth-creating function attracted writers especially and led to such masterpieces as the *Aeneid*. In the last quarter century however—and if we include the great precursors, the period would be extended to a full century—the leading literature has been one of demystification.

It has abolished myths of all kinds, first in the sphere of history and social relations, conventions and manners, then in the realm of illusions, hopes, all means of taking comfort. Literature set out to demystify metaphysics, history, and then human nature. Later still it demystified all the means and instruments it had used, ending with language.

The process of destruction and purification has been taken up most violently by the theatre since the war—first of all in matters of ideology, as in the case of some American writers and Sartre or even Brecht, who is in fact much more ambiguous than one would think from some of the things written about him. Then the so-called theatre of the absurd quickly destroyed most of the traditional means used in drama; it showed bare existence on an almost bare stage. Have we arrived at the limit of the process of destruction, or at the limit of "naked" theatrical theatre?

One might ask which theatre is the most truthful. To my mind the answer could be the circus: a circus in which genuine lions devour genuine Christians. We can now start measuring the gradations of theatrical illusion. Genuine lions and genuine Christians, but now the lions only pretend to devour the Christians; false lions and genuine Christians; and finally false lions and false Christians, that is to say, *Androcles and the Lion*, by George Bernard Shaw. Actors can eat real food and drink real drinks out of real plates and glasses, sitting by a real table; or they can sit by a real table, with real plates and glasses, but the plates and glasses are empty, imaginary drinks are drunk, non-existent food is eaten. And then there can be the situation where even the glasses and plates are imaginary. It is an amusing detail that in the theatre, where every activity can be mimed and all real gestures can be replaced by make-believe, there is one activity that so far as I know is never shown as an imaginary one: if an actor lights a cigarette, the cigarette is invariably real.* Even

* I have just heard of Robert Head's *Sancticity* (printed in TDR 22) where a cigarette is mimed.

on the rock bottom of the absurd. I must admit that I find this alarming.

Discussions on the future of the theatre, abstracted from an understanding of the function and role of literature in the contemporary world, serve little purpose. When the dignity of literature consists in demystification, when the ideology of criticism consists in the criticism of ideology, theatre has to perform both these functions: demystification and criticism. Both its raison d'être and its dignity consist in this.

Even in the least realistic theatre the actor smokes a real cigarette. Theatre, as Eric Bentley has written, is, like literature, a stripping of the soul, a tearing off of masks. But the soul, writes Bentley, has no eyes, breasts, hips, or knees. Theatre is a unique art in which the misery of metaphysics and the metaphysics of misery have to be shown through a living man who speaks to or acts with another living man. The theatre of the absurd has tormented souls or consciences. The theatre of cruelty wants to torment bodies; it wants to break the last taboo after the verbal, the metaphysical, the ideological—the taboo of the body, of man's physical nature. But what does it actually mean to torment bodies on the stage?

The most classical definition of theatre, that of Aristotle, asserts that it is an imitation of action. This seems to be true, but only in a particular manner: the imitation of an action by another action, the imitation of a body by another body. I like to call this the paradox of the striptease: a girl who strips doesn't only take off her clothes; at the same time she plays a girl who takes off her clothes. Nevertheless, at the end of the imitation the girl who plays a woman taking off her clothes stands naked on the stage. But what about torture and murder? The hero who was killed on the stage remains alive.

The paradox of the theatre raises not only theoretical questions, but practical ones as well. What is the difference between playing love and making love? "If intercourse were necessary in a play," Kenneth Tynan once said, "I would not hesitate to stage it." This is possible, but obviously only in England.

Films can be naturalistic, shocking, even obscene—they can be realistic, but they are never real. They do not exist *now!* They are only pictures of something that happened in the past and in another place. And we can never be sure that it really happened at all.

But a performance in the theatre is always in the present— it is here and now. In the theatre we are always witnesses or even co-stars. In films voyeurism is possible. We do not belong to the same reality; we are like a man who looks furtively from the dark street into a lighted window. In the theatre we belong to the same reality; it is the same time and space for the actors and the audience. We are present. If there is an orgy we should not just look at it—we should participate in it.

Orgy is very old and has always been connected with ritual and myths. It is not accidental that for Antonin Artaud, as for Peter Brook and many modern directors, the theatre of cruelty was and is closely connected with the theatre of liturgy and ritual. But what is the meaning of ritual? A ritual is first a form, a strict repetition of some gesture or words, and the significance of the gesture can be magical, symbolical, or even social. This significance is connected with what we can call in the words of Lévi-Strauss a "code"—a religious, magical, or social code in the society. But I should emphasize that ritual is always a repetition of words or gestures.

The Mass is a ritual, a repetition of sacred words and gestures. What would happen if a Mass were played on the stage? An actor on the stage does not *play* a priest saying a Mass, he *mimes* the gestures of the priest. As such the performance is not a ritual, but a profanation of the ritual, and this seems to be the real function of liturgy in the theatre of Genet.

Every liturgy and ritual, from liturgical dance to the presidential oath or a church wedding, is always a great mime and a great ballet. To make a sacred sign is to repeat a sacred gesture. The priest, or even a man who swears on a Bible, also performs a kind of mime. But the *theatrical* mime of a sacred mime played on the stage by an actor is shocking—it is a demystification of ritual. And now we approach the second paradox of the theatre and a new meaning of modern "theatrical" theatre.

The theatre is an imitation of an action by another action, the imitation of a body by another body. How far can we go with the imitation of love, violence, sacrifice, or murder? In the *naturalistic* theatre we can use a real pistol, but the bullet must always be false—the man who is shot does not really die. But there is also another theatre. An actor can have no pistol, his hands are empty, he only mimes an action of shooting and killing. The shot here is only a symbol—I prefer to use another word, is only a sign. This difference between "to act" and "to mime" seems to me to be of the utmost importance. I discovered this for the first time while analyzing the scene of the would-be suicide of Gloucester in *King Lear*. After his eyes have been gouged out Gloucester wants to throw himself over the cliffs of Dover into the sea. He is led by his own son, who feigns madness. Both have reached the depths of human suffering, but on the stage there are just two actors, one playing a blind man, the other playing a man who plays a madman. The madman leads the blind man. He leads him to a non-existent hill. There is no hill, there are only the illusions of the blind man, who, the mad son suggests, is on top of a hill. The father does not jump into the abyss; he merely tumbles on the stage. There is no suicide in *King Lear*, there is only the parable of suicide as in medieval morality plays. It occurred to me that this was a great pantomime. Edgar is supporting Gloucester; he lifts his feet high, pretending to walk uphill. Gloucester too lifts his feet as if expecting the ground to rise, but underneath his feet there is only air. The stage is bare, the cliffs are created only by words, the jump is a mime of a suicide. This kind of parable can be realized only on the stage; in narrative fiction it has no meaning. Gloucester's jump is both imaginary and concrete, meaningful and meaningless. This is probably the best example of naked "theatrical" theatre. The interpretation of this striking scene in terms of literary criticism without regard to its theatrical particularization is poor and inadequate.

Let me take another example. The central theme of the love stories in *Twelfth Night* and *As You Like It* is the disguise of a girl as a boy. But again the full and complex significance of this disguise has its realization only on the stage. Viola on the stage becomes Cesario and Rosalind changes to Ganymede. Viola-Cesario is a girlish boy for Orsino, and a boyish girl for Olivia. Viola-Cesario is the "master mistress" of the Shakespearean sonnets. I cannot give here the full explanation of the philosophical and aesthetic significance of Shakespeare's neoplatonism; I would like only to point out that in both plays we can find the eternal triangle of sex ambiguity that is exposed in the sonnets. This triangle is composed of a man, a boy, and a woman.

But Viola *is* Cesario; they have the same body. What is more, in a deep sense of Shakespearean parable, Sebastian also has the same body as Viola. The theatre is an imitation of an action by another action, of a body by another body. On the level of physical action—on the level of bodies—Viola-Cesario is either boy or girl, and the sense of ambiguity depends upon who takes this part—a boy, as on the Elizabethan stage, or a girl, as in modern times. If we choose a boy for the part of Viola or Rosalind the happy ending is illusory, the triangle of the Shakespearean sonnets remains unsolved, and the real meaning of *As You Like It* and *Twelfth Night* is a delusion. If we cast a boy for these parts, we have both acting and miming. Or, more precisely, we have a boy who mimes a girl who plays a boy. I am fairly sure this is the only way to render the full Shakespearean ambiguity.

"Without an element of cruelty at the root of every spectacle," wrote Antonin Artaud in *The Theatre and Its Double*, "the theatre is not possible. In our present state of degeneration it is through the skin that metaphysics must be made to reenter our minds."

To mime a Mass is a profanation, but to mime love is also
a profanation. The greatest of all profanations is to mime
an opposite sex or an opposite race; this is a major theme in
the theater of Genet: whites play Negroes, Negroes play
whites, boys play girls. The stage identifies the bodies and
the feelings, wrote Artaud. To play love is to imitate love,
but to mime love is to demystify love, to mime power is to
demystify power, to mime ritual is to demystify ritual. To
mime a priest, a chief, a hangman is one of the few serious
provocations still possible in the modern theatre. For Artaud
the profanation of ritual was the real function of the theatre
of cruelty. "The theatre is the only place in the world," he
said, "the last general means we still possess of directly affect-
ing the organism and, in periods of neurosis and petty sensuality like the one in which we are immersed, of attacking this
sensuality by physical means it cannot withstand."

(1967)